P9-DXJ-746

THE WRITER'S GUIDE TO QUERIES, PITCHES & PROPOSALS

THE WRITER'S GUIDE TO QUERIES, PITCHES & PROPOSALS

Moira Anderson Allen

ALLWORTH PRESS
NEW YORK

© 2001 Moira Anderson Allen

All rights reserved. Copyright under Berne Copyright Convention, Universal Copyright Convention, and Pan-American Copyright Convention. No part of this book may be reproduced, stored in a retrieval system, or transmitted in any form, or by any means, electronic, mechanical, photocopying, recording, or otherwise, without prior permission of the publisher.

05   04   03   02   5   4   3   2

Published by Allworth Press
An imprint of Allworth Communications
10 East 23rd Street, New York, NY 10010

Cover design by Douglas Design Associates, New York, NY

Page composition/typography by SR Desktop Services, Ridge, NY

ISBN: 1–58115–099–7

Library of Congress Cataloging-in-Publication Data:

Anderson Allen, Moira.
  The writer's guide to queries, pitches & proposals / by Moira Anderson Allen.
     p. cm.
Includes index.
  ISBN 1-58115-099-7
1. Authorship--Marketing. I. Title.
  PN161 .A55 2001
  070.5'2--dc21

                                                                    2001003492

Printed in Canada

TABLE OF CONTENTS

ACKNOWLEDGMENTS

A great many people helped with the development of this book. While most of them are named in the sections to which they contributed, I'd like to take a moment to thank them here. Thank you, Robin Catesby, Amy Chavez, C.J. Chilvers, A.C. Crispin, MaryJanice Davidson, Maryo Ewell, Debbie Farmer, Lynn Flewelling, Huw Francis, Sharon Ihle, Mary Rose, Amy Shojai, Victoria Strauss, Rebecca Vinyard, and Kelleen Zubick. Without you, this book would not have been possible! Thanks also to Tad Crawford of Allworth Press, who helped in the development of the concept, and to my very patient husband, Patrick, who has reviewed and re-reviewed every chapter—and still only shudders slightly when I hand him another sheaf of manuscript pages.

INTRODUCTION

The first question an author must answer when writing a book like this is, who is this for? Is it for beginning writers who have yet to write their first query? Or is it for more experienced writers?

The answer is, *both*. If you are a beginner in the writing and publishing business, this book will guide you through the process of locating and contacting markets for your work. It will show you how to create a query that tells an editor exactly what he or she needs to know about your article idea, how to pitch your first novel, how to propose a nonfiction book, and more. It will help you get started, no matter where you want to start.

If you are an experienced writer, this book will help you branch out into new areas, expanding your business and your sales. Often, the only thing holding a writer back from new markets is a lack of understanding of how to approach those markets, and that is what this book is designed to provide. So, if you've decided to take your career to the next level—to write a book on your area of expertise or send off that novel you've been writing in your spare time—this book will show you how.

But why a book that covers so many different topics, when a variety of books are already available on each individual topic? Perhaps the answer lies within the question: Why have eight books on your shelf when you can find the answers you seek in one? (You'll also find some tips that I don't believe are covered in any other book.)

When an author makes a promise like that, the first question a *reader* might ask is, How can you provide so much information on such a range of topics? Do you really know all this stuff? Well, I've done a lot in the twenty years that I've been writing—edited a national magazine, worked as a technical writer, freelanced as a corporate editor and newsletter developer, edited a Web site and e-zine, sold three nonfiction books, and published more than two hundred articles and columns. But I certainly haven't "done it all"—nor have I done everything discussed in this book.

That posed a certain challenge. I like to write about what I know, and this book proposed to cover a great many things I *don't* know firsthand. So, how could I present useful information on areas that I'd never explored as an author, without simply recycling what others have already written?

The answer: Find the folks who *do* know. The result is a book that is more than one writer's perspective, one writer's experience. It is a collection of perspectives from a variety of experienced authors, each offering tips from their own fields of expertise. To cover the question of how to write a novel synopsis, I obtained an example of a synopsis that *worked,* from a successful novelist—along with an analysis by a workshop instructor to explain exactly *why* it worked. Another novelist shares her tips on drafting query letters to editors and agents. A freelancer based in Turkey shares insights about selling a nonfiction book proposal to international publishers. An international columnist explains how to sell international columns. And so on . . .

The wonderful thing about talking to writers who *know* is how quickly they can demystify areas and processes that formerly seemed impenetrable and vague. They remind us that we can go where they have gone; that if they can do it, so can we. And then they tell us how.

So, if there's a particular type of market you've been itching to break into, chances are that you'll find the tools you need to get started within these pages. You can read this book one of two ways: from cover to cover, or by selecting the topics that you want to know more about. Each chapter is designed to stand alone, so that you won't have to read chapter 2 to understand chapter 8. (I do recommend, however, that everyone take a look at "the basics" outlined in chapter 1.) So dig in—and then get out there and start pitching!

Moira Allen
Chesapeake, VA
moira@writing-world.com

1

THE PERFECT PITCH: TEN STEPS TO A WINNING PROPOSAL

The life of the professional writer is getting tougher. Good markets are becoming harder to find, and to break into. Other markets vanish overnight without a trace—or change the rules without warning, imposing rights-grabbing contracts while offering little in return. Editors are flooded with inappropriate manuscripts and queries—often to the point that they no longer bother with rejection letters, but simply ignore material they don't want. Publications that were once friendly to freelancers are now closing their doors to unsolicited submissions, making it harder than ever to make a sale.

As a writer, however, your toughest challenge isn't coldhearted editors or grabby contracts. It's the competition. Each year, more and more writers enter the marketplace. Many don't have a clue as to how to proceed, which accounts for the overwhelming number of badly written manuscripts and queries editors receive every day. Others, however, are good—and that's the problem: There's always more good writing than there are markets for that writing.

To compete with the thousands of "good" writers in the marketplace, you have to be able to develop queries and proposals that are more than simply "good." They have to be great. They have to rise *above* the competition. They have to stand out in every respect: content, preparation, and presentation. They have to be as nearly perfect as you can make them.

The chapters that follow will discuss ways to craft "the perfect pitch" for a variety of markets. This chapter, however, will discuss essential steps and requirements that are basic to every proposal. Following these steps will give you the best possible chance of beating the competition—and making a sale.

STEP 1: RESEARCH THE MARKET

Proposals and queries aren't generic; there's no such thing as a "one-size-fits-all" pitch. Editors prefer proposals that are tailored for their publication, their audience—and they can usually tell when a writer has never seen that publication. Before you start to draft that query or proposal, therefore, you need to familiarize yourself with your target market. This usually means taking several steps:

READ THE GUIDELINES

Writers today have a profound advantage over writers four or five years ago: We no longer have to send out SASEs (self-addressed, stamped envelopes) and wait weeks for a publication to send us its contributors' guidelines. Nor do we have to rely on outdated, inadequate market listings in printed guides. Many publications now post their guidelines on a Web site, or make them available by e-mail autoresponder. With such lightning-fast technology at our fingertips, there's absolutely no excuse for *not* reviewing a publication's guidelines before sending a query.

This should be your first avenue of research. With luck, you'll be able to determine exactly what a publication does and doesn't want. Guidelines generally specify the desired word count for submissions, whether the publication accepts unsolicited submissions or requires writers to query first, and how to submit (e.g., by e-mail, by surface mail, with electronic files, etc.). Often, they will offer tips on style and presentation—e.g., "No first-person accounts." They may also provide a list of topics to cover and topics to avoid. They may even provide a description of the publication's target audience (e.g., "upscale travelers between twenty and forty-five, with incomes of $100,000 or higher").

Unfortunately, not every publication offers such detailed guidelines. Many leave you guessing, or wondering exactly what the editor means when he or she says, "We're looking for crisp, exciting writing." And some, of course, don't provide any guidelines at all. Which leads to the next step.

REVIEW THE PUBLICATION/PUBLISHER

Again, writers today have an advantage: Many periodicals now post material online. Even book publishers may post sample chapters of new releases, which is a good way to determine the type of style or subject matter that the publisher is currently seeking.

It's still a good idea to go beyond the Internet when researching a publication or publisher, however. If you're considering querying a print periodical, try to find a copy in your local bookstore or newsstand. Compare it to other periodicals on similar topics. What are the differences? Chances are, two magazines on the "same" topic won't be the same at all.

For example, while there are four major dog magazines on the market, each has a very different focus: *Dog World* focuses primarily on an audience of dog breeders and exhibitors, while *Dog Fancy* focuses on pet owners (and discourages breeding). *AKC Gazette* is almost exclusively for breeders and features fairly technical medical articles, while *Bark!* is for the "upscale" pet lover and tends to show pictures of dogs wearing rhinestone collars or living in Manhattan penthouses. These differences aren't apparent in the brief listings available in *Writer's Market* (which doesn't list the *Gazette* at all), and only two of these publications post contributor guidelines online.

Looking at a publication can also tell you whether you want to *be* in that publication. Do you really want your thoughtful article on women's health to be surrounded by ads for horoscopes and sex aids? Will your piece on "baking for the kids during the holidays" find a home in that magazine for young, primarily single, working women?

If you're researching a book publisher, again, don't rely on guidelines alone to help you choose. Check the publisher's online catalog to see what titles (and authors) it actually publishes. This will help you discover, for example, that your gritty police procedural may not fit with a publisher's lineup of "cozy" mysteries. It will also tell you whether the publisher accepts work by relatively unknown authors, or whether it only publishes "big names."

Check your nearest bookstore for more details about a potential publisher. Pick up a few of its books and look through them. Do you like what you see? Does the cover attract your attention, or make you want to put the book back on the shelf—face in? Do you like the interior design, font, paper quality, and artwork, if any? Would you want to see your own title produced the same way? If not, keep looking.

CHECK THE TERMS

Another question to consider before launching a query or proposal is what your target market can offer—and what it expects from you in return.

One of your first questions will probably be about money. How much does the market pay? When does it pay? If you're pitching a book, what kind of royalties will you be offered, and can you expect an advance? What are those royalties paid *on*: cover price or net sales? A publisher that offers 7 percent on the cover price will actually pay you more than one that offers 15 percent of net (the amount the publisher receives after bookstore and distributor discounts).

Money, however, is only part of the question. Another vital issue is the rights you'll be expected to grant to the publisher. More and more periodical publishers are asking writers to give up all rights, often with no corresponding increase in pay. Even if a market pays "well" for all rights, you should still ask yourself whether you can be absolutely certain that you'll never want to use or resell that material again—or whether you want the publisher to go on profiting from it (e.g., by selling it online) while you never receive another penny.

STEP 2: RESEARCH THE COMPETITION

One of the key questions you'll need to ask before submitting a query or proposal is, Has it already been done? Has a similar article been published by that magazine (or by one of its competitors)? Is a similar column already available in syndication? Has the publisher already produced a book on your topic, or on something very close to your topic?

Researching the competition is absolutely vital when pitching a book proposal. If, for example, the publisher you're targeting has just issued a book about shape-shifting dragons who play rock music in New York, don't expect them to want another manuscript on the same theme. If you're pitching a nonfiction title, you'll be expected to discuss exactly how your book compares to the competition—which means that you'll need to know what else is available on the topic.

Fortunately, you can conduct this much of this research during Step One. By reviewing the titles on the shelves, or in a publisher's online catalog, you'll be able to determine whether that publisher has recently produced any titles similar to yours—or whether a title produced years ago is still a popular seller. You'll also be able to determine what competing publishers are producing, which can work to your advantage in your proposal. (A publisher may be more willing to accept a book that could compete favorably with a title issued by another publisher.)

Checking the competition for a magazine article can be a little more difficult. The primary question you will want to answer is whether the magazine has published a similar article (or even one on a topic close to yours) within the past year or two.

Fortunately, many periodicals now list their back-issue index online. This will give you a list of titles of previously published articles, even if you can't review their contents. Also, many magazines issue an annual index at the end of the year, so if you want to request a sample copy, try to request the December issue.

STEP 3: FOLLOW THE GUIDELINES

This is one of the easiest and most important steps to follow when pitching a query or proposal—yet it is one of the most-often ignored. Many amateur writers suppose that *their* article, story, or proposal will be the "rule breaker"—the one that is so good that the publisher will just have to accept it, even if it breaks every "do" or "don't" in the publisher's guidelines.

This means that you can instantly elevate your proposal above the slush pile by simply following the publisher's guidelines. So, before you send that pitch, be sure that you:

- **Send it to the right person.** Nothing says "I haven't read your guidelines" like mailing a query to an editor who left the company two years ago. Generally, a publication's guidelines will give you the name of the editor you should contact. In some cases, you may have to choose between multiple editors—e.g., one for feature articles, one for departments. Be sure you've chosen the right person! If in doubt, call the publication and ask.

- **Observe the limits on word count.** Don't bother asking a magazine to consider a query for a 3,000-word article if they accept nothing longer than 1,800 words. Similarly, don't propose a 200,000-word book to a publisher who doesn't publish anything longer than 100,000 words. In some cases, you may also need to observe the minimum word count: If a publication says that it publishes articles "between 750 and 1,500 words," don't try to sell them something that's only 500 words.

- **Stick to the rules.** If a publisher says, "No first-person accounts," don't send a first-person account. If it says, "No stories told from the pet's point of view," don't send a manuscript ostensibly written by your poodle. If it says,

"No humor or poetry," don't send humor or poetry. This may sound simplistic—yet it's the rule most often broken by new writers.

- **Understand the audience.** Often, a publisher's guidelines will describe the target audience in terms of age, gender, occupation, interests, and even income. Make sure that your proposal fits into the parameters of that audience. For example, if a magazine targets younger women, an article on retirement communities won't sell—but you might be able to pitch a piece on how to start planning for retirement at twenty-five.

- **Prepare your manuscript correctly.** Most publishers expect writers to understand the basics of manuscript format: double-spaced, wide margins, readable font, etc. Some, however, have specific guidelines. For example, while most editors don't care what font you use as long as it is readable, there are some who want manuscripts to be submitted in Courier (i.e., resembling a typed manuscript). Many publications have very specific guidelines regarding how to submit materials electronically, such as the type of format or word-processing program you must use. Pay special attention to guidelines about how to query by e-mail: If the publisher says "no attachments," never send an attachment. Again, following this simple rule will cause your query to stand out over the dozens that not only ignore the publisher's guidelines, but are prepared by writers who have not learned the basics of manuscript format.

- **Send what the publisher asks for.** If the publisher requests clips, send clips (presuming you have them); don't just refer the editor to your Web site. If the publisher asks for three sample chapters, send three sample chapters and no more. If the publisher asks for a certain number of pages of your novel (regardless of how many chapters that may be), send that number of pages. If the publisher wants a copy of your resume or CV, send it. Don't, however, send anything the publisher has not requested (e.g., unwanted clips or samples, letters of recommendation, reviews, etc.). Never assume that you can improve your case by sending something that the publisher doesn't want.

STEP 4: PREPARE YOUR MANUSCRIPT PROPERLY

When editors are asked for advice on how to "beat the odds," the very first piece of advice they always give is "proofread, spell-check, and format your manuscript properly." Editors are deluged with improperly formatted submissions and submissions riddled with spelling and grammatical errors.

While good spelling and punctuation aren't enough to sell your idea, they *will* set your proposal apart from the majority of the slush pile. Proper format and a "clean" manuscript send the message that you are a professional—even if you've never sold anything in your life. And this is exactly the message you want to send.

Before you send out a query or proposal, therefore, be sure that you have not only run it through your computer's spell checker, but that you have also proofread it visually. Remember that a spell checker won't catch errors in word usage—"there" for "their," or "half" for "have." Errors like these are a dead giveaway that you haven't bothered to proofread your work.

If you have any doubts about your grasp of grammar and punctuation, be sure that the grammar-checking function of your word processor is turned on when you spell-check. This can be a handy tool for catching incomplete phrases, faulty punctuation, etc. Grammar checkers can give faulty results when it comes to style, however, so don't rely on them to actually improve the quality of your writing itself.

If you aren't sure how to format a manuscript properly, find out before mailing anything to an editor. Writer's Digest Books offers an excellent book on manuscript format, and you can also find information on this subject online (see the resource listing at the end of this chapter). Note that different types of proposals may require different formats—for example, a fiction synopsis may be either single- or double-spaced—so check with the publisher or agent for their preferences before submitting.

STEP 5: SEND AN SASE

If you actually want a response to your proposal, be sure to include an SASE (unless, of course, you're submitting via e-mail). If you would like to have your materials returned, send an envelope large enough to hold them, with sufficient postage to cover their return. (If your package weighs more than one pound, however, it's best to simply include a #10 stamped envelope for the publisher's response, as stamped return envelopes weighing more than a pound must now be taken to a post office for delivery.)

If you are submitting to a publisher outside your country, be sure to include at least two IRCs (international reply coupons) for a response. If you can obtain correct postage for that country, that's even better. If you live outside the United States and are submitting material to a U.S. publisher, you can purchase U.S. postage online at *www.stampsonline.com*. (At the time of this writing, it is possible to send a one-ounce letter or SASE from the United States to Canada or Mexico for 60¢, and 80¢ for most other countries.)

If you would like confirmation that an editor or agent received your query or proposal, include a self-addressed, stamped postcard for an immediate response. Just type a line on the back that reads something like:

Dear Author,

We have received your manuscript, "title," on (Date): _____.

We hope to be able to respond to your manuscript by (Date): _____.

(Signed): _____

The second line is optional, but useful if you'd like an estimate of when you can expect to hear from the editor or agent.

STEP 6: FOLLOW UP APPROPRIATELY

The question that plagues every writer when submitting a query or proposal is, How long do I wait for a response? The first and most obvious answer is, As long as the guidelines tell you to wait.

Most publishers provide an estimate of how long it takes them to reply to a query or proposal. Wait until that amount of time has elapsed before following up, even if you've submitted by e-mail. (E-mail submissions are often answered more quickly than surface mail, but don't assume that you can get an instant response to your query just because it's physically possible.) I also prefer to wait at least an additional two weeks before sending a polite inquiry—usually by the same medium as the original proposal (e.g., if a query was sent by e-mail, follow up by e-mail; if it was sent by surface mail, follow up by surface mail). See chapter 2 for more details on following up on an article query, and other chapters for specifics on following up on various other types of proposals.

Never be afraid to follow up on a submission. Many newer writers fear that they will anger an editor or agent by following up, and thus ensure that they are rejected. This is not true. Editors and agents are familiar with the standard courtesies and protocols and will not think you are "overeager" or unprofessional for following up. Quite often, they may simply be so busy that your material has gotten lost in the shuffle, and a follow-up is just what is needed to bring it back to their attention.

STEP 7: BE PROFESSIONAL

This really isn't a step; it's a state of mind. It isn't a matter of how many works you've sold, or how well known you are in your field. It's a matter of how you conduct yourself: A new writer without a credit to his or her name can appear every bit as professional as a writer who has published a dozen novels.

It is remarkably easy to appear professional (so easy, in fact, that it's a wonder that so many writers fail to do so). All you have to do is the following:

- **Learn the basics.** Understand how business is conducted in this industry, and act accordingly. Dozens of books have been published on the basics of the writing profession. You can also find this information on dozens, if not hundreds, of writing Web sites (where the information is absolutely free). To locate some of those sites, see the resource listing at the end of this chapter.

- **Be courteous.** No matter how tempted you are to send a nasty letter to an editor who has taken months to respond to your query, control yourself. This is more true today than ever, as editors are more in touch with one another via the Internet than ever before—which means that word can quickly spread about "problem" writers. The good news is that word also spreads about *good* writers. If you make a positive impression on editors, even when they reject your material, you're likely to make a good name for yourself.

- **Don't reveal your amateur standing.** If you've never published anything before, don't say so. Don't describe yourself as a mother of three, as someone who has always yearned for publication, as a writing student, etc. Don't tell a publisher that your family, friends, or instructors all think you're wonderful. Instead, behave as if writing, and submitting material, is the most natural thing in the world to you—and publishers are likely to believe you!

- **Don't argue, and don't complain.** When you begin to send out work, you *will* be rejected. Sometimes, it may seem that you are rejected for no good reason. Sometimes, you'll get a letter that makes you wonder if the editor even read your query or proposal, as the reasons given for rejection seem to bear no relation to what you actually wrote. When such things happen (and they will), you will not accomplish anything by asking the editor to reconsider—and you certainly won't accomplish anything by sending a nasty letter to the editor questioning his or her ability to read above the second-grade level. In short, even when editors and agents don't behave professionally toward *you,* it is still in your best interest to behave courteously toward *them.*

STEP 8: EXPECT AND ACCEPT REJECTION

Rejection happens. It happens a lot. It happens to everyone—to experienced pros as well as beginners.

Often, your work will be rejected for reasons that have nothing to do with quality. Some of the common reasons for rejection that aren't based on the quality of your work include:

- **Not enough space.** If a magazine can only publish ten articles per month and receives five hundred, 490 of those articles will be rejected—even if they are excellent. Most magazines also have a standard "mix" of articles each month. Thus, if a magazine publishes one medical article every month and it receives three high-quality pieces, two will be rejected.

- **Something similar is already on file.** When you come up with the "perfect" idea for an article or book, don't assume that you're the only person to have thought of it. Often, your proposal will be rejected because a similar piece is already on file that hasn't been published yet, or because something similar has been assigned to another writer. (Never assume, by the way, that if your query is rejected and you subsequently see something on a similar topic from that publisher, that they "stole" your idea. It is very common for editors to receive multiple queries on very similar topics.)

- **Something similar was recently published.** "Recently" usually means "within the past two years." It's just not possible for a writer to obtain every back issue of a publication (unless you're a subscriber), so you often can't determine whether your topic has been covered or not.

- **Something similar was recently published by the competition.** Often, editors don't want to try to compete with another high-quality book or article that is already on the market. Thus, if a book on your topic already dominates the market, you may have a tough time convincing an editor to accept yours, no matter how good it is.

- **The timing is wrong.** "Timing" is one of those subtle, intangible concepts: "I might have bought this a year ago, but I just don't feel like buying it now." Editors' tastes change, and so do the tastes and interests of readers. As editors are usually buying well in advance of publication (as much as six to twelve months for magazines, and as much as two to three years for books), editors aren't just thinking about what is selling *today*, but about what they believe will sell *tomorrow*. So, even though your topic may be "hot" right now, it may still be rejected, simply because the editor doesn't think it will be hot in two years.

- **Indefinable issues of taste.** Sometimes your proposal won't appeal to an editor simply because your writing doesn't match that editor's taste. That doesn't mean your writing is bad; it simply means that it isn't for everyone. Since that's true of every writer—*no* writer has 100 percent worldwide appeal—it's nothing to fret over. Eventually, you'll find the right match.

STEP 9: HONE YOUR SKILLS

Of course, there is always the possibility that your work is being rejected on the basis of quality. No one who writes articles or books about writing likes to come out and say, "Hey, you know, it's possible that your work needs *work*!" But it *is* possible, and you need to be able to accept that possibility—especially if you are experiencing rejection after rejection. Good writers are those who know there is always room for improvement.

There's a little-known secret in the editing business: The worse a writer's work, the less an editor will say about it. This may sound harsh, but look at it from an editor's perspective: Editors are not in the business of trying to train or educate unskilled writers. They are in the business of locating *skilled* writers who can contribute quality material. If an editor feels that a writer's work isn't even *close* to measuring up to that publication's standards, that editor will generally send nothing more than a form rejection. However, the closer a writer is to being publishable, the more likely an editor is to add a personal note to a rejection, perhaps encouraging the writer to try again, perhaps offering a specific comment on areas that need improvement. If an editor suggests a single area for change or improvement, this often means that very little is standing between you and publication.

However, this certainly doesn't mean that every time you receive a form rejection, the editor thought your work was abysmal. The majority of editors *never* make personal comments on rejections, no matter how good a writer's work may be. You can't assume, therefore, that if you're not getting personal rejections, you're no good. However, you *can* assume that if you *are* getting personal notes on your rejections, you're impressing editors, even if you aren't selling your work—*yet*.

Author Lynn Flewelling notes in chapter 15 that it's also important to watch for patterns in your rejections. If five editors reject your stories for five different reasons, this doesn't give you much information. If, however, five editors all say that you need to improve your grammar, or you need to spell-check more carefully, or your work needs to be more organized or less "chatty," this is a good indication of a problem area that needs work. Keep in mind that you are never obligated to follow another person's advice on how to write. If your goal is to sell your writing, however, seeking out and following *good* advice is often a wise idea.

So, if you are starting to feel that you could paper your walls with rejection slips, and you're beginning to wonder whether the problem lies in your writing, find out. Join a critique group that focuses on your type of writing—or join several, and see what type of feedback you receive. Sign up for an online writing course. Do whatever you can to improve your skills.

And finally . . .

STEP 10: KEEP TRYING

Rejection is inevitable. Success is not. However, failure is guaranteed to anyone who gives up after the first rejection, or the third, or the tenth. It isn't hard to find accounts of well-known writers who experienced dozens of rejections before going on to become millionaires.

The true secret of "the perfect pitch" is to find the perfect match—and that may not happen on your first try, or your second, or your tenth. You may have to go back and retool your proposal; you may have to run your material by a critique group; you may have to take some courses to improve your skills. But no matter what you do, the only way to sell your work is to keep trying—and trying, and trying, and trying.

CHAPTER 1 RESOURCES

REFERENCES
The Writer's Digest Guide to Manuscript Format, Writer's Digest Books.

USEFUL WEB SITES
Writing-World.com
www.writing-world.com
Contains a wealth of information on every aspect of the writing business, including a hefty section on "how to get started." At last count, the site offered upwards of 175 feature articles, three columns, 400+ links, and a free biweekly e-mail newsletter.

A Quick Guide to Manuscript Format (by Moira Allen)
www.writing-world.com/basics/manuscript.html

How Online Critiquing Can Help Your Writing (by Moira Allen)
www.writing-world.com/skills/critique.html

MORE BASIC WRITING SITES
Authorlink
www.authorlink.com
Links to publishers' guidelines; articles on writing; writers' organizations; and "The Writer's Store," where authors can post material available for sale.

The Eclectic Writer
www.eclectics.com/writing/writing.html
A number of resources, including many useful articles on various aspects of writing.

Forwriters.com
www.forwriters.com
Though this site tends to emphasize resources for writers of speculative fiction, it has something for everyone, including an excellent research section.

Misc. Writing
www.scalar.com/mw/index.html
Offers a number of excellent resources, including a comprehensive "FAQ" that answers most of a new writer's "getting started" questions. Also has links to writing resources, newsgroups, etc.

Preditors and Editors
www.sfwa.org/prededitors/
Categorized links to a wide range of resources, including agents, publishers, articles, associations, and more.

Pure Fiction
www.purefiction.com/menus/writing.htm
Among other resources, this site has good lists of editors, publishers, and agents.

RedInkWorks
www.redinkworks.com/writing_tips.htm
Links to a selection of good articles from various writing/authors' sites.

Resources for Writers

www.geocities.com/dboals.geo/write.html

Browsing this site (part of the History/Social Studies Web Site for K–12 Teachers) is like exploring a used bookstore: You never know what treasures you'll find in the way of fascinating, useful, and unusual links. For research, be sure to check its history and sociology links, which include a range of primary resources (such as journals and original documents).

WriteLinks

www.writelinks.com

This site offers one of the largest collections of links for writers on the Web. It also hosts critique groups, editing and tutorial services through "The Friendly Pencil," and a free newsletter.

The Writer's Center

www.writer.org/resources/resource.htm

Offers a number of useful articles (including a guide to scams), plus a dictionary of basic writing, editing, and publishing terms.

Writers.com

www.writers.com

Classes, workshops, a message forum, fun quizzes, a monthly newsletter, and other resources.

Writer's Toolbox: Internet Resources for Writers

www.writerstoolbox.com

Links, chat, and articles.

Writers Write

www.writerswrite.com

Links, critique groups, a writing "university," contests, job listings, book promotion services, classifieds, a guidelines directory, and the *Internet Writing Journal*.

Zuzu's Petals Literary Resources

www.zuzu.com

A particularly useful site if you're looking for lists (such as magazines, newspapers, libraries, associations, etc.). Unfortunately, many lists are text-only (no hot-links).

Section 1
_____

QUERYING PERIODICALS

2

WRITING THE (ALMOST) PERFECT QUERY

Perhaps the most common form of writing "pitch" is the query letter. This is the first, and often only, opportunity you have to convince an editor that you have something to offer. Hence, a query can be the "make-or-break" point of your writing career. Nearly every other type of proposal or pitch in this book involves some type of query, so mastering this skill is vital.

WHY QUERY?

Many writers wonder why editors would rather see a query than a finished article. How can a one-page letter demonstrate the quality and content of a 2,000-word piece? Wouldn't an editor be able to make a more informed decision if he or she could read the entire article?

Queries also add an extra delay: You have to wait for a response to your query before you can receive a response to the article itself. Wouldn't eliminating the query cut the waiting time in half? In addition, most of us prefer to write about a topic when it is fresh in our minds, but by the time we receive a response to a query, we've usually gone on to other things. Isn't it more logical to write the article at once?

These are all valid concerns. However, the primary issue is not whether a query is "better" than an article. The issue is that in most cases, writers don't have a choice. Editors today are inundated with badly written, inappropriate manuscripts. In response, many are closing their doors to unsolicited submissions. The better-paying or more prestigious the market, the more likely it is to insist on queries. Other publications pay less for unsolicited material than assigned material, which means that querying first can increase your income—in some cases by hundreds of dollars. In short, queries are no longer optional; often, they are a writer's only chance of making a sale.

BENEFITS FOR ALL

Queries benefit writers *and* editors. Perhaps the most obvious benefit to an editor is a query's length: it's easier to review a one-page letter than a ten-page manuscript. Queries enable an editor to determine, almost at a glance, whether a writer:

- Can write effectively
- Has a coherent, well-thought-out idea
- Has a basic grasp of grammar and spelling
- Has read the publication
- Has an idea that fits into the publication's content
- Has the expertise or credentials to write the article
- Approaches markets in a professional manner (a factor that doesn't necessarily depend on writing experience)

Queries also save time for the writer. Writing a single-page query is a much smaller investment in time and effort than writing an entire article. By querying first, you avoid wasting time and research on an article that may be rejected—perhaps because the editor already has a similar article on file or has run something like it in the past, or for any of a dozen other reasons that have nothing to do with the actual quality of your work.

A query also gives the editor a chance to give you feedback on your idea before you write the article, so you can tailor that article precisely to the needs of that market and audience. An editor might want a longer article than you proposed, or a shorter one. The editor might want you to include interviews with certain experts, or to provide specific information in a sidebar. Querying saves you from having to make time-consuming revisions to your material, and ensures that the editor receives exactly what he or she desires.

Sometimes, a query can result in a completely different assignment. If an editor is impressed by your credentials and writing style, but can't use the idea you've proposed, he or she may approach you with an alternate suggestion. When this happens, it often opens the door to a long and productive relationship.

Finally, it's much easier to set up interviews when you have a firm go-ahead from an editor. Experts are far more willing to talk to you if you have an actual assignment and can explain exactly where the material will be published. It also prevents you from wasting an interviewee's time when you don't know whether you'll be able to find a market for your article or not.

ESSENTIALS OF AN EFFECTIVE QUERY

Take another look at the things an editor can determine from your query. The goal of a query is to make a positive impression in each of those areas. If you miss even one, you risk rejection. It may seem impossible to cover all those bases in a single page, but it can be done. All you need is five basic components:

- The hook
- The pitch (or offer)
- The body
- The credentials
- The close

Each component is vital, but none is especially difficult. Most involve little more than common sense and the ability to write effectively.

THE HOOK

Like an article, a query should grab an editor's attention from the very first line. Indeed, many writers use the first line of their proposed article to open their query. That first line, the "hook," should also demonstrate your ability to write effectively and interestingly—and it should also demonstrate that you are familiar with the publication you are targeting.

A hook can be a single sentence or a brief paragraph. Hooks come in all forms; some of the most common include:

The "Problem/Solution" Hook

One way to "hook" the editor is by demonstrating exactly how the information in your article will benefit the reader. A good way to do this is to define a problem common to many of the publication's readers—and then propose an article that will help solve that problem.

Don't just state what your article is about. Show how the topic relates to the reader— *why* it is a problem. For example, if you are writing about cancer in pets, don't just say, "I want to send you an article about cancer in pets." Instead, demonstrate the significance of this topic to the reader: "No diagnosis is so dreaded by pet owners as the word 'cancer'." Then, explain how your article can help: "Fortunately, if an owner knows how to spot the signs of cancer early, this diagnosis doesn't have to mean the end of hope."

Following are examples of some successful problem/solution hooks:

- The pet magazine market is an ideal place for newer writers to "break in." However, it is constantly flooded with inappropriate submissions. To break in, one must understand what these magazines want, and what they won't accept. ("Writing for Pet Magazines," sold to *Byline*[1] [see chapter 3, figure 1 for full query].)

- For anyone who enjoys decorating with antique or delicate quilts, care is a vital concern. Most of us realize that we can't just pop Granny's handmade quilt into the washing machine or douse it with bleach, but what are the alternatives? How can we protect fine fabrics from further dirt and damage? ("Caring for Quilts: How to Preserve a Perishable Heirloom," sold to *Traditional Quiltworks* [see chapter 3, figure 2].)

---

[1]Available online at *www.writing-world.com/freelance/pets.html*.

• Writing is a solitary endeavor. Day after day, night after night, freelance writers make time with computers, often to the detriment of human contact. We forget that "solitary" does not mean "isolation." ("Networking: The Key to Balance in a Writer's Life," by Terri Mrosko, sold to *Inklings* [See chapter 3, figure 3].)

Be sure that your problem actually does affect (or at least interest) a large percentage of the publication's audience! By doing so, and by offering a solution appropriate to that audience, you provide solid evidence of your familiarity with the publication.

The Informative Hook

This type of hook typically presents two or three lines of useful or intriguing information (such as facts or statistics), followed by an explanation of how it relates the target audience.

To open a query on cancer in pets, for example, you might say, "Every year, XX percent of America's pets will be diagnosed with cancer. Of those, XX percent will die within the first year. But you can beat those odds by taking advantage of new treatments and technologies that significantly prolong a pet's life . . . "

Here's an example of an information hook:

Thanks to a translation glitch, Microsoft was forced to pull its entire Chinese edition of Windows 95 from the marketplace. Microsoft recovered—but that's the sort of mistake few small businesses can afford! ("How to Localize Your Web Site," sold to *Entrepreneur's Home Office* [see chapter 3, figure 4].)

For this type of hook to work, your information must actually be interesting (and relevant)! Your goal is to intrigue the editor with information that may not be commonly known, not to bore the reader with a host of statistics.

The Question

A problem/solution hook or information hook can also be posed as a question, such as:

• Did you know . . . ?

• What would you do if . . . ?

• Have you ever wondered . . . ?

Your goal is to capture the editor's attention with an intriguing question to which (presumably) he or she may not know the answer. However, such a hook also poses an inherent risk: If the editor's answer to "Did you know?" is "Yes," or if the editor's answer to "Have you ever wondered?" is "No," your hook may fail. Save this hook for unusual items; don't use it for obvious questions.

The Personal Experience/Anecdote

A personal-experience hook can be used to demonstrate that you have personally solved the problem or lived through the experience you intend to write about. This hook is effective when querying publications that commonly use first-person articles, articles with lots of anecdotes, or articles that have a more informal or personal tone.

Here are some ways to work your experiences into a query:

- Last summer, our beloved fifteen-year-old cat succumbed to cancer. Along the way, we learned a great deal about this disease and how it affects cats. ("Answers to Cancer," sold to *Cats Magazine* [see chapter 3, figure 5].)

- As a full-time freelancer, I also teach writing classes. During a recent query letter critique, one of my students raised her hand. "I feel like I know how to write a good query," she said hesitantly. "But I keep worrying about sending them out. What will I do if I actually get an assignment?" She seemed surprised that I could relate to her fear . . . ("Conquering Writers' Anxiety," by Kelly James-Enger, sold to *Inklings* [see chapter 3, figure 6].)

- Forget-me-nots. I love their wistful name. I love their tiny blue flowers. And yes, I love that growing them is as simple as pie. ("Forget-Me-Nots: Simply Unforgettable Spring Flowers," by Mary Rose, sold to *Fine Gardening* [see chapter 3, figure 7].)

Don't use this type of hook for markets that do not use personal experience articles, first-person articles, or anecdotal material.

The Attention-Grabber

The purpose of this type of hook is to make an editor sit up and take notice—hopefully long enough to read the rest of your query. It can range from a snippet of dialogue to an evocative declaration:

As I fell from the top of Yosemite's El Capitan, I wondered if my life would truly flash before my eyes—or if I would stop screaming long enough to notice.

Such a hook must be truly "grabby." It must also lead to an appropriate article. If your "El Capitan" hook leads to an article about illegal parachuting in Yosemite, it might lead to a sale; if it was just a bad dream brought on by indigestion (and you're actually pitching an article about foods to avoid before bedtime), you might want to try something else.

Hooks to Avoid

Certain hooks scream "amateur" and are guaranteed to speed your query to the rejection pile. These include:

- **The personal introduction.** Never begin with a line like, "Hello, my name is John Smith, and I'd like to write an article about . . . " Don't give the editor irrelevant personal information, such as, "I have been a writer for seven years, and I'd like to offer you a piece on . . . ," or, "I am a housewife and mother of three lovely children, and have recently decided to pursue my life-long dream of writing . . . ." Unless your hook actually calls for a personal experience, keep yourself out of it.

- **The "suck-up" hook.** Don't bother telling editors how much you enjoy their publication; prove it by offering an appropriate query. Editors aren't impressed by queries that proclaim, "I've been a subscriber to your magazine for twenty years, and I have the perfect story for you . . . "

- **The "bid-for-sympathy" hook.** Never tell an editor that this is your first attempt to get published, or that you need to sell this article to put food on the table. A query that begins "I am an unpublished mother of three" simply alerts the editor to the fact that you don't know what you're doing.

- **The "I'm perfect for you" hook.** Don't sing your praises ("I am a high-ly experienced professional and will be an asset to your magazine") or those of your article ("I know your readers will love this piece"). Don't tell an editor that your article is "good" or "informative" or whatever. Your query is a sales tool; it's not a press release. If you can't demonstrate the value of your article (or your writing ability) in the query itself, no amount of hype will help.

- **The "I'm an amateur" hook.** Never announce that you haven't been published before, or that you have tried to sell this same article to twenty other magazines, or that you're not sure how to write a query. Proclaiming your amateur status will not cause an editor to treat you more kindly or cut you some slack. Also, never tell an editor that your writing teacher suggested that you submit a piece for publication, or that your friends all think you're the next Erma Bombeck. Be professional, even if you haven't sold anything before.

- **The "I hope you're smarter than they are" hook.** I've never grasped the logic of telling an editor that other publications have already rejected the article you're proposing. Generally, such queries imply that all those *other* editors were dumb—but that you're hoping *this* editor will be smart enough to recognize a good thing when he or she sees it. In reality, editors trust the judg-ment of other editors: If you reveal that your work has already been rejected several times, an editor will suspect that there may be a good reason for this.

Finally, make sure you choose a hook that matches the style of your target publication. If the publication never uses personal experiences or first-person accounts, don't use the personal-experience hook. If a market never publishes statistical information, don't load your hook with facts and figures. If the publication uses a conservative style, don't offer an overly dramatic "attention-grabber." Use your hook to demonstrate that you are familiar with the publication's style and tone—and that you know how to write for that particular audience.

THE PITCH

Once you've "hooked" the editor, it's time to move on to the pitch. This usually appears in the next paragraph, though it may sometimes appear in the same paragraph as your hook.

Your "pitch" describes what you are offering. Often, you'll start by explaining how your article will solve the problem or answer the question posed in your hook. It's also the place to offer a working title for your article and a suggested word count. (Though a title isn't necessary, it can help the editor grasp your concept.)

Here are some of the pitches that followed the hooks listed above:

- I'd like to offer you a 1,500-word article titled "Internationalizing Your Online Market." The article would discuss how small businesses can take advantage of "localizing" agents to tailor their products and market strategies to the international marketplace." (Article published as: "How to Localize Your Web Site.")

- "Forget-Me-Nots: Simply Unforgettable Spring Flowers" is an exuberant, thousand-word profile detailing . . . ("Forget-Me-Nots: Simply Unforgettable Spring Flowers.")

- Cancer is not an immediate death sentence for a cat; some forms of cancer can be managed medically to prolong a cat's life with little or no discomfort. However, it is vital to recognize the presence of cancer early, and discuss options and treatments with a veterinarian as soon as possible. To help your readers do just that, I propose a 2,500-word article on "Cancer in Cats." ("Answers to Cancer.")

Before you start your pitch, be sure that you've checked the publication's guidelines. Don't offer a 2,000-word article to a publication that only publishes shorts!

THE BODY

The body is the largest section of the query and the section with the greatest power to make or break a sale. It is usually two to four paragraphs in length and presents the details of the article you are proposing.

An editor wants to know exactly what your article will cover. That means you must know the answers to the questions you plan to address—and have a working outline of your article in mind.

A good way to summarize your proposed article is to divide it into logical subtopics. The longer the article, the more subtopics you are likely to include. For example, if you are writing about cancer in pets, a 700-word article would probably cover only one topic (e.g., "the warning signs of cancer"). A 2,000-word article, however, might cover three to five subtopics (e.g., "common types of cancer," "warning signs," and "treatments"). If you have too many subtopics, your article will appear too generalized, without enough in-depth information in each area. If you have too few, your word count may seem inflated. One way to determine if you have the right balance is to divide the word count by the number of topics: A 2,000-word article with five subtopics gives you 400 words per topic.

List those topics, with a brief description of each, in the body of your query. Here's how I outlined my "Cancer in Cats" article:

My article will cover:

- The types of cancers most common in cats (including mammary tumors and cancers of the mouth, lips, and gums—some of which are preventable!).

- How to recognize the signs of cancer early (what is that lump?).

- The symptoms and progression of various types of cancer (weight loss, diminished appetite, coughing, and wheezing can all be signs of cancer).

- The types of treatments available, pros and cons of different treatments, how treatments can affect a cat's life expectancy and quality of life, and how to find treatment (not every city has an animal cancer clinic).

Some writers like to use bullet points to set off their subtopics. Others use plain paragraphs. In some cases, the entire body of your query may fit into a single paragraph, like the following:

The article covers techniques of hand-cleaning delicate quilts to avoid damaging fragile fabrics and prevent fading and staining. It discusses ways to remove spot stains (including blood spots and rust stains from needles and other metal contact). It also discusses ways to mend damaged quilts without destroying the integrity of an heirloom piece. Finally, it discusses the best ways to store or display quilts in order to preserve and protect them. ("Caring for Heirloom Quilts.")

There is no rule as to the best presentation style. You don't want an editor to become bogged down in a twenty-line paragraph, however, so try to make your letter visually appealing as well as informative. Make sure that the editor can determine what you are offering quickly and easily.

Mistakes to Avoid

Since the body of a query is a writer's only opportunity to describe the article, writers make two common mistakes: not saying enough and saying too much. Here's how to avoid these errors:

- **Don't use your query as a fishing expedition.** Don't write a query when you don't actually have an article in mind, but simply want to discover whether an editor has an interest in a particular topic or subject area. (See chapter 4 for exceptions to this rule.) Also, don't query simply to let an editor know that you are available for assignments, unless you have already worked with this editor. Impress the editor with your ideas and material first; then, after you've sold two or three articles, you can ask for assignments.

- **Don't tease.** Don't tell editors that they will have to read your article to find the answers to the questions you've posed. Answer those questions in the query itself. Editors will want to know exactly what you have to say on a topic before asking to see your article.

- **Don't raise questions to which you don't have the answers.** A common error is to promise that, once you have been given the assignment, you will find out the answers to the questions you pose in your query. This, however, indicates that you don't already have those answers. Don't say, "I will interview experts to try to find out the best solution for Problem X." Since you can't provide details about the solution, an editor will not be able to determine whether the results of your research will be useful.

- **Don't clutter your query with data.** An editor wants to know the *type* of information your article will cover—but not necessarily the facts and figures themselves. If you're covering cancer treatments, for example, explain that you will cover specific therapies and name them—but don't go into detail about how they work. Save that for the article.

- **Don't overdescribe your article.** Some writers try to cram chunks of their article into the query. Avoid this temptation! Your query is not a condensed version of your final article; it is a summary of that article. Think of it as a description, an overview. (If you have trouble summarizing what your article is about without using portions of the article itself, try explaining the article out loud to another person without actually looking at the text.)

THE CREDENTIALS

Besides wanting to know what your article is about, editors also want to know why *you* are the best person to write it. (Sometimes this section can be very creative!)

Credentials do not necessarily have to include writing credits. Often, other credentials (such as professional experience) are more important. You should also check the publication's guidelines, and bylines of other authors in the publication, to determine what credentials are most valued by that publication. Relevant credentials are most likely to include:

- **Professional experience.** If you work (or have experience) in the field about which you are writing, this is often the best credential of all. Many editors would rather work with an expert who is a mediocre writer than work with a good writer who may not have sufficient knowledge of the subject. For example, Mary Rose sold her article on forget-me-nots on the basis of being an experienced gardener (which she demonstrated by submitting photos of her garden); it was her first article sale. Some publications, in fact, will accept material *only* from experts.

- **Academic degrees or training.** If you have a degree or specialized training in a field, that is often enough to convince an editor that you can write about it. Some types of publications (including academic and scientific journals) accept material only from writers who have the necessary academic credentials.

- **Teaching experience.** If you teach about the subject you're proposing, you can probably convince an editor that you have the ability to communicate effectively about that subject—and, therefore, write about it.

- **Personal experience.** If your article is about personal experiences, or personal self-help topics, you may be able to sell it on the basis of your own experience. For example, if you're writing about finding a retirement home for an elderly relative, you may be able to pitch that article on the basis of having gone through this experience yourself. On the other hand, you may have difficulty pitching an article on child-rearing techniques simply on the basis of having been a parent. Keep in mind that personal experience will not substitute for professional credentials in publications that prefer articles written by experts.

- **Writing experience.** Different publications place different levels of value on previous writing experience. Some insist upon it; others don't care. Some editors are only interested in whether you have written on relevant topics; for example, a history publication may not be impressed by the fact that you've sold several articles to gardening magazines. If you have written only fiction, that may not help you sell a nonfiction article (unless it is *about* writing fiction), and vice versa. Also, the less professional your writing experience, the less it will help you. Being "published" in arenas that are considered equivalent to "self-publishing" (such as the now-defunct Themestream site) won't help you at all. If your publication credits are limited to nonprofit newsletters or post-it-yourself Web sites, it would be better to focus on other credentials.

- **Interviews.** If you don't have the right credentials yourself, one way to sell your article is to interview other experts who *do* have the necessary credentials. This is often the ideal solution when you can't demonstrate relevant expertise.

The best place to list your credentials is usually in the last, or next-to-last, paragraph of your query, right after the body. Here are some examples:

- As Webmaster of *www.musicphotographer.com,* it has been my job to connect music writers and photographers with the markets that need their work. This is the only site devoted to music journalism on the Web. I'm also writing the first guide on the topic. Reviews for my last book, *The Van Halen Encyclopedia,* are available at Amazon.com. ("How to Write for the Music Market," by C.J. Chilvers, sold to Inkspot [see chapter 3, figure 8].)

- I currently have over seventy-five articles published in the *West Life,* the *Plain Dealer,* and the *News Sun* newspapers; magazines, including *Women as Managers* and *Asthma Magazine;* and e-zines, such as *Inscriptions* and the *Writing Parent.* I specialize in career and business management articles. ("Networking: The Key to Balance in the Writer's Life," by Terri Mrosko, sold to *Inklings* [see chapter 3, figure 3].)

THE CLOSE

Use your closing paragraph to thank the editor for taking the time to consider your proposal, and make a final "offer" to help close the deal. I usually use this paragraph to provide an estimate of when the article can be delivered, if assigned:

> If you'd like to see the article, I can have it in your hands within thirty days of your go-ahead. Thanks for your time and attention; I look forward to hearing from you.

The close can also be used to encourage the editor to follow up with questions, or for clarification:

> Interested in this topic for *Inklings?* As a self-employed writer who often struggles with writing-related anxiety, I believe I can bring a unique perspective to this piece. Let me know if you have any questions about this story idea, and thank you for your time. ("Conquering Writers' Anxiety," by Kelly James-Enger.)

Closes like these show professionalism and courtesy—two factors that always appeal to overworked, underappreciated editors!

FORMAT

The presentation of your letter is nearly as important as its content. A badly formatted letter (typed on erasable bond with a faded ribbon and smudged with corrections) will not inspire an editor to read further. It's no use arguing that appearances shouldn't matter and that content is all that counts; editors assume that if you can't handle the basics, you won't be able to handle the more important stuff either.

A well-formatted query includes the following elements:

- **A decent letterhead.** If you have a computer, you can design a basic letterhead simply by printing your name and address at the top of the page in an

attractive (but not overly fancy) font. You can also design an inexpensive letterhead online at iPrint.com (*www.iprint.com*), or choose from a range of
templates and designs. Or, ask your local print shop to design and print a letterhead for you on quality paper.

- **A business-style body.** If you aren't familiar with terms like "block" or
"modified block," don't worry. Just follow the examples in chapter 3. Always
include a blank line between paragraphs, and don't indent more than five
spaces (if you indent at all).

- **Contact information.** Your letterhead should include full contact information, including your full name (or pen name), address, telephone number,
fax number (if any), and e-mail address (if any). It isn't necessary to include
your URL; include that in your credentials section if you wish to refer an editor to your Web site.

- **A formal salutation.** Unless you know the editor personally, don't use first
names. If you're not sure whether the editor is male or female, use the editor's
title (Dear Editor Johnson:).

- **Clean, spell-checked copy.** A query riddled with typos won't lead to a
sale. And don't rely solely on your computer's spell checker; visually proofread
your query as well. If you're using a typewriter and make errors, type a fresh
copy.

- **Quality paper.** Always use a paper that is at least 20-pound bond. Some
writers use fancy textured bonds or colored papers for queries, on the theory
that this will help them stand out from all the plain white paper on an editor's
desk. Don't get too fancy, however; stick with subtle colors (such as ivory, gray,
or parchment). Never use colored inks, and avoid those tempting papers with
pretty borders or decorative designs that you can find in office supply stores.
Never use erasable paper.

- **An SASE (self-addressed, stamped envelope).** Don't use a #9
(insert) envelope for your SASE; use a full-size business envelope (#10), fold-
ed in thirds. Be sure it has adequate postage. (If you are submitting to a publication in another country, don't put your own country's postage on the SASE;
include International Reply Coupons [IRCs] instead. One IRC is usually sufficient for postage between the United States and Canada; two are advisable for
correspondence between other countries.)

CLIPS

Many editors request clips, which are copies of previously published materials. The key word
here is "published"—never send unpublished material as a clip!

It is always best to send clips that are relevant to your target market, if you have them. If you're pitching to a gardening market, send gardening clips. If, however, you don't have relevant clips, send the very best clips you have (e.g., from the most prestigious publications). Even a gardening editor will probably be somewhat impressed by a clip from *Smithsonian Magazine,* even if it's on a completely different subject.

It is not a copyright violation to photocopy your own articles (even if you've sold all rights) for use as clips. You are not trying to "publish" that material (unless you're submitting them as reprints); you're simply using them as examples of your writing ability. Don't bother making color copies, unless the clips also include examples of your own photography.

Many writers now struggle with the question of how to present electronic clips. Somehow, a printout of an article published online doesn't look the same as a printed page. Such work is every bit as valid, however, if it comes from a reputable publication. Be sure that your printout includes the name of the online publication, if possible.

Writers whose work appears primarily online are often tempted to refer editors to the location of that material. This is becoming increasingly acceptable, but use caution. If an editor asks for clips, send at least one hard copy, and then refer the editor to the URLs of other work. (See chapter 4 for tips on sending clips with e-mail queries.)

Don't send clips of unpublished work, or work that has only appeared on your own Web site or a self-publishing Web site. No matter how good these materials are, they are not considered "published" by current editorial standards. It's also better to avoid sending clips from amateur publications, such as office or nonprofit newsletters, unless they directly relate to your proposal or support your credentials. Don't send copies of letters to the editor; these are not considered publications. Remember, a bad clip is worse than no clip at all!

And what if you *have* no clips at all? Don't despair. Most editors will consider the merits of your query first, and your samples second. (To be honest, many editors just don't have time to read clips, even though they request them.) If your query is strong enough and you can offer appropriate credentials, the lack of clips won't necessarily ruin your chances, unless the publication specifies that it works *only* with published writers.

RESPONSE TIME

I usually allow another two weeks over the published response time before following up on a query. Then, it's time for a polite inquiry as to the status of your proposal. Usually, this should be sent via the same medium as your original query—if you queried by e-mail, use e-mail. If you queried by surface mail, use surface mail. Your inquiry should simply ask whether your query or proposal was received, and if it was, when you might anticipate a response. Send a copy of the original query, so that the editor won't have to dig it up out of the file; this will also encourage a more immediate reply.

If you still do not receive a response after another two to three weeks, you may wish to send a more urgent follow-up—e.g., "I would like to know whether this query is still under consideration, so that I may send it on to other markets if it is not." It's also not out of line to call the editor or agent at this point, and ask (*very* politely) whether your proposal has been received and whether it is being reviewed or considered for acceptance.

Sadly, more and more writers are reporting that they no longer receive any response from editors who don't intend to use their material. Many editors are no longer bothering to send out rejection letters, even when you enclose an SASE. Besides being discourteous, this is profoundly frustrating for writers, who have no sure way of determining the status of their material.

If you still receive no response to your second or third inquiry, your best bet is usually to assume that your material is *not* being considered. It is then advisable to send a final letter to the editor, formally withdrawing your material from consideration. This letter can be phrased very simply:

> Dear (Editor):
>
> As I have not received a response from your office regarding my query for (article title) that was submitted on (date), I am assuming that you are not considering this material for publication, and am hereby withdrawing the material from consideration. Thank you for your time and assistance.

This "withdrawal" letter is important, as it protects you from the appearance of having submitted material to two publications simultaneously. If the first editor or agent *does* finally respond to your query after you've sent it somewhere else, the second editor won't feel that you've violated publishing protocol.

The ability to write a good query is one of the most important skills a writer can develop. A good query shows that you can write and that you are a professional—qualities that may result in an assignment even if the editor can't use your original proposal. Think of a query as your letter of introduction: If you make a good impression, you are likely to be invited back. If you make a bad impression, you may find that door forever closed.

And if the door doesn't open, don't panic. Repolish your query, tailor it for another market, and send it out again. It can often take two or three tries before you find the right article for a particular market—or the right market for a particular article. Eventually, if you are persistent and professional, your work *will* find a home.

3

QUERY LETTERS THAT WORKED

O n the following pages, you'll find a selection of queries that led to article sales. Some are my own; others are queries that I've received (and accepted) as managing editor of the Inkspot Web site and *Inklings* newsletter. These (and the query from Mary Rose) are used with the permission of their authors.

Please note that while I have included editors' names on most of these queries (though not the actual addresses of the publications), many of these editors are no longer at those publications. Please do not use these queries as "guidelines" for submitting to the publications themselves.

Figure 1: Query to *Byline*

Moira Allen

address • city/state/zip
phone • fax
e-mail

March 10, 1997

Marcia Preston, Editor
Byline
(address)
(city/state/zip)

Dear Ms. Preston:

The pet magazine market is an ideal place for newer writers to "break in." However, it is constantly flooded with inappropriate submissions. To break in, one must understand what these magazines want, and what they won't accept. I'd like to offer you an 1800-word article on how to write for the pet markets, covering the following topics:

• The types of articles pet markets are hungry for (e.g., care, training, health, breed), and how to write them even if you're not an "expert."

• How to win assignments from the major pet magazines (and even how to be considered for a column).

• The types of articles pet magazines don't want to see, and why ("my first puppy," "the day my cat died," talking pets, etc.).

• How to turn a personal experience article into a marketable service piece.

• Understanding the different markets (including why all dog magazines are not the same), what they expect, what they pay, and what you can expect from them.

I'm the ideal person to write this article, as I was the editor of *Dog Fancy* for two years and am thoroughly familiar with all the major pet publications. I have been writing for the pet markets for more than ten years and am a member of the Dog Writers' Association of America. I am the author of the award-winning *Coping with Sorrow on the Loss of Your Pet* (Alpine, 1996). I also teach professional and creative writing at two local colleges, including a class on this topic.

If you'd like to see the article, I can have it in your hands within 30 days of your go-ahead. Thanks for your time and attention; I look forward to hearing from you.

Sincerely,

Moira Allen

Figure 2: Query to *Traditional Quiltworks*

Moira Allen

address • city/state/zip

phone • fax

e-mail

Editorial Team
Traditional Quiltworks

Dear Editors:

For anyone who enjoys decorating with antique or delicate quilts, care is a vital concern. Most of us realize that we can't just pop Granny's handmade quilt into the washing machine or douse it with bleach, but what are the alternatives? How can we protect fine fabrics from further dirt and damage?

To help your readers answer this question, I would like to offer you a 1,900-word article titled "How to Care for an Antique Quilt." The article covers techniques of hand-cleaning delicate quilts to avoid damaging fragile fabrics and prevent fading and staining. It discusses ways to remove spot stains (including blood spots and rust stains from needles and other metal contact). It also discusses ways to mend damaged quilts without destroying the integrity of an heirloom piece. Finally, it discusses the best ways to store or display quilts in order to preserve and protect them.

An earlier version of this article appeared in *Quilt* in 1988. I am offering second serial rights to the article, which has been revised and updated. I have been freelancing for more than 18 years, and my articles have appeared in *Quilt, Omni, Writer's Digest, Dog Fancy,* and many other magazines.

If you are interested in this article, I can have it on your desk within a week. Thank you for your time and consideration; I look forward to hearing from you.

Sincerely,

Moira Allen

[NOTE: Normally, one would address a query to a specific editor. However, this particular publishing group prefers queries and submissions to be addressed to the "Editorial Team"—a fact I verified by phone before sending the query.]

Figure 3: Query to *Inklings* (sent via e-mail)

```
Moira Allen
Managing Editor, Inkspot

Dear Ms. Allen:

Writing is a solitary endeavor. Day after day, night after night,
freelance writers make time with computers, often to the detriment
of human contact. We forget that solitary does not mean isolation.

There is a human side to writing, and freelance writers need to
ensure that we stay in touch with others. We need to make it a
point to pursue this contact. The human side of writing entails
interaction via:

Networking--Essential to marketing your ideas, products, and services.

Editors--Learning to make direct contact now and then to enhance
the quality of your work.

Interviews--The writer must interject the human element into their
articles through direct contact and information from others.

Family and friends--Don't neglect this important contact, even on
your busiest days.

My article will highlight the importance of the human side of
writing and offer suggestions and insight on how to work this
essential element into your day. It doesn't matter what stage your
writing career is at; we all need human contact.

I currently have over seventy-five articles published in the
_West Life_, the _Plain Dealer_, and the _News Sun_ newspapers;
magazines including _Women as Managers_ and _Asthma Magazine_;
and e-zines including _Inscriptions Magazine_ and the _Writing
Parent_. I specialize in career and business management articles.

Please let me know at your earliest convenience if you are
interested in this article.

Thank you for your consideration.

Terri Mrosko
Communications Services
Media/Business/Editorial
(e-mail/phone/fax)
Writing samples: (URLs of online publications listed)
```

[NOTE: This query is formatted for e-mail and contains no bullets, italics, or other formatting that would cause problems in an e-mail message.]

Figure 4: Query to *Entrepreneur Magazine*

Moira Allen

address • city/state/zip
phone • fax

December 17, 1996

(Editor's name)
Entrepreneur Magazine

Dear Ms. (Editor):

Thanks to a translation glitch, Microsoft was forced to pull its entire Chinese edition of Windows 95 from the marketplace. Microsoft recovered—but that's the sort of mistake few small businesses can afford! Yet, thanks to the Internet, international markets are suddenly only a few keystrokes away. Just about any home office entrepreneur with a computer and a modem can create a Web page that may be accessed around the world. If those keystrokes are wrong, however, that same page can drive international business away.

I'd like to offer you a 1,500-word article titled "Internationalizing Your Online Market." The article would discuss how small businesses can take advantage of "localizing" or "internationalizing" agents to tailor both their products and their marketing strategies to the international marketplace. Localizing includes not only translation assistance, but advice on "cultural correctness" in both one's product and marketing approach. For example:

• When is a mailbox not a mailbox? "Standard" computer icons often reflect images that are incomprehensible or offensive to other cultures—including images of American-style mailboxes that may have no counterpart in the market you're trying to reach.
• When are pictures of babies offensive? In Moslem countries, the display of bare body parts (even diaper-clad babies) is unacceptable, even when considered modest by Western standards.
• Is it really black and white? In the West, black is the color of funerals and white is the color of weddings. But in Asia, white symbolizes mourning and death, while red symbolizes marriage.
• Does anybody know what time it is? Depending on your market, it could be 3:30 P.M., 1530, 15h.30, 15.30, or 15:30. Times, dates, and currency expressions vary widely throughout the world!

My article would describe the types of services available from a localizer, the costs involved, and how to find such services. It will highlight "internationalizing" a Web page to make it more effective, "culturally correct," and user-friendly in the international market. The article will include an interview with Sol Squires, president of Twin Dragons, who will share some of the blunders that can be avoided with localization help.

When even the smallest of businesses are capable of offering products and services via computer to the international marketplace, business owners need to know how to avoid the pitfalls of this type of marketing. I believe this article would be timely and useful to your audience; if you agree, I can provide the piece within thirty days of your go-ahead. Thanks for your time; I look forward to hearing from you.

Sincerely,

Moira Allen
Encs.

Figure 5: Query to *Cats Magazine*

Moira Allen

address • city/state/zip
phone • fax
e-mail

Annette Bailey, Editor
Cats Magazine
(address)
(city/state/zip)

Dear Ms. Bailey:

Last summer, our beloved fifteen-year-old cat succumbed to cancer. Along the way, we learned a lot about this disease and how it affects cats.

Cancer is not an immediate death sentence for a cat; some forms of cancer can be managed medically to prolong a cat's life with little or no discomfort. However, it is vital to recognize the presence of cancer early and discuss options and treatments with a veterinarian as soon as possible. To help your readers do just that, I propose a 2,500-word article on "Cancer in Cats." The article would cover:

• The types of cancers most common in cats (including mammary tumors and cancers of the mouth, lips, and gums—some of which are preventable!).
• How to recognize the signs of cancer early (what is that lump?).
• The symptoms and progression of various types of cancer (weight loss, diminished appetite, coughing, and wheezing can all be signs of cancer).
• The types of treatments available, pros and cons of different treatments, how treatments can affect a cat's life expectancy and quality of life, and how to find treatment (not every city has an animal cancer clinic).

The article would include information on cancer treatment from Dr. Alice Villalobos, head of the Animal Cancer Center in Hermosa Beach, California, and from the local veterinarian who assisted me during my own cat's illness.

You are already familiar with my qualifications as a pet writer from our previous correspondence (former editor of *Dog Fancy* and associate editor of *Cat Fancy,* author of *Coping with Sorrow on the Loss of Your Pet,* etc.). If you are interested in the piece, let me know and I will be able to provide it within thirty days of your response. Thanks for your time and consideration; I look forward to hearing from you.

Sincerely,

Moira Allen

Figure 6: Query to _Inklings_ (sent via e-mail)

Dear Moira:

As a full-time freelancer, I also teach magazine writing classes. During a recent query letter critique, one of my students raised her hand. "I feel like I know how to write a good query letter," she said hesitantly. "But I keep worrying about sending them out. What will I do if I actually get an assignment?"

She seemed surprised that I could relate to her fear. Although my work has appeared in more than twenty-five magazines, including _Woman's Day_, _Good Housekeeping_, _Family Circle_, and _Fitness_, I still experience pangs of anxiety when I'm working on a new assignment. Am I doing enough research? Does the story flow well? Does my lead capture the reader's attention? It's only when the piece is accepted (and the check is on its way!) that I completely relax--only to start obsessing over my next assignment.

Yet, I'm not alone--every writer I know struggles with "writer's anxiety." "First, you're anxious if you don't have work, but then when you do, you're anxious about making it the best you can," says full-time St. Louis freelancer Kris Rattini, who's written for _Family Money_, _Family Circle_, and _Boy's Life_. "If it's a new editor, it's just intensified because you want to make a good impression and get more assignments."

"I Think I Can, I Think I Can: Conquering Writers' Anxiety" will examine why even successful writers struggle with this feeling and include ways of coping with--and overcoming--this common malady. I'll interview psychologists and successful full-time freelancers about the best ways to dispel anxiety; while I estimate 1,000 words for this story, that's flexible depending on your needs.

Interested in this topic as a feature for _Inklings_? As a self-employed writer who often struggles with writing-related anxiety, I believe I can bring a unique perspective to this piece. Let me know if you have any questions about this story idea, and thank you for your time.

Best,

Kelly James-Enger
(e-mail/phone)

Figure 7: Query to *Fine Gardening*

Mary Rose
(address)
(city/state/zip)   (phone)
_____

_____, Editor
Fine Gardening
(address)
(city/state/zip)

Dear Ms. _____:

Forget-me-nots. I love their wistful name. I love their tiny, blue flowers. And yes, I love that growing them is as simple as pie. Beneath rose shoots shriveling from blight, my forget-me-nots cheerfully ignore fungi brought on by yet another wet Washington spring. But in spite of their simple nature, forget-me-nots have shown up in some pretty sophisticated places: Monet grew them at Giverny, Jefferson planted flocks of them at Monticello, and Lady Chatterly's gardener found an unusual spot to strew some.

"Forget-me-nots: Simply Unforgettable Spring Flowers" is an exuberant, thousand-word profile detailing:

• Historical background
• Varieties and colors
• Usefulness in formal, cottage, and native gardens
• Growing requirements
• Cautionary measures

Your encouraging response to a query of mine prompted me to share my love of forget-me-nots with you. I look forward to your reply.

Sincerely,

Mary Rose

[NOTE: This is an example of a follow-up! Mary had submitted a previous query that was rejected, but with an encouraging personal note; she followed up immediately with a new query that was accepted. Her bullet list also mirrors the publication's guidelines. By the way, Mary's query (which was developed in a writing class I taught) gave me the format idea for my own letterhead.]

Figure 8: Query to Inkspot (sent via e-mail)

C.J. Chilvers

May 16, 2000

Moira Allen
Associate Editor

Dear Ms. Allen,

Imagine meeting your favorite rock stars, probing their innermost thoughts, and making money in the process. Few writing markets can compete with the lure of the music market. Yet, with the hundreds of resources available to aspiring writers, coverage of the music market is almost nonexistent.

This is quite mystifying when you consider just how large the music market is. After all, there are hundreds of magazines, dozens of record labels, thousands of fanzines, and countless Web sites devoted to the subject of music that are starved for content.

What I propose is an article for your newsletter that will show your readers how to break into the music market. The article will include:

- How to get backstage and photo passes
- How to land the interview
- What editors in this market are looking for
- Which markets are closed to freelancers
- Which markets are eagerly seeking freelance material

As Webmaster of www.musicphotographer.com, it has been my job to connect music writers and photographers with the markets that need their work. This is the only site devoted to music journalism on the Web. I'm also writing the first guide on the topic. Reviews for my last book, _The Van Halen Encyclopedia_, are available at Amazon.com.

I hope to hear from you soon. Thanks for your time.

CJ Chilvers

[NOTE: This query is formatted for e-mail and contains no bullets, italics, or other formatting that would cause problems in an e-mail message.]

4

QUERIES THAT BREAK THE RULES

Editors are rarely impressed by writers who break the rules. A query written in blue ink on pink paper won't lead to an assignment. Nor will a five-page query describing a ten-page article. Editors much prefer to work with writers who can demonstrate, through a well-crafted query, that they understand how business is done in the publishing world.

Nevertheless, some types of queries are, by definition, rule-breakers—or are at least governed by a different set of rules. Most notable among these is the e-mail query, which bypasses not only the rules of format listed in chapter 2, but some of the rules of style and content as well. You may also be able to break many of the rules in that chapter when querying editors to whom you have already sold material.

Rules should never be broken out of ignorance, however. A writer who doesn't understand the rules will simply appear unprofessional. The key is to know the rules first—and then understand how and when to bend them.

E-MAIL QUERIES

A few years ago, only a handful of periodical publishers listed in *Writer's Market* provided e-mail addresses. Now, nearly every publisher in that directory does so. While many magazine editors still prefer queries to be sent by surface mail, more and more are expressing a preference for e-mail queries.

Among electronic publications (such as e-zines and e-mail newsletters), the preference for electronic queries is almost universal. Many will not even consider (or post an address for) surface-mail queries.

E-mail queries have obvious advantages. They save postage, and they save time. When you hit the "send" button, you know your query will reach the editor in seconds rather than days. Since the editor does not need to draft a formal response on official letterhead to answer your query, you may also receive a response more quickly (often within days rather than weeks). If the response is positive, that enables you to start work on your article right away; if it is negative, it allows you to move on to other markets almost immediately.

E-mail queries also have disadvantages, however. A common complaint among editors is that writers often don't bother to prepare e-mail queries carefully. Many seem to be written too quickly, with little attention to style or presentation—as if the speed of the medium inspires haste in the writer. Many are not proofread carefully (and not all e-mail programs offer spell checkers). Editors also find that e-mail queries often tend to be less formal, more chatty (and sometimes even "cutesy"), than traditional queries—qualities that are rarely endearing in a query in any form. Just because a query can be transmitted instantaneously, that doesn't mean a writer should consider this an invitation to dash off a quick note to an editor and hit "send."

Editors also encounter more impatience in writers who query by e-mail. Your query may arrive within seconds—but that doesn't mean the editor is going to read it, let alone respond to it, the moment it arrives. Few things annoy an editor so much as a writer who starts nagging for a response within days (or even hours) of sending an e-mail query. E-mail queries often do encourage faster responses than surface-mail queries, but a magazine's published response times still apply.

While e-mail queries contain many of the same elements described in the previous chapter, they also contain unique elements that need special attention. Understanding these elements can mean the difference between an assignment and a very fast rejection.

ELEMENTS OF THE E-MAIL QUERY

The Header

With e-mail, you can't impress an editor with nice paper or a snappy letterhead. Instead, you must rely on a few lines within your header to provide vital information about yourself and your query. Your header is your first impression; make sure it's a good one by putting the right information in each of these sections:

- **To:** As with a surface-mail query, it's important to address your query to the right person at the right address. Try to locate the exact e-mail address of the editor you wish to contact. Don't send your query to a general "info@" or "letters@" address; it may not be routed to the correct editor, or even to the editorial department at all.

- **From:** You probably wouldn't think of signing a traditional query with a name like "Crystal Windsinger" or "Rafe Moondragon." If you use such a nickname to communicate online, however, it may slip into your query by mistake. Be sure to set up an alternate, professional "personality" in your e-mail program that includes your real name and a professional-sounding e-mail address.

- **Subject:** Include the word "Query" in your subject line, along with a brief (two- to three-word) description of your proposal—e.g., "Query: Cancer in Cats" or "Query: Writing for Pet Magazines." Never leave this line blank. Avoid cuteness or excessive informality. A subject line like "May I have a moment of your time?" looks too much like spam and could cause your query to be deleted. (Granted, one writer did send me a query with the subject line "Of Confetti and Green Sunsets" and got published anyway—but not until her second try!)

The Text

The safest way to handle the text of an e-mail query is to treat it just like a traditional query, with all the essentials (hook, pitch, body, credentials, and close) described in chapter 2. Such an approach will rarely go wrong.

However, one of the advantages of e-mail is its ability to save time—and many editors find that they prefer e-mail queries to be shorter and more concise than surface-mail queries. One reason for this is that an editor likes to be able to read an entire letter without having to scroll through a long "page." The less scrolling an editor must do to read your query, the better.

Consequently, many writers are turning to brief, one- to three-paragraph e-mail queries. The hook is often eliminated entirely; writers often begin directly with the pitch, followed by a single paragraph of description, and closing with a summary of the writer's credentials. Here's an example of an e-mail query I received from a regular contributor to Inkspot:

Hello! I promised you a query, so here you go.

"Flash What?" is an exploration of the (at-first-glance) strange medium of flash fiction. The article does not attempt to define the form, as flash is virtually undefinable, but it does identify the many styles of flash and its many names. I cite such writers as Lila Guzman and Pamelyn Casto and their thoughts on the form. Following this, I segue into a general how-to segment on writing flash, listing three essential questions every flash writer must ask. Once that's finished, I close out with market listings and other resources.

With flash fiction becoming more and more prevalent in the literary community, especially the online publishing world (whole zines are devoted to the medium), I think that this piece is very useful to Inkspot's many readers who double as fiction writers.

"Flash What?" is about 1,220 words long. I'll be happy to send along the full piece if you are interested.

Thanks! Looking forward to your reply.

Jason Gurley

When crafting an e-mail query, therefore, give serious thought to ways that you can condense your information into a compact summary that the editor can view within a single screen. Just be sure that your summary actually covers all the points that you wish to make!

Credentials and Clips

It's perfectly acceptable to list your credentials in an e-mail query, just as you would in a traditional query. Many writers, however, also use this opportunity to provide a link to a Web site where editors can learn more about the writer's qualifications, or perhaps view writing samples. Others list that information after their signature, or in their signature block (see below). You can't be certain, however, that an editor will actually check the sites you list, so it's wise to state your credentials explicitly, and offer Web sites as a source of additional information.

One frustration many authors feel with electronic queries is the impossibility of including clips. (Never send copies of your published articles as attachments to an e-mail query!) Once again, URLs are usually the best answer. If you haven't developed an author Web site yet, consider doing so, if only to post samples of your published work where they can be viewed by editors who are considering your proposals.

The Address Block

In a traditional query, your name and address and other contact information would go at the top of the page (or be incorporated into your letterhead). In an e-mail query, it should go at the bottom, below your typed signature:

Jane Smith
1042 Gloriana Lane
Whippet, IL 60606
(555)123–4567
(555) 123–4568 (fax)
janesmith@isp.com

The Signature Block

You may wish to use a standard signature block to include your Web site and any special credentials you'd like to list. This is a good place, for example, to list a book title that you've published. It's not such a good idea, however, to include your mailing address and other contact information in a signature block, as you don't want that information to accidentally be transmitted in other types of e-mails.

Avoid overly cute signature blocks, or blocks that involve graphic elements. Save the cats, dancing weasels, and emoticons for more personal correspondence.

Format

There is little you can do to improve the standard, boring format of an e-mail query. What you can do, however, is ensure that your attempts at style don't make an e-mail query even harder to read! If, for example, you type your query into a word-processing program (like MS Word) and use certain types of characters (e.g., long dashes, curly quotes) that you would use in a normal (nonelectronic) query or submission, your text may come across looking like this:

Yet I,m not alone~every writer I know struggles with ,,writer,s anxiety‰. ,,First you,re anxious if you don,t have work, but then when you do, you,re anxious about making it the best you can,‰ says fulltime St. Louis freelancer Kris Rattini, who,s written for Family Money, Family Circle, and Boy,s Life. ,,If it,s a new editor, it,s just intensified because you want to make a good impression and get more assignments.‰[1]

To avoid this type of gobbledygook, be sure to observe these basic guidelines:

- Single-space your text.
- Double-space between paragraphs; don't indent.
- Avoid long blocks of text. Use short to medium-length paragraphs.
- Don't use bullets; they rarely show up as bullets on the receiving end.
- Don't insert any format commands (such as bold, italics, or underlining). Use asterisks to indicate *boldface*, and underscores to indicate _italics_ or _underlining_. (In a query, there should be little need for either.)
- Turn off "smart" ("curly") quotes, or do a search/replace that converts such quotes (and apostrophes) to straight quotes. Otherwise, your quotes will generally be converted into other characters in transmission and make your e-mail extremely hard to read.
- Don't use keyboard commands to create a long dash, or "m-dash" (—). Instead, use two hyphens to indicate a dash, like this: (--). (Text is easier to read if you leave a space between the words and the dashes.)
- Don't use any other special character keys—including accents, tildes, etc.
- Avoid emoticons, such as :) or <g>. Save these for more personal correspondence.
- Never use HTML or other special types of formatting. Don't insert graphics. Don't use colors (either in your fonts or your background).
- Use a readable font—at least 10pt. or, preferably, 12pt. Arial and Courier are good fonts for e-mail queries; Eudora uses Mishawaka as a default font, which is also very readable. Make sure your font size is set to "normal." If you're not sure how your font looks to others, e-mail a test message to a friend and ask for an evaluation.

---

[1] Translation: "," = apostrophe; ~ = "m-dash" (long dash); ,, = left-hand smart quote; ‰ = right-hand smart quote. Some keyboard and "special" characters can produce even more bizarre characters than these when transmitted by e-mail; this text is at least readable (and the query *was* accepted).

Attachments

In a word, don't. Many editors will simply delete unsolicited attachments unread—and with the number of viruses circulating on the Internet, attachments are becoming more unwelcome than ever. Your query should be contained entirely within the body of the e-mail itself. The same applies to submissions; never send an attachment unless you have cleared it with the editor first and determined what type of file to send. Also, turn off any functions in your e-mail program that generate automatic attachments, such as vCards. (It's also a good idea to periodically check your e-mail for viruses so that you don't inadvertently pass along unwanted problems with your queries.)

QUICK-PITCH QUERIES

A quick-pitch query allows you to bounce an idea off an editor to see if there is any interest, without investing a great deal of time in the query itself. Again, this generally works only with editors who already know your work and know that you can deliver whatever you promise (though some will ask you to submit a more detailed query if they are interested in the idea).

Here are some examples of quick pitches I've received (and accepted) from regular contributors to Inkspot:

- Would you be interested in an article on Spanish writing sites for Global Writers' Ink online? I think it would be good for Global Writers' Ink's image to address topics relating to writing in another language, without posting an article in another language . . . I could do one on French sites, too, if you're interested.

- I have another article that just went through proofing, and I think it might be something Inkspot's readers would be interested in.

  The title is "Researching That Agent—Online," and it's approximately 1260 words. It's an informative piece that deals with successfully researching a prospective agent's career, track record, and biographical information and then using that information to your benefit in a strong query letter. The piece suggests great reference sites and unheard-of-but-better-than-the-rest search engines, as well as association sites, and makes five suggestions for using the gleaned information in a query letter without stepping over the line.

- Whether it's local, regional, or national, or low paying, medium, or high paying, knowing the appropriate market to target and when to move on is an important step in a freelance writer's career. Are you interested in a 1,000-word article that outlines steps to moving up levels within the different market ranks? The article will include advice from writers at different levels in their careers and how they target the appropriate market.

All of these queries were submitted by e-mail, which is the ideal mechanism for quick-pitch queries. Many of the pitches I receive from regular contributors run no more than three to five lines. However, note that each still contains all the necessary information an editor needs to make a decision—provided the editor *already* knows that the writer is capable of delivering what he or she promises. Since such queries are easy to read and reply to, quick pitches are likely to receive quick responses.

MULTIPLE-PITCH QUERIES

A multiple-pitch query offers an editor a selection of several article ideas rather than just one. Such a query usually suggests from two to ten topics, with a paragraph of detail apiece.

This type of query is, by definition, a fishing expedition—and as I mentioned in chapter 2, fishing expeditions are usually *not* appropriate when you are making contact with an editor for the first time. This type of query should only be used with an editor that you have already worked with—preferably several times. The editor needs to know, without question, that you are capable of fleshing out any of the suggested topics, even when the query itself doesn't provide nearly the level of detail of a traditional query. This type of query enables the editor to pick and choose from a selection, and such a query can often result in more than one assignment. (Rarely, however, will an editor accept every idea on your list.)

Here's an example of a multiple-pitch query I submitted to Inkspot:

Dear Debbie,

We've talked about several articles recently, and I wanted to find out whether you are interested in any/all of these:

1) Author chats—are they useful? I've talked to several authors who have given "chats" online. This article would discuss whether an author chat is worthwhile and how to make the best of one.

2) Teaching writing classes offline. This piece would discuss how to teach a writing class in a "real world" environment.

3) Teaching writing classes online. The follow-up to the previous article would discuss how to teach a successful online writing class.

4) Giving a talk—this would fall under the category of "promotion." I'd like to include information on how to prepare for a talk, and also information on the technical side— how do you give a good presentation? What will your listeners want to hear? What about handouts, outlines, charts, etc.? I think this would be most effective as a longer article on Inkspot (rather than an *Inklings* piece)—and it could be broken into two parts, one on technical presentation and one on personal preparation.

5) How to obtain a teaching job—this might make a good *Inklings* piece, on how to find (and land) a job at a community college or similar organization. It wouldn't discuss "how to teach," but, rather, how to locate places to teach, submit a proposal, etc. (This and #2 might make a good two-part series.)

6) What if your work is stolen? I would like to talk to the National Writers Union and other sources to find out what recourses you actually have if your work turns up somewhere else (as mine did in Northern Lights). What steps should you take? What rights do you have?

7) How to develop a "business plan." Since I've just done this for 2000 (and found it an amazingly "focusing" process), I thought it might make an interesting article, perhaps for January.

8) International copyright—someone recently wrote to me and wanted to know about copyright protection when sending his manuscript to a publisher in another country. Would this be worth researching for *Inklings*/Inkspot?[2]

In many cases, an editor will respond to a multiple-pitch query with a request to flesh out one or more of your pitches into a full-fledged query. In this case, you won't need to worry about a hook or credentials (assuming the latter have been established); instead, concentrate on the body of the query, explaining exactly what will be covered and how the article will be organized.

As the examples above illustrate, even queries that break the rules don't *really* break the rules—at least, not the important ones. Whether you submit a quick-pitch or multiple-pitch query, and whether you submit by surface mail or e-mail, you must still offer a query that is sound, well-written, well-thought-out, appropriate for the publication, and professional. The goals of your query remain the same: to demonstrate that you can provide exactly what an editor is looking for.

---

[2] If you're curious, I sold topics 1, 4, 6 and 7. Topic #5 became chapter 19 of this book.

5

NEWSPAPER QUERIES
by Amy Chavez

Newspapers publish letters to the editor, travel stories, features, op-ed pieces, and more. In addition to regular staff members and reporters, newspapers use freelancers to help fill their papers with fresh, new material every day. Many newspapers also have a Sunday magazine, inserted into the regular Sunday edition, with local features about the city and its goings-on. The Sunday magazine will have a separate staff from the newspaper and should be queried accordingly.

You can query multiple newspapers simultaneously, as long as the readership of the papers doesn't overlap. (You can be pretty safe by using the hundred-mile rule: if two newspapers are within a hundred miles of each other, query only one at a time.) Most newspapers will not care if the piece has already been published in a newspaper outside of their hundred-mile radius, since their readers will most likely not have seen it.

This means you can make money over and over for the same piece. Newspapers can also be a great reprint market for articles that previously appeared in other media such as newsletters, magazines, or books, as long as the content is appropriate for that particular newspaper's readership.

HOW TO READ THE MASTHEAD

Newspapers rarely publish guidelines, but you can quickly find out who is in charge by reading the masthead. The masthead is the section of the paper that lists the managing editor, the editor-in-chief, the editors, and other staff members. Larger newspapers will have a different editor for each section, such as a news editor, sports editor, features editor, etc. If an editor is listed for the section you wish to submit to, send your query to the appropriate editor.

Smaller papers may list only the editor-in-chief or the managing editor. In that case, send your query to one of them, or call the paper to find out who would be most appropriate to query for your article idea. While you're on the phone, ask if you might be able to speak with the person to run your idea past them first.

The Annual Editor & Publisher International Year Book (available at most libraries) lists addresses and editors of U.S. and Canadian daily newspapers, as well as alternative newspapers and specialty newspapers covering topics such as parenting, seniors, ethnic groups, and real estate. *The E&P Year Book* also gives you valuable information on how often the newspaper is published (daily, weekly, bimonthly), its circulation figures, whether the paper has a Sunday magazine, and a list of the paper's weekly sections and special editions.

Weekly sections focus on subjects like food, entertainment, business, education, church, etc. For example, the weekly food section may be on Mondays, the entertainment section on Tuesdays, etc. Weekly sections often have their own editors. Special editions are published at specific times of the year and have seasonal or popular themes. Example titles of special editions include: spring, bridal, back-to-school, health care, baby, home improvement, and holidays.

Knowing what weekly sections and special editions a paper offers will enable you to time your query and target your audience so that you'll have a better chance of acceptance. If you have an article idea that you think would fit into a paper's special edition, call the newspaper and ask them what month the special edition appears, so you can get your query in about six weeks before the publication date. Also, be sure to ask for the name of the editor in charge of that edition.

MAKING CONTACT

With the exception of some travel articles or ongoing series of articles, newspaper items are usually short enough (roughly 500–1,500 words) that most editors prefer you send the article along with your query. (To put it another way, your query also serves as your cover letter.) Newspaper editors are very busy and work with daily deadlines, so the shorter and more to-the-point your query is (about half a page is enough), the better your chances of making a sale. Your query letter should briefly state why you think the article is relevant to the readers of that particular paper.

Don't bother sending clips with your query, as most editors are too busy to look through them. However, you should note in your query letter if you have been published before, and where. You can include an SASE if you wish, but many editors don't have time to respond unless they actually want to accept your article. Don't expect a rejection on unwanted material; in most cases, it will simply be trashed.

Most newspapers don't encourage telephone inquiries. However, if you feel strongly that you need to talk to an editor before you query, especially if the query is about something timely, such as pressing news, go ahead and call. You may also be able to call the editor of a smaller, local paper in your area. If you do call, however, make sure that you make it worth the editor's time to talk to you. Don't waste time with idle chit-chat.

Some editors still prefer surface-mail queries, while others prefer e-mail queries. Check the newspaper's home page for a list of e-mail addresses of the editors of the print edition. If the e-mail address of the editor you want to query is listed, it should be safe to query by e-mail.

OP-ED, TRAVEL, AND FEATURE ARTICLES

The newspaper sections most open to freelancers are the op-eds, travel articles, and feature articles (including profiles). Although newspapers don't all call their feature section by the same title, look for this type of article in sections with names like Living, Weekend, or Style. Regular features such as book or restaurant reviews, music, and theater are usually assigned to staff or reporters.

The easiest area to break into newspapers is through the op-ed pages. The op-ed page showcases opinions of about 400–800 words and is open to a wide variety of subjects and styles. With op-ed pieces, you must send the completed article. Along with the article, send a short cover letter explaining why you wrote the piece. The cover letter is also a good place to cite any credentials you may have that would give credibility to your piece. If you write an opinion piece about a current issue on the education ballot, your piece will have more weight if you happen to have a background in public policy. If you write an opinion piece on the Israeli-Palestine conflict, it will help the editor to know if you lived in Israel for several years. However, if you have no special background related to the piece, that's okay, too. Also, don't limit yourself to newsy items. The op-ed section is a good place to submit humor and satire. You can even submit a section from your published book here. In the op-ed section, anything goes!

Features and travel articles require a little more expertise. You'll be expected to demonstrate more knowledge of your subject matter, and more professionalism in your query.

THREE WAYS TO MAKE YOUR QUERY IRRESISTIBLE

1. **Give it a local slant.** Unless you're querying a national newspaper such as the *New York Times, USA Today,* or the *Wall Street Journal,* your story will have a much better chance of being accepted if it has a local slant. This can be hard to do if you're writing from another state, but there are things you can do to give an otherwise-generic story a local slant. For example, if your story is about a small town in the United States, then perhaps your story would have relevancy to readers of other small-town newspapers. Or, if you wrote a feature story about the Amish in Ohio, you could do a little research and tell readers where they can buy Amish goods in their town. Or perhaps you may be able to find an Amish person living near that town whom you could highlight in a sidebar to your article. Your sidebar would be different for each paper, focusing on a different person. Mention any local slants in your query letter.

2. **Look for tie-ins to newsworthy events.** Travel sections require some type of tie-in to current news or local events. Even international travel can be

relevant if you can think of a proper tie-in. If you want to write about your recent trip to Poland, for example, and you find out that your town is having an international food festival next month, you could write about Poland and inform readers that they can see traditional Polish costumes and sample the delicacies you describe in your article by attending the International Food Festival. Do a little extra research and find out if there are any other events, such as Polish dancing or a Polish crafts booth, at the festival. In your query, tell the editor how beautifully your piece will fit in with the articles that his or her staff will be writing about the International Food Festival.

Vietnam is just starting to open up to tourism, which makes Vietnam newsworthy and a good possible candidate for a travel article. If, after doing some research, you find that cheap flights and bargain seaside accommodations abound, tell the editor in your query that you'd like to tip off readers to this undiscovered paradise.

Editors are also always looking for local travel articles. Look for travel trends, such as the recent surge in adventure travel, and write an article about local places to go for adventure. In your query letter, tell the editor that your article highlights places locals can go for thrills without leaving the state.

3. **Offer photos.** If you have decent photos to go along with the article, this will help sell your story. Don't send the photos with your query, though, because you may not get them back. Instead, mention in your letter that photos are available on request. Some newspapers pay extra for photos; others do not.

Your Local Paper Route

If you're just starting out and don't have the confidence to query newspapers, you'll be glad to know that there is a way to get published without having to write a polished query letter. Many papers have a section that openly solicits readers' stories. These sections pay very little, if at all, but are easier to break into and do not require a query letter. Read your newspaper carefully for a column or section that is devoted to reader essays on a special topic (such as women's issues, traveling, parenting, or anything people share in common). At the bottom of the story, you will find a note inviting readers to send their stories. You may find this the perfect way to break into newspapers and to start a relationship with a newspaper editor.

Most freelance newspaper writers start by publishing in their local newspapers. Since bigger newspapers are inundated with submissions, you're much more likely to find a place for your work in your local paper. Furthermore, your local paper will be more open to your ideas and opinions and is a great place to start making contacts. After you've found success at home, you can query bigger, more prestigious papers with a polished query letter that includes mention of your previously published articles.

SECTION 1 RESOURCES

GENERAL
iPrint
www.iprint.com
You can design your own letterhead or business stationery on this site, or use iPrint's templates.

No Clips? Don't Despair; Here's an Alternative (by Moira Allen)
www.writing-world.com/basics/clips.html
What to do if you don't have clips to submit with a query.

WRITERS' GUIDELINES
These sites will help you locate guidelines for various types of print and online publications, as well as addresses for queries.

AcqWeb
www.library.vanderbilt.edu/law/acqs/email-ad.html
AcqWeb offers an "international directory of e-mail addresses of publishers, vendors, and related professional associations, organizations, and services." A good place to look for markets.

Guide to Online Guidelines
www.snafu.de/~gadfly/

Market List, The
www.marketlist.com
Covers speculative fiction markets (e.g., SF, fantasy, horror).

Markets for Writers
www.chebucto.ns.ca/Culture/WFNS/markets.html
Includes links to a number of resources for finding Canadian markets.

SFF Net: Ezines and Rags
www.sff.net/sff/ezines.htp
Paying and nonpaying electronic markets.

Spicy Green Iguana
www.spicygreeniguana.com
More than 200 links to SF, fantasy, and horror magazine publications.

Working List of Speculative Fiction Markets
www.bayarea.net/~stef/sf-markets.txt
Text listing of all major speculative fiction markets (URLs listed but not linked). Probably one of the most comprehensive guides available on the Web. (Last updated February 1999.)

Writer's Digest
www.writersdigest.com/guidelines/indexbody.htm

Writer's Guidelines (The Write Markets Report)
www.writersmarkets.com/index-guidelines.htm
A listing of paying markets, updated daily, from the publisher of *The Write Markets Report.*

Writers' Guidelines Database
http://mav.net/guidelines/

Writer's Place, The
www.awoc.com/Guidelines.cfm

Writers Write
www.writerswrite.com/guidelines

MAGAZINE AND NEWSPAPER LISTS

General

Christian Periodical Publishers
www.colc.com/pubbook/key.htm
Christian magazines, book publishers, and religion editors at secular newspapers.

Links to Media and News Resources Around the Globe
www.uct.ac.za/depts/politics/intnew.htm
Links to international journals, broadcast media, lists, magazines, newspapers, online resources, and "other."

Michigan Electronic Library: News, Media, and Periodicals
http://mel.lib.mi.us/news/News-Journal.html

Newsletter Access Directory
www.newsletteraccess.com/directory.html
Searchable directory of newsletters (online and off).

Yahoo! (Australia)

http://au.yahoo.com/news_and_media/magazines

Links to Australian and New Zealand publications.

Yahoo! News and Media

http://dir.yahoo.com/News_and_Media/By_Region/

Search for newspapers and online media by region.

Magazines

Electronic Newsstand (Enews)

www.enews.com

Links to thousands of magazines, searchable by title and category.

BCAMP: The B.C. Association of Magazine Publishers

www.swifty.com/bcamp/index.html

Another place to start searching for markets in Canada is this site, which offers information on more than 200 British Columbian publications (including e-zines).

British Magazines

www.britishmagazines.com

Dubbed "The UK's largest online magazine store," this site offers an extensive listing. Unfortunately, it gives minimal information about each title and does not link to the magazines' Web sites. However, it does offer the opportunity to purchase individual copies of various titles rather than an entire subscription, which makes it useful for ordering sample copies.

Canadian Magazine Publisher's Association: Magazine Index

www.cmpa.ca/magindex.html

Listings of Canadian publications, by title and by subject.

Council of Literary Magazines and Presses

www.clmp.org

A great place to hunt for literary magazines and presses; includes an extensive member directory.

Free Magazines

www.freesitex.com/magazine.html

A list of magazines that offer free sample copies or subscriptions.

Little Magazines
www.little-magazines.co.uk
Names, addresses, subscription rates, and submission guidelines to over sixty U.K. "little" (e.g., literary) magazines.

Magazines of Europe
www.travelconnections.com/Magazines/Europeindex.htm
For magazines from other parts of the world, go to *www.travelconnections.com/Magazines/*

NewsDirectory.com
www.newsdirectory.com
Links to thousands of magazines, searchable by title and category. Also offers links to international media, searchable by title, category, or country.

Newsdirectory.com: Worldwide Magazines
www.newsdirectory.com/news/magazine/world

WebWombat: Online Magazines
www.webwombat.com.au/magazines/
An Australian search engine that offers extensive listings of magazine home pages around the world, including many non-English publications.

Yahoo: Magazines
http://search.yahoo.com/bin/search?p=magazines

Newspapers

1500+ U.S. Newspapers and Their Links
www.zuzu.com/helpful/new-add.htm
Exactly what it says.

AJR NewsLink
http://ajr.newslink.org/mag.html
Huge list of links to newspapers around the world, plus a smaller list of popular magazines.

Editor and Publisher Interactive
http://emedia1.mediainfo.com/emedia/
The site index for *Editor and Publisher* offers links to a variety of magazine and newspaper indices.

Fleet Street Online
www.fleet-street.com/top.htm
Links to U.K. newspapers.

International News Links
http://inkpot.com/news/
Links to newspapers with an online presence around the world.

Journalism.Net
www.journalismnet.com/papers.htm
Lists publications by region.

Media UK
www.mediauk.com/directory/

Mercator
www.aber.ac.uk/~merwww/allang.htm
This is a fascinating site that links to resources related to "minority languages in the European Union." Look here for links to newspapers, media, newsgroups, and more for such languages as Asturian, Basque, Ladin, Occitan, etc. The page is offered in English, Welsh, and French.

Newspaper Association of America
www.newspaperlinks.com/home.cfm
Links to Canadian papers, international papers, U.S. dailies, press associations, and other newspaper-related sites.

Newspapers.com
www.newspapers.com
Lists and links to U.S. and international newspapers, college newspapers, religious papers, online news services, and more.

PPPP.Net: The Ultimate Collection of News Links
http://pppp.net/links/news/

Transitions-Online Newsstand
www.transitions-online.org/newsstan.html
"Newsstand" for newspapers and other media from Central, Eastern, and Southeastern Europe, Russia, Transcaucasia, and Central Asia. Indicates whether information is available in English, and how current the archives are.

US Newspaper Links.com
www.usnewspaperlinks.com/ncnews.html
A huge collection of links to U.S. newspapers and radio stations, searchable by state.

Writer's Guidelines Database: Small Newspapers
http://mav.net/guidelines/newspapers/smallpapers.shtml

PUBLICATIONS THAT LIST MARKETS
Byline
www.bylinemag.com
Monthly print magazine with Web site.

Inscriptions
www.inscriptionsmagazine.com
Also free, *Inscriptions* is a weekly e-mail newsletter that covers market lists, contests, and job listings for writers, along with excellent articles.

Kazoodles
http://klockepresents.com/KaZoodles.html
A biweekly list of links, updates, markets, and announcements for writers.

musicjournalist.com
www.musicjournalist.com/
A newsletter and Web site offering writing tips and market information for writers covering the field of music.

The Writer
http://writermag.com
Monthly print magazine with Web site.

Writer Online
www.novalearn.com/wol/marketplace.htm
This monthly e-zine covers many different types of writing, including playwriting, PR, business writing, and a monthly column in "writing for international markets" by Michael Sedge.

Writer's Digest
www.writersdigest.com
A monthly print magazine, with information and markets posted on the Web site as well.

Writers Weekly

www.writersweekly.com

A weekly e-mail newsletter listing markets and jobs for writers, plus links to online articles and columns.

Writing for DOLLARS!

www.awoc.com

A monthly newsletter offering tips and markets.

Writing World

www.writing-world.com/newsletter/index.html

This biweekly newsletter includes a markets section focusing primarily on electronic markets, and includes only those that pay at least $20 for features.

Section 2

COLUMNS AND SYNDICATION

SELLING A COLUMN

Your mother thinks you're the next Erma Bombeck. Your friends embrace your advice with the same awe they'd accord Ann Landers. You can't count the number of times you've been told, "You should write a column."

And perhaps you should! Columns offer many benefits. A column announces to the world that a publication regards your work highly enough to make you a regular rather than an occasional contributor. Columnists are generally regarded as experts, which can help you in your quest for other assignments. Columns also provide a steady income: you know that you'll be receiving a regular check, for a regular amount.

Getting a column assignment, however, is not easy. Most publications have limited space for columns, and the competition for that space can be fierce. Because columns build reader loyalty, editors generally prefer to hold onto existing columns as long as possible, which means that opportunities for new columns are rare. To win one of those spaces, it's vital to do your homework so that you can prepare a truly dynamic proposal package.

CHOOSING A MARKET

The first question you should ask yourself is, Where do I want to publish my column? You may already have an answer—you'd like your column to appear in a favorite magazine, your local paper, or a noteworthy Web site. If you don't, take a moment to consider some of your options.

NEWSPAPERS

Newspapers represent by far the largest market for columns. Even the smallest regional papers generally run a few columns, often by local authors. Larger papers run a mixture of local and national (syndicated) columns. While weekly papers feature weekly (and sometimes monthly) columns, daily papers usually offer a mix of weekly and daily columns. Weekend editions often feature columns that don't appear during the week—including review and "local event" sections. Some newspapers also feature rotating monthly columns, with a different author featured each week.

Newspapers also offer the widest variety of content for a single publication. Regular sections may include health, cooking, lifestyle, women's issues, religion, books, movies, local events, travel, and more—and each of those sections may have several column opportunities. (For example, a weekly cooking section might include a column on healthy recipes, a column on regional specialties, a column on diet and weight loss, a column on baking, a column on vegetarian cooking, etc.) Since newspapers are based on regional readership, they seek material that will appeal to a broad cross-section of the public, which improves your chances of breaking in.

The downside of newspapers is that many offer very low pay for columns. Smaller newspapers may pay as little as $15 to $25 per column. While larger papers pay more, you still won't get rich writing for a single newspaper. However, as newspaper readership is regionally based, you can often sell the same column to more than one (noncompeting) paper. (See chapter 7 for tips on how to self-syndicate your column.)

MAGAZINES

While most magazines run a selection of columns, this market can be much more difficult to penetrate. Of all publications, magazines are the most limited in the amount of space they can offer columnists. When a column slot does come up, magazine editors generally turn first to their stable of regular contributors to look for a new columnist. The best way to get a shot at a magazine column, therefore, is to *become* a regular contributor, thereby establishing yourself as a reliable writer who can be counted on to produce quality material on deadline and with a minimum of fuss. Once you have contributed several pieces to the magazine, you may wish to pitch a column idea to your editor; even if the idea isn't accepted, you'll have planted the idea that you are interested in writing a column when an opportunity becomes available.

Magazine columns generally offer better pay than newspaper columns, though that pay is usually monthly rather than weekly. The downside of working for magazines is the possibility of editorial interference—while some editors let columnists write about whatever they wish (within the constraints of the column topic), I've also worked with editors who attempt to micromanage a column by dictating topics, style, and even what they want you to say about specific topics. Be sure, therefore, that you can work comfortably with a particular editor before you offer to do so on a monthly basis.

ELECTRONIC PUBLICATIONS

The number of electronic publications available to writers—e-zines, newsletters, "content" Web sites, and more—is increasing daily. Such markets often defy conventional description.

Your first thought might be to look for e-zines or e-mail newsletters that cover your interest area, but that's just the tip of the electronic iceberg. Many commercial sites (such as online pet-supply stores) offer extensive content sections to attract visitors and feature a number of regular columns. Other sites focus on pure content and offer thousands of articles and columns.

Finding these sites can be a challenge, but breaking in is often relatively simple. Online, space is far less limited than in print, so electronic publications can often afford to run more columns. Columns are usually archived, so readers can locate not only your current offering but everything you've written to date.

Payment for online columns varies widely—anywhere from $15 or $20 to $300 or more. E-mail newsletters generally offer the lowest rates (and seek columns that are usually no longer than 750 words). E-zines tend to fall within the mid-range, while commercial and content sites generally pay higher rates. There are no rules, however; judge every site on its own merits.

Most electronic publications ask only for electronic rights to your column (though there are exceptions), which leaves you free to market the same column elsewhere in print.

COLUMNS AND CREDENTIALS

What kind of column do you want to write? While the potential for topics is virtually infinite, most columns fall within one of five basic categories: how-to/informational, advice, op-ed, review, and humor. Each requires a certain set of credentials.

HOW-TO/INFORMATIONAL COLUMNS

Look in any publication, and you're likely to find one or more columns that teach you how to do something. In your local newspaper, you'll find gardening columns, cooking columns, health columns, parenting columns, and a host of others. Larger papers often feature columns on managing finances, buying and selling real estate, improving/maintaining/decorating your home, caring for your pet, and even more esoteric subjects. Travel columns tell you where to go, what to see, how to get there, and how to save money. Self-help columns tell you how to improve your personal life and relationships.

Magazines offer a similar array, tailored to the subject matter of the publication. A health magazine might offer columns on fitness, diet, or alternative health care. A pet magazine may offer tips on training, medical care, and behavior. A more general women's magazine may host columns on fashion, beauty, household hints, health, and a dozen other topics.

To break into the how-to column field, you need to know how to do something and how to do it well. Unlike a freelance article (for which you can interview experts), a column generally relies on your expertise, your credentials. Don't try to write a gardening column if you've never picked up a rake! However, if your keyboard is covered with muddy fingerprints from your last potting escapade, a gardening column might be perfect for you—especially if you have the ability to explain complicated techniques and concepts in simple, easy-to-follow terms.

ADVICE COLUMNS

Advice columns often overlap with how-to columns in that they, too, offer instruction. Advice columns are based on reader questions—"Dear Abby" and "Ann Landers" being perhaps the best-known examples. Though such columns are popular, most publications offer only a few advice columns (compared to the number of how-to columns), making this a more difficult field to break into. It's especially difficult to penetrate the personal self-help advice column market, as Abby and Ann are widely syndicated to even the smallest newspapers.

To pitch an advice column, you need to be able to demonstrate two things: your credentials for giving the advice and your personal appeal as a columnist. Readers need to know why you're qualified to answer their questions—and your answers need to be sufficiently interesting to *other* readers (the ones who read your column for information or entertainment, but who don't write in) to build a following.

Often, specific credentials will be required for an advice column. An editor seeking a parenting columnist, for example, is likely to require someone with a degree in psychology. A medical advice columnist will usually be expected to have a medical degree. Similarly, a pet-health column will typically be written by a veterinarian. Before you attempt to pitch an advice column, therefore, be sure you have the necessary credentials to answer that first question: What qualifies you to give this advice?

OP-ED COLUMNS

Everyone has an opinion—and op-ed (opinion/editorial) columns have long been a staple of newspapers and general-interest magazines. Op-ed columns can cover just about any topic: politics, world events, social issues, special interests, even personal topics. Newspapers and general-interest magazines are more likely to seek op-ed pieces on issues of interest to the largest possible audience (e.g., politics, current events, social issues). Smaller publications, such as local and regional newspapers, may feature op-ed columns that relate directly to local events (or local perspectives on larger issues). Special-interest publications feature op-ed pieces that relate to those interests. Finally, many publications offer opportunities for op-eds on purely personal matters.

To sell an op-ed column, you generally need more than an interesting opinion. You also need to give the reader (and an editor) a reason why your opinion should be heard. Sometimes this is a matter of credentials or experience: If you have twenty years' experience in international affairs, your opinion on world events might be a hot commodity. Sometimes it is a matter of demographics: Do you speak for a particular group that seeks a voice? Sometimes, it's as simple as being local—and being able to offer an opinion that is representative of your community. The primary question an editor may ask of a would-be op-ed columnist is, What segment of my readers will want to hear what you want to say? To pitch an op-ed column, you may need to explain not only what you are speaking about, but whom you are speaking *for*. (For more information about op-ed pieces, see chapter 5.)

REVIEW COLUMNS

Just as nearly every publication has some form of how-to column, nearly every publication also offers some type of review column. Subjects most commonly reviewed include:

- Books, movies, and music
- Arts, events, and (live) entertainment
- Products (including computer products and games)
- Restaurants (and other "on-the-town" locations)
- Travel destinations and accommodations

Some publications offer reviews in only one or two of these areas; others offer review columns in all these areas and more. For example, a pet magazine is likely to feature reviews of products and books relating to pets. A travel magazine may feature reviews of destinations, accommodations, restaurants, and even books on travel. A computer publication is likely to seek reviews of new software, hardware, and possibly books. A local newspaper is likely to seek reviews of local attractions (such as restaurants), movies, books (including books by local authors), and anything else that will appeal to the audience of that area. Online publications also offer review columns, while a handful of sites consist of nothing *but* reviews. The larger and more general the focus of a publication, the broader its range of review columns—and the greater the possibility that you may be able to break in with a column that covers something not currently reviewed by that publication.

The good news is that this type of column often requires no special credentials. Review columns blur the line between information and entertainment; while their stated purpose is to inform readers about the quality of a product or event, many such columns are popular simply because of their style. Consequently, for most consumer publications, all that is required is an ability to discuss a book, product, or event intelligently and interestingly.

The bad news is that because no special credentials are required, this is often the first place that would-be columnists look for work. Review columns offer an extra appeal: the fun, even the glamour, of being able to do things you would do anyway (read books, watch movies, eat out), and then get paid to write about them. To earn a space, you'll have to ensure that your column rises above the competition.

Finally, don't imagine that review columns are a ticket to free movies, free dinners, free travel, or free books. Most such products are sent directly to publications, not to reviewers—so you have to obtain a column slot before a publication will pass those products on to you.

HUMOR COLUMNS

Humor columns are among the hardest to launch, for several reasons. First, humor columns generally fall into the category of entertainment, and most publications devote only a limited amount of space to pure entertainment (rather than information). Second, what is funny to one person (or writer) often isn't funny to another—it's tough to tickle an editor's funny bone, and even tougher to build a reader following. Third, the market is already saturated; if your local paper already carries Dave Barry, it's not likely to want or need a second humor column. The fact that most of us know the major humor columnists by name is an indication of how few such columns exist (or become successful). That doesn't mean you shouldn't try; it simply means that you should not expect humor to offer you an easy entry into the world of columns.

OTHER COLUMNS

The categories listed above are certainly not the only possible types of columns; they are simply the most common. Other types of columns do exist.

One such column is the "slice of life"—personal glimpses into your own world, your life, your thoughts and feelings. These, however, are tough to sell—you have to find a way to convince the editor, and reader, that your life is not only worth writing about but worth reading about. (Your opinions, on the other hand, might fit into the op-ed category.)

Another tough sell is a purely informational column (as opposed to a how-to column)—e.g., a column that offers facts, but no tips on how to apply those facts to one's own life. While certain special-interest publications may offer purely factual columns, these are hard to find in more general-interest markets. If you want to write this type of column, see if you can present it in a how-to format—e.g., if you're writing about azaleas, remember that most people aren't that interested in the history or botanical details of the flower, but would be more likely to want to know how and when to plant them and what varieties to choose for the garden.

THE BASIC COLUMN PROPOSAL

No matter where you hope to sell your column, your basic proposal should include the following elements:

- A query
- Three to six sample columns
- Clips of other (relevant) published work
- Supporting material (optional)

THE QUERY

A query for a column is very similar to that for an article. However, instead of proposing a single piece, you are proposing an ongoing series—so the goal of your query should be to present a rationale for why the target publication would want to cover your subject on a regular basis.

Instead of going into detail about any single column, therefore, your query should present an overview of the nature and purpose of the entire column. Describe the subject, and explain why this subject is of sufficient importance (or interest) to merit ongoing coverage.

The Hook

The goal of your hook is to establish not only that you have a worthwhile subject to cover, but a subject that is too large to be handled in a single article. Your hook should also offer convincing evidence that a large number of the publication's readers would be interested in this subject on an ongoing basis.

Any of the types of hooks listed in chapter 2 can serve this purpose. Suppose, for example, that you are proposing a column on natural health alternatives to a general-interest women's publication. Any of the following hooks might pique an editor's interest:

- **Problem/Solution:** Many women today are becoming increasingly frustrated with the limitations of "traditional medicine." Often, traditional techniques—or harried HMO doctors with not enough time—just don't seem to answer women's questions or meet their needs. More and more women are seeking alternatives—and seeking accurate, helpful information to guide them toward those alternatives.

- **Informative:** Natural remedies have become big business. No longer confined to strip-mall "health stores," they now line the pharmacy shelves of every supermarket. Now, more than ever, women are in need of accurate, reliable information on the products competing for their health dollars—and on how to safely incorporate natural health care into their lives.

- **Question:** Are you bewildered by the array of natural products on your local supermarket shelves? Do you wonder whether these products are safe, whether they can actually meet their claims, or how to choose between them? If so, you're not alone; thousands of women face the same decisions every day.

- **Personal Experience/Anecdote:** When I had my first baby, I wasn't prepared for the violent reaction I would have to XXX drug. Yet it was all my doctors could offer. The next time, I vowed to be prepared; I studied alternatives and found natural solutions that eased my pain without ruining my health. Since then, I've talked to many women who wished they had the same options . . .

- **Attention-grabber:** Nature can be the death of you—even when it's attractively bottled in a supposedly "safe" product on your supermarket shelf. While natural remedies offer a host of helpful alternatives to traditional healthcare, it's vital to know what you're doing—what's in that bottle, how much you can safely take, whether it actually works, and how it might react with other natural products.

The Pitch

Your hook should lead directly into your pitch—and your pitch should clearly describe the type of column you are proposing. Be sure to include a catchy but descriptive column title in your pitch; a good title helps fix your idea in an editor's mind.

Your pitch should include two additional pieces of information: the length of the column and its frequency. If you're pitching to a monthly magazine, the frequency is predefined; however, if you're pitching to a newspaper or online publication, you should state how often you expect your column to appear. If possible, include the section of the publication in which your column would fit—for example, the "Tuesday Health Section" of your local paper.

A good pitch to follow the hooks above might read:

> I'd like to offer you a [monthly, weekly] column covering the many facets of natural health care. Titled "Natural Health," this column would fit well within your "To Your Health" section. It would run between 750 and 1,000 words, and cover such topics as: [List topics]

The Body

The body of a column query should list a selection of topics that would be covered in your column. A bullet-point list often works well for this:

> My column would cover such topics as:
>
> • Traditional home remedies: which ones work, and why
>
> • How to read and understand the labels of "natural" products
>
> • Why "natural" doesn't necessarily mean "safe," and how to use such products safely
>
> • Understanding the health claims of natural products: what they're based on, whether they're true
>
> • Product interactions: knowing which natural products can be taken together and which can be harmful
>
> • Teas, tisanes, and distillations: how to best prepare a natural remedy
>
> • Natural remedies for pregnancy and childbirth problems

Be sure to provide enough information on each point to ensure that the editor can clearly determine what the column will be about.

The Credentials

As I mentioned above, columns are generally based on the writer's personal credentials. You'll be much more able to sell a column based on your own skills, education, expertise, or experience than on interviews with other experts. Columnists dispense wisdom, counsel, and advice; readers expect them to be experts in their own right. Since an inaccurate column can damage the credibility of the entire publication, editors will want to be sure you have the credentials to qualify you for the job.

The Close

The final paragraph of your query should offer a potential start date for your column. If appropriate, it may be the place to specify your terms—the rights you are offering and, in some cases, the fee you expect. In most cases, however, you'll leave these matters to be negotiated after the editor approves the column idea.

SAMPLE COLUMNS

Unlike an article proposal, a column proposal only *begins* with the query letter. The heart of your proposal will be the columns themselves—the proof that you can deliver what your proposal promises.

Most editors expect to receive at least three, and sometimes six, sample columns with a proposal. Needless to say, these should be your best work; this is your first and only chance to demonstrate both the value of your information and the quality of your writing style.

Format your columns as you would an article submission, with each column beginning on a separate page. If your column is likely to require fact checking (or if the publication routinely fact-checks columns and articles), provide a list of references with each column. (One way to do this is to provide footnotes throughout the column. These are strictly for editorial use and will be removed when the column is actually printed.) Add a brief "about the author" bio to the end of your columns.

Don't use the same topics for your sample columns that you've listed in your query. Your query should present a list of topics that goes beyond your samples, to demonstrate that you have plenty of material for an ongoing column.

CLIPS

Good clips are often essential to make the sale. While your column may demonstrate that you can write well, your clips demonstrate that you write well enough to have been accepted and published, preferably by reputable publications. Be sure to select clips that relate in some way to your column. If you don't have clips that relate directly to the subject matter, use clips that relate to the general type of column you're proposing—e.g., if you're offering a how-to column, send along clips of other how-to articles that you've written, even if they aren't on the same subject.

Your clips needn't necessarily be from consumer publications, or even work for which you were paid. If you are basing your column on professional or educational credentials, and have contributed to professional journals or in-house publications at your place of employment, these may be sufficient to help establish your expertise (and demonstrate that you have written about your subject before).

A published book makes an excellent clip. Being able to state that you are the author of a book on your column subject is one of the best ways to establish your expertise and authority. If you can, send the publisher a copy of the book itself. Otherwise, send a photocopy of the cover, one or two chapters, and copies of any especially favorable reviews (particularly reviews that have appeared in reputable publications).

SUPPORTING MATERIAL

In addition to your query and sample columns, you may wish to provide some supporting material to back up your credentials. Such optional material might include:

- A publications list (highlighting publications relevant to the column)
- An expanded author bio
- A photo (you will often need a photo to run with the column, but many writers prefer to send in such a photo only after the column has been accepted)

THE SUBMISSION PACKAGE

Unlike article queries, column proposals should generally be submitted by surface mail, for two reasons. First, you are submitting a large package, which would create a very long e-mail message—something an editor might be unwilling to read online and equally unwilling to print out. Second, column proposals do not lend themselves to a quick response (the only quick response possible would be "no," which is not the answer you want), which eliminates the primary value of submitting by e-mail. Submitting a paper package by surface mail enables an editor to review your submission thoroughly and perhaps pass it around to others before making a decision.

Submit your column package in a professional manner. Use a 9" × 12" mailing envelope so that your materials will arrive flat and unrumpled, and include an SASE for the editor's response. (A letter-size SASE should be sufficient; just indicate that you don't need to have the materials returned.) Be aware that it may take longer to make a decision on a column proposal than it would on a regular article query; wait at least six weeks before following up.

The exception, of course, is when submitting to electronic publications. When submitting to an online market, you should send your proposal by e-mail unless the market's guidelines indicate otherwise. Unless the market indicates a willingness to accept attachments (most don't), include everything in the body of a single e-mail. Make sure that you have saved your material as a text-only file and have checked for any "odd characters" that can result from "smart quotes" and other special formatting. (See chapter 4 for a list of rules to observe when formatting an e-mail query.) Often, you can avoid submitting actual clips and simply refer the editor to a Web site that offers some of your previously published (and preferably relevant) material.

The final stage of the process involves negotiation. Once an editor decides to accept your column, you'll need to negotiate an acceptable contract and rate of payment. What constitutes "acceptable" in either category can vary widely from writer to writer and publication to publication. Keep one thing in mind: If you have any thoughts of moving on to syndication, you'll need to retain the rights that enable you to do so. But that's another chapter!

SELF-SYNDICATING YOUR COLUMN

Once you've been writing a column for a few months, you may want to consider the next step: marketing that column to more than one publication. This is particularly appropriate for newspaper columns, as newspaper readership is generally based on region rather than interest—and thus rarely overlaps. You can often sell the same column to newspapers in different states, or even papers in different counties or cities within the same state, as long as you are certain that there is likely to be little reader overlap.

Many writers dream of national syndication, but this is considerably harder to achieve, at least in the beginning. (See chapter 8 for more information.) It's usually easiest to start by marketing your column to an ever-expanding list of newspapers until you've built enough of a following to justify a larger distribution. In short, you'll want to begin by syndicating *yourself.*

"Self-syndication" simply means offering a column on a nonexclusive basis to several different publications that are not in direct competition with one another. The best place to start is with local and regional newspapers. Because the distribution of such newspapers is generally limited to a specific town, city, county, or region, such a paper will not be concerned with the fact that your column also appears in the next county or even the next city. (See chapter 5 for Amy Chavez's explanation of the "hundred-mile rule": don't submit the same material to two newspapers within a hundred-mile radius of one another.)

CHOOSE A TOPIC

The previous chapter discussed several types of columns. If your goal is to self-syndicate, you'll want to choose a subject that crosses regional boundaries—or that can be sold to a variety of publications within a certain geographical area.

Some topics, such as health tips or parenting, are universal (or at least tend to work well within the bounds of your own country; other countries may have different health systems or different ideas about parenting). Other topics, however, tend to be more localized. If you're writing a gardening column, for example, you'll need to tailor it to the region you're familiar with, addressing the issues of climate, soil conditions, plant types, etc. that apply to that region. It would be difficult to sell a column on Northwest gardening tips to a newspaper in Arizona. The subject of your column, therefore, will often be the first consideration in determining where to market it.

The farther afield you choose to market your column, the less commonplace it should be. While you may be the only person writing about parenting for your hometown paper, thousands of other writers are covering this topic for other publications throughout the country. To break into a wider market, therefore, you'll need to develop a column that contributes something unique within the field—something that will enable it to compete with other columns that address similar topics.

The same applies to review columns. Reviews of books, movies, and music may cross regional boundaries (if you can create a compelling reason for an editor to buy *your* reviews rather than those of a local or nationally known reviewer). Reviews of restaurants and events, however, tend to be much more localized (though you might be able to pitch such a column to a travel page as a destination piece).

In short, don't waste too much time trying to export a column that has only a limited local value. Focus, instead, on ways that you can give your column a broader appeal—or consider launching an entirely new column that you can market to multiple publications from the start.

SELECT YOUR MARKETS

You might be amazed to discover how many local newspapers exist in your state or region. You can locate such newspapers through any of the dozens of electronic "newsstands" on the Web (see section 1 resources for a list of online guides to newspapers and magazines). You can get even more detailed information about many papers through the *Gale's Directory of Media Publications,* which can be found in the reference section of your local library. While researching newspapers online is easier, *Gale's* has the advantage of providing important information about circulation, frequency, and editorial staff. If you have decided, for example, that you only want to target newspapers that are distributed daily and have a circulation of over 20,000, you may wish to turn to *Gale's.*

Amy Chavez notes another resource in chapter 5: *The Annual Editor & Publisher International Year Book.* Available in most libraries, the *Year Book* "lists addresses and editors of U.S. and Canadian daily newspapers, as well as alternative newspapers and specialty newspapers covering topics such as parenting, seniors, ethnic groups, and real estate. *The E&P Year Book* also gives you valuable information on how often the newspaper is published (daily, weekly, bimonthly), its circulation figures, whether the paper has a Sunday magazine, and a list of the paper's weekly sections and special editions."

Prescreening newspapers by content and circulation is a wise precaution. You don't want to waste time or money submitting columns to weekly shoppers, or papers that are clearly too small to have any budget for freelance (or at least nonlocal) submissions. In addition, if a city or region is served by more than one newspaper, you won't want to submit to both simultaneously.

Some regions are served both by local papers and a larger state or big-city paper. Since you don't want your column to appear in both (or more accurately, your editors won't appreciate it if your column appears in both), you'll need to decide which to target first. This may not be as easy a decision as it sounds. While a big-city paper may pay more (and will reach a larger audience), it is also likely to demand more rights (or even all rights)—and is also more likely to want to post your material on its Web site, which can further limit your ability to distribute that column elsewhere. Smaller papers, though offering lower pay, may be less demanding of rights and less likely to have a Web site.

DEFINE YOUR TERMS

Your basic syndication submission package should include a simple description of the terms you are offering, including:

- Column length (usually 750–1,000 words is best)
- Column frequency (daily, weekly, biweekly, monthly)
- Rights offered

Rights are a key issue in self-syndicating a column. Indeed, you should start thinking about rights long before you consider self-syndication; you should think about this issue when you sell your very first column to your very first paper.

Markets of all types are placing increasing demands on writers for their rights. More and more publications (including small-town newspapers) want writers to sign over all rights to their columns, or even produce them as work for hire (which means that the newspaper owns the copyright to the material from the beginning). You may find that publications that pay as little as $10 to $50 per column still expect you to fork over all rights to that piece.

If you have any intention of selling your work elsewhere, you must ensure that you retain the rights to do so. Typically, you will want to offer a newspaper "one-time nonexclusive rights" to your column, perhaps with the guarantee that the column will not appear in a competing publication. An alternative is to offer "exclusive regional rights," and define "region" as narrowly as possible. The region should be limited to the area of the newspaper's general readership; if the paper is read only in Yakima, Washington, for example, don't let it restrict you from selling the same column to another paper in Seattle or Tacoma.

In some cases, a newspaper will want "first" rights. This may work if your first column sale is to your local paper—it gives you the ability to resell that column a week later to all your other markets. Since only one publication can ever be "first," however, think carefully before granting this option.

Don't be tempted to accept more money for "all rights." The goal of self-syndication is not to earn a huge amount from any single publication, but to gain the widest possible distribution for your piece. Payment for columns is always fairly limited—you're not likely to get an offer above $500 from even the largest paper. If you can sell the same piece to twenty newspapers that offer $50 apiece, you've already doubled that figure—and quite possibly doubled your readership as well. (If you have hopes of moving on to national syndication, readership figures will be vital to your success. It is better to be read not just by a large number of people, but by a large number of people distributed across a wide range of markets.)

Finally, you'll want to determine a minimum rate you're willing to accept. Some small newspapers still offer as little as $10 per column—but that amount can add up quickly if you can sell your column to several papers. Debbie Farmer, who syndicated her column "Family Daze," sets her fee by a standard formula: 50¢ per thousand subscribers.

PREPARE YOUR PACKAGE

Self-syndication has one downside: expense. Most newspapers still prefer to receive column proposals by surface mail rather than by e-mail. This means that to pitch your idea to a wide range of markets, you'll have to invest in postage, printing, and envelopes.

Your submission package will be much the same as that described in the previous chapter, including:

- A cover letter describing your proposed column (be sure to list the terms you are offering)
- Three to six sample columns
- Clips
- Supporting materials, if desired
- An SASE, or
- A self-addressed, stamped postcard that provides "check boxes" for an editor's response

Many editors prefer a postcard to an SASE, as it enables them to quickly check off the appropriate response, rather than having to prepare a formal letter of acceptance or rejection. Your postcard might read something like this:

Date: _____

Dear (Your Name):

Thank you for submitting your proposal for a column titled "Natural Health Tips for Seniors."

_____ We would like to use this column on a weekly basis. We will pay you a fee of $_____ for one-time, nonexclusive rights (per your guarantee that the column will not appear in a directly competing publication).

_____ We regret that we cannot use your column.

(Signed) _____

Editor's Name: _____

If you plan to submit your column to a large number of newspapers, you'll probably want to have all your materials printed in bulk. Have your cover letter printed on a good-quality paper stock; your clips and column samples can be printed on plain 20-pound bond. Most print shops will also be able to print your return postcard. To save costs (and weight), print your clips double-sided.

FOLLOW UP AND MOVE ON

If you don't hear anything from your top prospects within a month of your mailing, don't hesitate to follow up. Often, material gets lost on a busy editor's desk, and a polite phone call may be all you need to close a sale. (In this case, a follow-up letter or card also stands a high risk of being lost in a shuffle of papers, so a phone call is actually a better follow-up mechanism.)

Don't be surprised if an editor wants to modify the terms of your agreement. Some may wish to suggest a lower price or a different word count. It's up to you to decide whether to accept such modifications. If you will be distributing your column to a large number of publications, attempting to tailor the material to each one individually may not be worth the effort. On the other hand, if you've received little response to your mailing, this can be a good way to build a solid relationship with one or two newspapers, which can lead to better rates and additional assignments later.

If you still don't hear anything after following up on your initial mailing, don't be surprised. Many newspaper editors simply do not respond to material they don't plan to accept, so you may never receive any word from many of your markets. Don't be insulted; simply move on to the next prospect.

Self-syndication is a wonderful way to build your portfolio. Be sure to ask for copies of the issues in which your column appears, or at least for a tear sheet of your column. Once you have a regular column with a local paper (even if it's not local to *you*), you can list yourself as a contributor or stringer to that publication. This may be just the stepping-stone you need to propel your column into the big leagues—such as national syndication.

HOW I BECAME A SYNDICATED COLUMNIST
BY DEBBIE FARMER

About two years ago, I decided I didn't have enough excitement, frustration, and uncertainty in my life, so I decided to become a syndicated family humor columnist.

I starting writing monthly family humor articles for the local Mother's Club newsletter while my children were napping. About six months later, I brought column samples to the editor of a tiny, independent newspaper, and the newspaper began running my column every two weeks.

I stayed with that paper long enough to generate several months' worth of clips and some fan mail, then approached the features editor of the larger daily newspaper. Now, I was competing with established syndicates who had professional columnists, but I offered the editor something she couldn't get elsewhere—a local family humor columnist.

The bigger daily gave my column a catchy name ("Family Daze") and started publishing it weekly. I finally began to take my writing more seriously. I figured out that the only chance I had of earning pay that reflected the hard work I put into each column was for it to be picked up by a major syndicate that could market it to hundreds, perhaps thousands, of papers. This became my goal—right along with every other freelance newspaper columnist in the world. But since ignorance can be bliss to a budding columnist, I was naïve enough to think that I could beat the odds.

I quickly learned, however, that I had a better chance of breaking into a major syndicate if I self-syndicated my column into as many papers as I could manage. I sent out packets to editors that contained a cover letter, publishing history, six column samples or clips, and a price/distribution sheet. I put everything into a folder with a clear cover that allowed my cartoon logo on the first page to show through.

Kathleen Purcell, who self-syndicated her column "The Corner Booth" to dozens of newspapers, suggests using a bright blue cardboard folder with a business card die-cut in the front cover, centered about one-third of the way down. She says, "I selected six of my favorite columns, dropped my photo (digitally) onto the upper left quadrant (just like it would appear in a real column), and ran them off on my printer. Those I put in the right pocket of the folder. In the left pocket I put my bio, list of papers where my column was running, cover letter, and three business cards (one for the editor, one for the secretary, and one to pass out to other editors at conferences). The cover letter explained how I billed, how much I charged (50¢ per thousand circulation, according to the newspaper's circulation figures published in *Gale's Directory of Media Publications*), when they could expect to receive columns, and how to contact me if they had a problem."

I also use a standard pricing formula of 50¢ per thousand circulation. This means that I receive amounts between $50 per column (from my local paper) to $1.50 per column (from my smallest independent paper). The average price range is generally $10–$15 per column. Of course, you have to find the marketing system that works best for you, your schedule, and budget.

Since everyone's pitching style will be different, do what's comfortable for you. I tried to keep my pitch short and sweet—preferably with no begging. Okay, just a little begging. I highlighted my publishing history, reader appeal, and professional awards.

Kathleen Purcell's pitch takes specifics of the publication into consideration. She says, "For small, community papers I said my column built reader loyalty, would *not* offend advertisers, supported community values, and appealed particularly to women with children (easily the bulk of their readership). For larger papers I said my column was unique, timely, built readership, and provoked discussion."

After two years, my persistence finally paid off. Well, almost. "Family Daze" is now published weekly in over two dozen newspapers, I've sold articles to national parenting magazines, and I have an offer pending with a national syndicate. It just goes to show that with a little bit of moxie, persistence, determination, and luck, you can successfully syndicate your newspaper column. Just don't quit your day job—yet.

How to Become a Syndicated Columnist

by Amy Chavez

Almost all column writers dream of becoming syndicated. Syndicates distribute your articles to newspapers and magazines, with the profits split between you and the syndicate. Representation by a major syndicate guarantees a wide readership for your work.

Getting syndicated is tough, though. Jay Kennedy, editor-in-chief of King Features, cautions, "Newspapers in general don't have enough space to cover all the news they would like to. They make hard decisions about what to print and what not to print." That means that your column idea really has to stand out.

How to Make Your Column Idea Stand Out

Make sure your idea is appropriate. Sidney Goldberg, senior vice president/editorial director at United Media, says, "Many submissions we get are inappropriate for syndication. Consider whether your idea might work better for a magazine. Magazines have a constant need to fill each issue with new material."

Magazines target niche audiences, whereas newspapers must appeal to a more general audience. Ideas that are appropriate for syndication are those that lend themselves to weekly or twice-weekly news or updates, such as a column about technology or stocks. Columns that provide a voice for a certain population of people are popular: Ted Rall (Universal Press) represents the voice of Generation X; Leonard Pitts (Tribune Media Services) speaks for African-Americans. Such opinion columns draw from the news, a never-ending resource for material. Advice columns on subjects such as personal finance, parenting, and relationships are also appropriate, while horoscopes and crossword puzzles are staples in syndication.

Unfortunately, all these topics have been taken. What you'll need to do is uncover a new idea that doesn't compete with anything already out there, yet isn't too narrow in scope. For example, a column on healthy, timesaving recipes for working mothers might be appropriate, whereas a column on cookbook reviews would be too narrow for syndication.

Since syndication slots are limited, competition for them is stiff. "There are a lot of good columnists out there, so to replace an existing columnist, your column idea has to be dramatically better," says Goldberg. That means your idea has to be fresh and new, offering something the syndicate doesn't already have.

This is not as easy as it sounds. "Although syndicates say they want new ideas in theory, some of them don't seem to want to sign them in reality," admits David Astor, an associate editor of *Editor & Publisher Magazine*. In other words, an appropriate idea is one that is new but not too risky. Your idea has to appeal to the conservative tastes of newspaper editors who will be buying the column.

SHOW THE NEED FOR YOUR COLUMN

If your material has already been published elsewhere, you've already proven that there is a need for your material. "Start trying to sell your column idea on your own," says Lee Salem, syndication vice president for Universal Press. "After you've signed up a few papers on your own, put a package together of some sample columns." The more papers you can sign up on your own, the better your chances are of convincing a syndicate there is a need for your column.

KEEP UP WITH THE TRENDS

In order to know what syndicates are looking for, keep up with the trends. "Syndicates and newspapers don't seem as interested in humor columns as they used to be," notes David Astor, who writes "Syndicate World," a weekly column about the syndicate industry for *Editor & Publisher Online*. That doesn't mean there isn't a lot of humor being syndicated, however. It's just been repackaged. "Click and Clack Talk Cars" (King Features), for example, is humor repackaged as car advice.

Another trend in syndication is "syndication packages." Syndicates are offering whole broadsheets containing several articles that newspapers can simply add as a section to their paper. Syndication packages can cover topics such as food, health, technology, parenting, and dozens of other areas. Knight Ridder/Tribune Information Services (KRT) offers a home, garden, and hobby package as well as a package called "New Voices," which focuses on diversity. Have you noticed the increase in popularity of car racing in the past few years? In response, some syndicates now offer weekly packages of NASCAR information.

When newspapers buy a package, they pay a set price for the entire section. This is good for columnists, because syndicates have to sign on more writers to fill the sections. The pay, however, can be less than a standard fifty-fifty split. Syndication packages tend to pay one set price for your article, no matter how many packages are sold.

Another recent trend is Web syndication. Not only are traditional syndicates going the way of the Web, but Web-based syndicates such as isyndicate! (*www.isyndicate.com*) have opened up new opportunities for writers to self-syndicate their columns. Still another trend among print syndicates is to distribute features internationally. Think of how a global audience might affect your syndication idea.

One more hint for keeping up with trends: Columns and comic strips are closely related, and most syndicates carry both. To spot new trends, look at the new cartoons. The Los Angeles Times Syndicate just picked up a comic strip featuring a nine-year-old girl who lives with her father. Universal Press Syndicate has a new comic strip called "Baldo," which features Latino characters and is available in both Spanish and English. How can these trends help you develop your column idea?

How to Approach a Syndicate

Before you send out your submission, do your homework. Doing so will save you time and prevent you from making costly mistakes that will only further delay your pursuit of syndication.

Get a copy of the *Editor & Publisher Syndicate Directory,* updated annually, which lists all the syndicates in the United States as well as all the names of syndicated columns and columnists (including those self-syndicated). (You can order it from E&P Online.) Contact names and addresses are listed for all syndicates, as well as their Web sites. By visiting syndicate Web sites, you can quickly find out what kind of columns they already carry. Since many columnists are self-syndicating their columns these days, knowing who these people are, what kind of columns they write, and where their columns appear will help you decide if your column idea should be pursued or not.

Read David Astor's "Syndicate World" at Editor & Publisher Online for industry gossip, current acquisitions, and editorial changes. This is also a great place to spot trends and opportunities.

Once you decide which syndicate to approach, be sure to read the submission guidelines (usually posted on their Web site). Most syndicates want to see about six sample columns. If your work has already been published in other places and you have received feedback from readers, include some copies of their letters in your package, recommends Salem. "Even negative letters are okay. Controversy and the ability to stir up people's emotions can be a good thing. Also, get a supportive letter of recommendation from the editor who runs your column."

Other things to include in your package are articles about you or your work that have appeared in publications, your publishing history, and a bio. Don't forget the SASE. Note that stamped packages weighing more than sixteen ounces must be taken to the post office for delivery, which can be a hassle; it's often better to simply send a letter-size envelope for a reply, and allow the editor to dispose of the rest of your materials. Overseas submissions cannot be returned in prepaid envelopes under any circumstances (you must include one or two International Reply Coupons with your self-addressed envelope).

It takes time and effort to put together an attractive package to send to a syndicate. But remember, the most important part of your package is your column idea. Sidney Goldberg sums it up rather poignantly: "If you have a good idea, don't send it. Send only absolutely phenomenal ideas!"

HOW TO BECOME AN INTERNATIONAL COLUMNIST
by Amy Chavez

Have you ever wanted to be a newspaper columnist with international exposure? Foreign newspapers use freelance columnists every day. You don't have to be a journalist. Here's a step-by-step approach to becoming a columnist for a foreign newspaper.

TARGET A NEWSPAPER

Any large public or university library will have current foreign newspapers. You can also research newspapers online by country at one of many electronic newsstands (see section 1 resources).

Selecting a newspaper will largely be determined by your expertise and the type of column you would like to write. If your interest is martial arts, for example, your target newspapers would probably be those in China, Japan, or Korea. Since each of these countries has its own style of martial arts, you could narrow your focus to one style and one country. If, however, you want to write a column about the latest fashion trends in New York City, you could query several different newspapers around the world.

Scan the newspapers for patterns. Do they get most of their international news from wire services such as the Associated Press and Reuters? Do they use syndicated columnists for politics, economics, and opinion pieces? If so, don't try to break into those sections; they're already taken. Most newspapers, however, also have a lifestyle or weekend section, where outside contributors are published.

Although the Sunday edition is the most prized spot for a columnist (because readership tends to be highest on Sundays), dailies use one or more columnists every day of the week. A columnist may write anywhere from one to five times a week, depending on the demand for that column's information. For a columnist who lives outside the country, once or twice a week is typical.

FIND A HOT COLUMN TOPIC

After you've developed a good sense of what kind of content a newspaper carries, look at what the newspaper doesn't have. Think of a new idea, one that isn't being addressed in the paper yet. Can you give advice on cross-cultural communication? Dealing with American businesses? Investing? Are you a marriage counselor with experience dealing with international marriages? Would you make a good international food critic? If you are scanning business-oriented newspapers, perhaps you could propose a column on how to deal with American businesses. Or consider a column that reviews the latest trendy restaurants in Europe—something that would be of interest to business travelers. If it's a business-oriented newspaper in Asia, perhaps you could give advice to businessmen on how to avoid cultural faux pas when dealing with American or European businesswomen. On the other hand, if you're scanning nonbusiness newspapers with large lifestyle sections, you might propose a column on wine-making or herbal medicine.

If you live in the host country or have inside knowledge about a country (e.g., you spent your childhood in a foreign country or you are married to someone from another country), perhaps you could write a column that bridges the cultural gap between the foreign population and the nationals. A column on cultural differences or intercultural communication, or even an advice column, might be appropriate. English newspapers abroad must appeal not only to native English speakers, but also to the population that reads English as a second language. Maybe you could write a column related to English-language learning, such as grammar usage or vocabulary improvement.

If you have no special experience or inside knowledge, submit lifestyle articles. There is almost always a need for articles on health, celebrities, and American pop culture.

PROPOSE YOUR COLUMN

If you happen to live in the host country, you can sell yourself with a local angle, such as, "I live in Japan, so I'm well aware of the problems Japanese people have in learning English." If you live outside the country, sell that angle—for example, "I live in New York, so I can bring you the most up-to-date New York fashion news," or "I live in France, so I can give first-hand information on martial arts trends in Europe."

Use your selling point in your query letter. Send a simple query letter and a proposal with three to six sample columns to the editor-in-chief. You'll find the name of the editor-in-chief on the newspaper's masthead. If an e-mail address is listed, e-mail first to see if it is acceptable to send submissions electronically.

SELL REPRINTS

Presuming you only sold the original newspaper first publication rights, you can then sell second (reprint) rights of your column to other publications. But don't try to sell the same articles to another English-language newspaper in the same country: That's a competing market. Look at magazines and other publications in the host country or in your home country that specialize in your subject matter. I've sold reprints to humor magazines, online magazines, book anthologies, U.S. newspapers, and even an ESL textbook.

Some publications don't accept reprints. Other publications, such as the *Utne Reader* and *Funny Times,* specialize in reprints. To find out if a publication accepts reprints or not, check their submission guidelines. See the resources at the end of this section for online collections of magazine and newspaper guidelines.

ONLINE SUPPORT

Being a columnist can be lonely. You'll want a community of writers to discuss issues with and get opinions from. Support groups for writers abound on the Internet, and most have subscribers from all over the world. One source is the Freelance Journalist Mailing List; another is BlueEar.com (*www.blueear.com*).

SECTION 2 RESOURCES

REFERENCES
BlueEar: Global Writing Worth Reading
www.blueear.com

Editor & Publisher Online
www.mediainfo.com

David Astor's "Syndicate World"
www.mediainfo.com/ephome/news/newshtm/webnews/syndicate.htm

How to Be a Syndicated Columnist, by Angela Adair-Hoy
(E-book available from *www.booklocker.com;* includes extensive lists of syndication contacts.)

You Can Write a Column, by Monica McCabe Cardoza (Writer's Digest Books)

SYNDICATES
Major Syndicates
Copley News Service
P.O. Box 190
San Diego, California 92112
www.copleynews.com
(newspaper columns, features, fillers)

Creators Syndicate
5777 West Century Boulevard., Suite 700
Los Angeles, California 90045
www.creators.com
(newspaper columns)

King Features
235 East 45th Street
New York, New York 10017
www.kingfeatures.com
(comics, columns, editorial features, cartoons)

Los Angeles Times Syndicate
Times Mirror Square
Los Angeles, California 90053
www.lats.com
(newspaper columns, comics)

Tribune Media Services
64 East Concord Street
Orlando, Florida 32801
www.tms.tribune.com
(newspaper columns, comics)

United Media
200 Madison Avenue
New York, New York 10016
www.unitedfeatures.com
(comics, cartoons, columns, features)

Universal Press Syndicate
4900 Main Street
Kansas City, Missouri 64112
www.uexpress.com
(newspaper columns)

Washington Post Writers Group
1150 15th Street NW
Washington, D.C. 20071
www.postwritersgroup.com

Newer Syndicates
DBR Media
P.O. Box 593548
Orlando, Florida 32859–3548
1–877–493–5360
www.dbrmedia.com

Paradigm, TSA
P.O. Box 111372
Stamford, Connecticut 06911–1372
Paradigm@Paradigm-TSA.com
www.paradigm-tsa.com

Self-Syndication
isyndicate!
www.isyndicate.com

NEWSPAPERS
See section 1 resources for sites with links to print and online newspapers.

Section 3

SELLING A NONFICTION BOOK

10

PREPARING A NONFICTION BOOK PROPOSAL

Take a look around any bookstore, and you'll quickly realize that the vast majority of books offered for sale are nonfiction. Nonfiction titles cross the spectrum of ideas and experience. Some appeal to a small, focused niche of readers; others have an audience of thousands.

The good news is that the nonfiction book market is fairly open to new writers, provided that you have a marketable idea and the skill to present it in a readable (and hopefully interesting) form. The even better news is that you can often sell your nonfiction book *before* you write it, by presenting a convincing proposal to the right publisher. This means you won't have to start writing without a commitment from a publisher (and quite possibly an advance). It also means that you can get feedback from the publisher before you start, so that your book is tailored specifically to that publisher's needs.

FINDING THE RIGHT PUBLISHER

The first step in selling a nonfiction book is to find the right publisher to sell it *to*. Locating an appropriate publisher means more than grabbing a directory of markets and looking in the topic index. Just because a publisher offers books on dogs, for example, doesn't mean that it's the right publisher for *your* dog book. You can waste a lot of time sending out proposals to inappropriate publishers—or save a lot of time by targeting the right publisher on your very first try.

Here are some steps you can take to find that publisher:

1) **Check your bookshelf.** Take a look at the reference books you use in the subject area you're writing about. Do certain imprints stand out? If so, these may represent publishers who produce the kinds of books *you* use for research—which means that your own book might fit well into their lineup. Make a note of any imprint that appears more than once on your bookshelf.

2) **Check a bookstore.** Browse through the shelves as if you were looking for titles you might want to buy in the relevant topic area. Again, do certain imprints stand out? Do you find that you pick up books by a specific publisher more often than any other? If so, this is another indication that the publisher matches your interest area—and that you might match the publisher's interests as well. While you're browsing, ask yourself these questions:

- **Do you like the look and feel of the publisher's products?** Is the paper of high quality? Is the cover attractive? Does it make you want to pick up the book and browse? Is the type easily read? Would you want your book to be presented in a similar fashion?

- **Does the book *look* like the book you're planning?** One thing to consider, for example, is illustrations: If the publisher likes to use lots of color photos, can you supply them? Conversely, if your book requires artwork and you see no illustrations in the books you're reviewing, will you be able to convince that publisher of the need for art?

- **Does the style and presentation match your own?** Pay attention to the language of the books you've selected. Do they match your style and tone? If you write in a conversational style, don't try to pitch to a publisher whose books are all written in a highly technical or academic style.

- **Do your credentials match those of the publisher's current authors?** Take a look at the authors' bylines and bios. Would yours be comparable? Or does this publisher require academic degrees or professional experience that you lack?

- **What is the price range of the publisher's books?** Does it match the buying range of your target audience? You may like the idea of presenting your work in glossy, coffee-table format, but will your audience be willing to shell out $30 or more to buy it? Or would you be better off with a publisher who offers more reasonably priced editions?

3) **Check the Web.** Once you've located two or three publishers who seem to be likely candidates, try to locate their Web pages. (Most of the larger publishers, and a good number of the smaller ones, now have Web sites.) On the publisher's Web site, you should be able to review the publisher's current catalog and submission guidelines. Take a look at that catalog: It will tell you not only what authors the publisher features, but also whether it has produced any titles similar to yours. If the publisher has recently offered a book much like the one you're about to propose, it isn't likely to want another (especially as the two books would be in competition with one another).

4) **Review the submission guidelines.** Make sure your proposal matches the publisher's requirements. Are you offering the right kind of information and supporting materials? Is your book the right length? (If it isn't, can you cut it back, or expand it, as needed?) Does your book fit into the range of desired topics? Make sure you know exactly what the publisher wants you to submit, and submit precisely those materials.

5) **Review the publisher's terms.** Most print publishers don't post copies of their standard contracts online (though most electronic publishers do); however, they will usually provide an overview of the basic terms they impose on authors. Make sure you aren't submitting your book to a work-for-hire publisher (or you'll lose the copyright). Make sure you understand what royalties are offered, on what basis (e.g., retail price versus net profits), and when they will be paid. Knowing these things in advance will prevent you from making the mistake of accepting a bad offer, just because you feel that any offer is better than none.

ESSENTIALS OF A PROPOSAL

Once you've found an appropriate publisher, your proposal must answer three basic questions:

- What is this book about?
- What is the market for this book or idea?
- Why are you the right person to write it?

To answer those questions, you'll need to prepare a package that consists of the following elements:

- **Overview.** This section is usually divided into several subsections, including:
  - Content—a general summary of what the book is about
  - Rationale—a discussion of the potential market for the book, as well as why it should be published *now*
  - Competition—a review of other books on similar topics
  - Format—the length and presentation of the proposed book
  - Market—how to reach your intended audience
- **Chapter-by-Chapter Outline.** This section provides a list of chapter titles and usually a brief (one-paragraph) description of each chapter.
- **Author Credentials.** This is where you'll answer the all-important question: Why are you the person to write this book? Your bio should be at least half a page to a page in length.

This chapter will offer some basic tips on proposal construction. The next will show you two examples of successful book proposals: Amy Shojai's proposal for *New Choices in Natural Healing for Dogs & Cats: Over 1,000 At-Home Remedies for Your Pet's Problems* (published by Rodale Press in 1999) and my proposal for *writing.com: Creative Internet Strategies to Advance Your Writing Career* (published by Allworth Press in 1999). Amy Shojai also agreed to be interviewed for this section.

THE OVERVIEW

TITLE

While your title may be the last thing you decide upon, it will be the first thing a potential editor sees when reviewing your proposal. Amy Shojai points out that a title "must not only describe the book and/or concept, but be that illusive thing that editors/agents describe as 'sexy.' In other words, the title must strike an instant chord of recognition with the editor. One of my favorites, still, is my book, *Competability: Building a Peaceable Kingdom Between Cats and Dogs.*" At the same time, she notes, "don't get too attached to titles, either. Editors change them all the time, often for something that's boring (after all the trouble you went to in finding a killer name!)."

CONTENT

What is your book about? Presenting a coherent, well-defined answer to this question is crucial to selling your idea. Your topic must be both broad enough to justify a book-length manuscript and specific enough to focus on a definable market niche.

For example, if you're a pet writer, you wouldn't want to pitch a book about dogs. That's far too broad a topic (as evidenced by the hundreds of dog books already on the shelves). Instead, focus on a more specific topic that you're qualified to write about, such as medical care of dogs, traveling with dogs, hiking with dogs, breeding dogs, training dogs, etc. Even then, you may need to narrow the field. Amy Shojai's proposal, for example, doesn't attempt to cover every aspect of medical care for pets, but focuses on natural health care.

The first part of your overview should offer a general summary of the content of your book. Don't go into excessive detail; instead, try to convey the general focus and purpose of your book, including the benefits it will offer to readers. (The concept of "benefits" is key: Your overview should clearly indicate what readers have to gain from your book.)

The overview for my proposal for *writing.com* defines the content of the book through a series of questions likely to be asked by readers, beginning with the question, "What do writers want to know about the Internet?" The overview continues with a promise to the publisher:

> **Writing in Cyberspace** is designed to answer these questions, and more. It is divided into three sections that correspond with the way most writers "experience" the Internet: *Exploration* (research), *Interaction* (using e-mail and networking), and *Creation*

(establishing an online presence). Each chapter highlights a particular aspect of the writing business and how that aspect has been affected (or can be improved) by the Internet.

Note that this is a fairly general description. While the questions themselves offer some detail about the book's content, most of that detail has been saved for the chapter-by-chapter outline that comes later in the proposal.

Amy Shojai explains that her book "examines the world of nontraditional medicine for dogs and cats, and offers real-world applications to the many health conditions that affect our pets." Note, again, that this is a very general overview of the subject matter. At the end of her proposal, however, she includes a "therapy thesaurus" that lists "(about) a hundred common dog and cat illnesses/conditions." That list is enough to give the publisher a clear idea of the topics to be covered (from acne to wool-sucking), without cluttering the overview itself with excess detail.

RATIONALE

Besides explaining what your book is about, your overview should also provide an idea of the audience for that book. "Back up the need for the book with stats," says Shojai. "Editors want numbers; don't just say 'everybody who loves pets will buy my book.' Tell them how many owners there are who have dogs who chew used bubble gum and would benefit from your book, *12 Steps to De-Gumming Da Dog*."

Shojai's approach is to offer broad statistics that define the potential of the market: "66.2 million cats and 58 million dogs are kept by Americans." She then narrows that market to the "most likely" readership: those who "welcome pets into their hearts and homes as full members of the family. This pet generation is eager to provide quality care for their furry families ... " She further defines the market by noting that the "national obsession with health and fitness" also applies to pets—and that a large number of pet owners are also interested in alternative health care options.

By highlighting a growing trend (the interest in alternative health care), Shojai also indicates why her book is *timely*. Her proposal conveys the impression that the time to target this market is *now*, while the trend is growing—but before the market is saturated with books on the topic.

Similarly, when I proposed *writing.com*, little information was available offline for writers who wanted to know more about online opportunities and resources. A year or so earlier, publishers might not have recognized the growing importance of the Internet to writers (I actually spoke to a publisher of writing books who felt that writers were not going to be very interested in the Internet!). Today, the market is saturated with information on this topic. Your proposal, therefore, needs to answer the vital question: Why publish this book *now*?

Though I've listed "Content" and "Rationale" separately, these should not necessarily be separate components of your overview. In most cases (as the sample proposals in the next chapter illustrate), they will be tightly interwoven. As you discuss content, you should also present your rationale for why this particular content will be important to your target audience at this particular time.

COMPETITION

Your overview should also discuss the competition that currently exists for your book. If you perceive little competition for your book (i.e., few books on the market on the same or similar topics), you may decide to cover this topic in your discussion of "Content" and "Rationale." If, however, your book faces steep competition (i.e., many books have already been published on similar topics), you may wish to break this out into a separate section, so that you can address the competition in detail.

Before you can discuss the competition, however, you must first research it. Hopefully, you've already done this before you started working on your book: It's vital to know what has already been written, so that you don't end up reinventing the wheel. Your publisher will also want to know that you've reviewed the competition and that you can offer something new and different.

Amy Shojai sums up the need to study the competition in a nutshell: "The competition section is vital; it's probably the most important part of any proposal. [It's a] balancing act here, though—I try to *never* slam the competition, but just to put my proposal in a favorable light compared to whatever might be out there. In this case, I felt that some of the competition was quite good—just way, way out of date, which meant my proposal was timely. Of course, I added lots of new elements the competition doesn't have, too."

Your discussion of the competition should list specific titles (including author, publisher, and publication date). It should then explain how your book differs from those titles: how it improves, differs from, or goes beyond what has been written before. For example, Shojai lists several representative titles in her proposal, then notes that while most of her competitors focus on single therapies, her book will present a range of approaches. She sums up her description of the competition by stating that "no book to date offers the comprehensive balance, positive approach, and step-by-step advice of *Healing at Home Naturally.*"

When I proposed *writing.com* to Allworth Press, one significant competitor was one of Allworth's own titles, *The Writer's Internet Handbook.* To demonstrate that my book filled a niche not addressed by the *Handbook,* I prepared a chapter-by-chapter comparison of the two books, noting the points that would be covered in my book but not in the *Handbook,* and also the points addressed in the *Handbook* that would not be covered in my book, to avoid overlap. My goal was not to suggest that my book was better than the *Handbook,* but, rather, that it would meet a different need in the market.

What if you can't identify any competition for your book? This is not necessarily a good thing! Shojai notes, "If there is no competition, find some. Put something in, even if it's a stretch, because if nobody has done the topic before, the publisher or editor will figure there's a reason—probably because it's not a salable idea. You *want* books on your topic to be out there and successful; that means you have a ready-made market. Then, it's a matter of making your book different enough, bringing something new to the table, to make the idea viable."

FORMAT

Even if your book is not yet written, your publisher will want an idea of its anticipated format. This section may be as short as a paragraph; it should list the book's title and subtitle, the number of words you anticipate, and any other information that will be relevant to the actual production of the book.

For example, Shojai's proposal notes that her book will be organized in two sections, the second of which will be in the form of a "thesaurus." She also mentions the use of sidebars, and an appendix that will include a glossary, directory, and resources. In my initial pitch for *writing.com* (below), I mentioned that:

> Resources are important and should be included, but I would prefer to see such references grouped together in sidebars or at the end of a chapter. (It can be frustrating to try to relocate a URL that is buried in a paragraph of text.) Ideally, I'd like to compile an updateable CD-ROM of writing-related links to accompany the text.

Be sure to mention any illustrations or other artwork that will accompany the book—e.g., charts, diagrams, figures, tables, line drawings, photographs, etc. If you plan to use color illustrations, make sure that the need for such illustrations is clear, as these will involve extra production costs.

MARKET

While you presented a rationale for the type of audience your book is likely to attract earlier in your proposal, you may also wish to add some specifics about how to reach that audience. Shojai, for example, lists a variety of pet and health magazines that target the same market as her book and cites circulation figures for each. She also provides a list of organizations that might be interested in her book (and, possibly, in promoting it).

This information isn't absolutely necessary at this point. However, keep it in mind— because you'll be asked to provide it if and when your proposal is accepted. By presenting it in your proposal, you'll have demonstrated, again, that you have done your homework and can offer the publisher not only a high-quality book, but valuable support in selling that book.

CHAPTER-BY-CHAPTER SUMMARY

While this may be the largest part of your proposal, in terms of pages and word count, it is the most easily explained. Simply provide a list of planned chapters and a brief (one- to two-paragraph) overview of the contents of each.

Of course, this may be more easily said than done. If you haven't actually begun to write the book, you may not have any idea how many chapters it will contain, or what will go in each. If you don't, guess. Your publisher will expect this information in your proposal—but will also understand that it isn't written in stone.

One way to develop such a summary is to work from your existing outline. If you haven't developed an outline yet, this exercise will accomplish two tasks in one. Dividing your planned content into chapters is a good way to determine the logical organization for that content—and also a good way to discover whether you have too much information in one area and not enough in another.

There are no rules about how many chapters a book can or should contain. However, if you're familiar with other titles in your subject area, you'll probably have a good idea of how many chapters those titles contain, on average. Ten is always a nice, round number. Five chapters or fewer may make your book seem too short, even if each chapter is packed with information; more than twenty chapters may make the book seem too long or unwieldy. (Remember, you can always adjust the number of chapters later in the writing process.)

Some writers, like Shojai, let chapter titles speak for themselves. Others (like myself) write expansive descriptions of each chapter. The next chapter offers examples of both approaches.

Author Bio

No matter how convincing an outline you put together, publishers will still have one "make-or-break" question: What are your qualifications for writing this book? How can you prove that you know what you are talking about?

Your bio should answer this question in the space of (about) a single page. It should be written in narrative format, and in third person—e.g., "John Smith is an award-winning decoy carver who has practiced—and taught—the craft for more than twenty years . . . "

Before you attempt to put together an author bio, be sure you know what credentials are *expected* of you by the publisher you're approaching, and by the market you are attempting to target. For example, if you're writing a scholarly treatise, you'll want to seek an academic publisher, and you'll be expected to have the right academic credentials. If, however, you're writing a book for a more general audience, you will want to find a publisher who can reach that audience—and who may be more interested in your writing ability than in academic degrees. In other words, research the market first!

A publisher is likely to expect credentials in one or more of the following categories:

- Educational background
- Professional background and expertise
- Personal experience and expertise
- Previous writing credits

If your book focuses on scholarly information, chances are good that you'll be expected to have academic credentials. For example, a book on military history or recent archaeological discoveries is more likely to sell if it is written by a qualified military historian or archaeologist. There are exceptions, but you're going to have to present a very convincing argument for your proposal if you don't have a publisher's first choice of credentials.

If your book focuses on business or technical information, you may be expected to provide relevant professional experience. For example, if you're writing a book on corporate management, you'll have a much better chance of selling it if you are a CEO, or at least an experienced manager. If you can combine that expertise with a degree in business management, so much the better—but the practical experience will, in this case, generally outweigh the academic credentials.

If your book addresses more popular how-to or self-help topics, you may be able to market your proposal on the basis of professional *or* personal expertise. For example, if you're writing about dog training, the fact that you've been a professional trainer for years would carry more weight than a degree in veterinary medicine. If you're writing a book on how to build your own sailboat, the fact that you've built three such boats in your garage (and, perhaps, sailed them around the world without sinking) will be more significant than a degree in engineering.

Personal *experience* can be a tricky credential. It is, of course, essential for a book that is, itself, an *account* of your personal experiences (e.g., a memoir or account of a specific life event). It is usually less helpful, however, in marketing how-to or self-help titles. A good guideline to consider is that the more impact your book might have on a reader's well-being, the more credentials you will be expected to have. While you might sell a book on fly-fishing on the basis of a weekend hobby, you may have trouble selling a book on child care if your only "credential" is having been a parent.[1]

Previous writing credits can be useful *if* they are relevant to the book you are proposing. Shojai, for example, cited the fact that she had already written ten nonfiction pet books and more than 250 articles on pet care. This might have been sufficient to sell her proposal, even without her professional credentials (veterinary technician, spokesperson for Purina brand pet foods).

If, however, your writing credentials don't relate to your proposed topic, they will carry very little weight. Rodale Press would probably not have been impressed if, for example, Shojai had written ten books on gardening. Writing experience is generally the last credential publishers look for; while such experience does indicate that you can write (and even that you can write a successful book), it doesn't necessarily indicate that you are qualified to write *this* book.

---

[1] Before someone writes to tell me that they know someone who sold a book on just that type of topic with no more credentials than I've mentioned, let me hasten to say that there are exceptions to every rule, and many books *have* been sold with virtually no author credentials. If you *don't* have the credentials, however, you will have to work that much harder to make the rest of your proposal convincing.

SUPPORTING MATERIALS

Your basic proposal package—overview, chapter-by-chapter summary, and bio—should provide all the information that an editor (or agent) would need to make a decision. In some cases, however, you may wish to include certain supporting materials, such as:

- **Resume or curriculum vitae.** Include this if it supports the credentials described in your bio. If it doesn't, omit it.

- **Publications list.** Again, if this supports your bio, include it. Or include an edited list that focuses on those publications that *do* support your proposal, leaving out those that are irrelevant. (You can title this "Selected Publications List.")

- **Writing samples.** Some authors (and publishers) discourage the inclusion of samples of previously published work. Include them only if they are relevant to your proposal—and include no more than three samples.

- **Business card.** It's always a good idea to include a professional-looking business card (or two) with your proposal, so that an editor or agent can easily contact you.

- **An SASE.** Need it be said? Yes, you should include an SASE with your proposal! If your entire proposal weighs less than one pound and you would like it to be returned, then include a manila envelope with enough postage for its return. More typically, however, you should simply include a stamped, self-addressed #10 envelope for the editor's or agent's response.

- **A reply postcard.** If you would like to know when your proposal was received, you can include a self-addressed postcard that the recipient can toss in the mail. Just put the name of the publishing house or agent on the reverse; the postmark itself will give you a date for delivery confirmation.

- **A product sample.** In very, *very* rare cases, it might be appropriate to include a "sample" of whatever it is you are writing about. For example, if you're writing a book on "how to create your own personalized greeting cards," it might be appropriate to include a sample card in your proposal package. I've heard of authors sending a batch of cookies along with a cookbook—but I'm not sure I'd recommend it!

Do not send any of the following:

- **Your photo.** The recipient doesn't need to know what you look like, your age, your race, or any other information that would be conveyed by a photo. Save the publicity shots until after your book has been accepted.

- **Testimonials or reviews.** If other folks have said nice things about your work, that's great—but don't share them with your editor or agent. Let your work stand on its own.

- **Irrelevant writing samples.** If a sample doesn't support the subject matter of your proposal in some way, don't send it—even if it's the only writing sample you have.

- **Anything unprofessional.** It's probably best that you don't include greeting cards, personalized bookmarks, business pens, or other "gifts" with your proposal. Don't try to rationalize that such objects will help "get an editor's attention." They may—but they won't improve your chances of selling your book.

One other item that you may not be expected to submit is sample chapters. In this, nonfiction proposals differ dramatically from fiction proposals. When submitting a fiction proposal, you will generally be expected to have completed the book—and thus you can be expected to have the first three chapters available to send with your proposal. A nonfiction proposal, however, may be submitted before you've written the first word of the book itself, and thus sample chapters are often not necessary. (Always check the publisher's or agent's guidelines to be sure!)

Even if you *have* written the entire book, however, a proposal is usually a far better way to market that book than sending out the entire manuscript. Don't expect your manuscript to speak for itself, no matter how good it may be. Instead, use your proposal as an opportunity to speak *for* your manuscript—to convince an editor that there is a market for your book and that it can beat the competition.

WHEN TO "PITCH" INSTEAD OF "PROPOSE"

A good book proposal can sometimes lead to an assignment that you don't expect. If all the elements of your proposal demonstrate to a publisher that you would be a good author to add to their "stable," but they can't use the book itself, you may be asked to present an alternate idea.

In this case, you'll often be asked to "pitch" rather than "propose." Most likely, the publisher will ask you to suggest two or three book topics, with a brief description of each. That description should cover content and rationale, but you won't need to go into details about the competition or attempt to develop an outline. You also won't need to provide the same level of detail about your own credentials, as you've already established those in your original proposal. (You may, however, need to provide a few lines to indicate why you would like to write, or are specifically qualified to write, the book you're now pitching.)

A pitch can take the form of a simple letter (formatted like a basic query). Often, the publisher may wish to receive this via e-mail, which is a good idea, as you want to get your pitch in as quickly as possible.

Following is a portion of the pitch letter I submitted to Allworth Press, after my initial book proposal to that publisher was rejected:

Dear Mr. Crawford,

Thank you for your kind words about my proposal, "How to Launch Your Writing Career." Yours is probably the most encouraging rejection letter I've ever received!

Thank you also for the invitation to suggest some additional book concepts for possible consideration. Following are three topics that I believe might be of interest to Allworth Press:[2]

1) Writing in Cyberspace: How to Build Your Writing Business Online

Thus far, most Internet books for writers (including Arco's recent *Writer's Guide to Internet Resources*) have been much the same. They discuss the basics ("This is a URL") and provide an overview of Internet resources of interest to writers.

I'd like to go beyond that and develop a book that focuses on "applications": specific ways in which writers can expand their business and sales and enhance their writing skills. Some recent topics I've explored include:

- How to research and market to international publications

- How to promote a book online

- How to get the most out of an online critique group

- How to protect one's electronic rights

Other topics that might be appropriate for this type of book include:

- How e-mail etiquette applies to electronic queries and submissions

- How to research a market online

- How to locate contacts and conduct e-mail interviews

- How to promote one's work through a Web site

- Participating in (or offering) online writing workshops and classes

- Pros and cons of writing for electronic markets (such as e-zines)

- Alternate markets (e.g., becoming a "guide" for a Web site such as Miningco)

---

[2]Only the pitch for *writing.com* is included here; I still hope to sell the other two ideas!

Resources are important and should be included, but I would prefer to see such references grouped together in sidebars or at the end of a chapter. (It can be frustrating to try to relocate a URL that is buried in a paragraph of text.) Ideally, I'd like to compile an updateable CD-ROM of writing-related links to accompany the text.

This could be the book that picks up where [Allworth's] Tim Maloy's *The Internet Research Guide* leaves off!

Thank you for the opportunity to pitch these ideas to you. I hope that at least one of them excites your interest. Please feel free to contact me by e-mail; I look forward to discussing these or other topics with you further. Thank you again for your interest in my work.

The request for a pitch can take you by surprise. You may not be prepared to suggest a topic other than the book you've already planned. But if a publisher makes such an offer, it's wise to do your best to come up with something, even if you feel you're really reaching for ideas. You never know when a quick pitch is going to result in a long-term relationship.

11

TWO SAMPLE
NONFICTION PROPOSALS

PROPOSAL FOR *WRITING.COM* (BY MOIRA ALLEN)

Note: The cover letter that accompanied this proposal has been omitted, as it was simply a follow-up on the "Quick Pitch" letter shown in chapter 10.

writing.com: Creative Internet Strategies to Advance Your Writing Career was published in August 1999 by Allworth Press. The original "pitch" title was "Writing in Cyberspace."

Writing in Cyberspace:
Overview and Rationale

What do writers want to know about the Internet?

For most, the answer is not "how to get connected" or "how to use e-mail." Nor is it "what's out there," although writers are always interested in new resources. What writers want to know is, "How do I use it?" Specifically, writers want to know how to use the Internet to improve productivity, find research material quickly and easily, increase markets and sales, and improve their writing skill.

The Internet is changing the way writers do business, not only with electronic media but also with traditional print markets. It is changing the rules—and writers of every level of experience, from beginner to seasoned professional, are asking the same questions:

• How will the Internet affect my future as a writer?
• How can I use it to locate new markets and increase sales?
• How can I build better research skills so that I can find what I want more quickly?
• How can I find a good online writing or critique group?
• When is it appropriate to use electronic queries, and how do they differ from traditional queries?
• How do I format a manuscript for electronic submissions?
• Do I have to learn to write "differently" for e-zines and electronic publications?
• How will the international nature of the Internet affect and improve my business?
• Am I in danger of losing my copyright if I post material online?
• How can I build a Web site that will increase my visibility and reputation?
• Should I "self-publish" my work online?

These questions haven't been addressed either by traditional writing books (which still provide little information about the Internet) or by existing "writer's guides" (which either focus on introductory basics or on lists of resources). Writers are eager for material that will help them write and sell more effectively—material that not only tells them what is available on the Internet, but how to use it.

Writing in Cyberspace is designed to answer these questions, and more. It is divided into three sections that correspond with the way most writers "experience" the Internet: *Exploration* (research), *Interaction* (using e-mail and networking), and *Creation* (establishing an online presence). Each chapter highlights a particular aspect of the writing business and how that aspect has been affected (or can be improved) by the Internet.

Writers will find the *Resource Appendix* particularly useful. This appendix doesn't simply list sites by name, but divides them into categories and provides a brief description of each site. It focuses upon the use of "jump sites"—data sites that provide links to a particular topic or subject area. For example, instead of listing individual author Web sites, the *Cyberspace* Resource Appendix will take the reader to central "author directory" sites, from which the reader can then search for authors by name or genre. The Resource Appendix will list not only important writing-related sites, but key "jump sites" in various research categories.

Writing in Cyberspace is written from the perspective of a writer. It asks the questions writers ask, and answers them with the information writers need to improve their sales and their skill. It dispels many of the myths that have surrounded the Internet ("It will replace books and make writers obsolete!") and demonstrates a host of new opportunities for writing success in the twenty-first century.

Writing in Cyberspace: Chapter Overview

Introduction: *Writing in Cyberspace* is like no other guide to the Internet. Instead of focusing upon Internet basics or providing lists of resources, *Cyberspace* emphasizes applications and "how-to's." Its three sections—Exploration, Interaction, and Creation—correspond to the way most writers experience the Internet, beginning with research and moving on to Web site development.

Chapter 1: Reshaping the Future
The Internet is changing the future for writers. It is opening new opportunities, including markets that will enable a writer to be "heard" around the world. It is also changing the rules—which is a source of tension for many writers, who have traditionally been taught never to break those rules. This chapter will cover:

• Why geography is no longer an issue for writers
• How "instant communication" can help writers increase productivity and cut costs
• The new rules and how they are changing the marketplace (both online and in print)
• The expanding marketplace and how to explore it
• How to become part of an international community of writers
• What is expected of writers (and what to expect) in the electronic marketplace
• Myths associated with the Internet ("It will replace books and magazines!")

Part I: Exploring the Internet

Chapter 2: Researching the Infinite Library
The key to effective research is understanding how the Internet "works"—how to impose a logical search system upon an uncoordinated, uncataloged mass of data. This chapter will discuss search strategies specifically tailored to the needs of writers, including those seeking information for nonfiction articles and books, and those seeking background details for novels and short stories. Topics include:

• Selecting effective key words and search terms
• Locating and using "jump sites" (data centers that list key links in a topic area)

- Determining the value of a site (and learning how to prescreen search "matches")
- Knowing when to keep looking and when to stop
- Using meta-search engines
- Using online bookstores, databases, forums, and other research sources

Chapter 3: The Electronic Marketplace

Today, the Internet has become the writer's marketplace. Magazines that have never been listed in *Writer's Market* host Web sites online, offering editorial guidelines and the equivalent of electronic "sample copies" (a real money-saver for writers). Electronic newsstands offer links to thousands of publications and make international publications as accessible as domestic markets. High-quality, paying e-zines and e-mail newsletters are also emerging in a variety of fields. This chapter addresses:

- How to use electronic newsstands to find domestic and international markets
- How to locate market information (including guideline databases and market newsletters)
- How to preview a magazine site before spending money on sample copies
- Exploring electronic markets
- Locating book publishers: learning their needs, backlists, and guidelines

Chapter 4: Protecting Your Rights

The downside of the emerging electronic marketplace is the threat to writers' reprint and electronic rights. Increasingly, print publications are attempting to lock in electronic rights or "all rights" against possible future electronic uses. This chapter (based on an extensive survey of e-zines and print magazines) will discuss current trends in the area of electronic rights, recent lawsuits on the issue, and ways writers can protect themselves.

Part II: Interacting on the Net

Chapter 5: The Basics of "Netiquette"

Is e-mail just another form of correspondence? For writers the answer is, *Yes and no.* Many writers fear that contacting editors by e-mail is too "informal"; many editors, on the other hand, prefer such correspondence. This chapter will discuss how e-mail can be used as an extension of the way writers currently do business, including:

- How to make "first contact" with new markets
- When and how to use e-queries and how they differ from traditional queries
- What to do about clips
- How to format and submit a manuscript electronically
- How to use attachments (and when to avoid them)
- How to maintain professionalism in electronic correspondence
- How to locate and interview experts and professionals
- How to conduct online surveys

Chapter 6: Writers' Groups and How to Use Them

Writers' groups online are a lot like writers' groups in the "real" world. However, they also have certain advantages: You don't have to drive anywhere, you can participate on your own schedule, and the donuts aren't stale. An online discussion or critique group can help you stay motivated, address specific questions, and provide useful feedback on your work. This chapter reviews:

- How to locate and join a listserv mailing list or mailing group (including how to select options such as "digest" and "repro")
- What to expect from a group and what the group will expect from you
- Netiquette basics, including a comparison of moderated and unmoderated lists
- How to choose a critique group and how to submit material
- How to write an effective critique (and assess those you receive)
- How to participate in a workshop or chat group
- How to use lists to network with professionals and find research contacts
- How to use forums and bulletin boards

Chapter 7: Online Writing Courses

The Internet offers dozens of writing classes, some for free, some for a fee. Find out what such classes involve and how they work in this chapter, which covers:

- How to locate online classes that relate to your interest or specialty
- How online classes work: lectures, discussions, and homework
- "Online Writing Laboratories" (OWLs) and other resources for writers

Part III: Creating a Presence on the Web

Chapter 8: Do You Need a Web Site?

Writers hunger to be heard, and one way to satisfy that hunger is to build a Web site. The wrong kind of site, however, can do more harm than good (posting unpublished works on a site, for example, virtually shouts "amateur"). First, a writer needs to determine a focus: Is the site intended to promote one's work and attract new readers? Is it designed to impress editors with expertise in a particular subject area? Or is it intended to help and guide other writers? This chapter discusses:

- Defining the goal of your site and determining its audience
- Content, content, content: the most important component of your site
- How to select, post, and exchange links
- How to promote your site and attract visitors
- How to monitor, maintain, and update your site
- How to handle site-generated correspondence
- Building forms and scripts into your site

Chapter 9: Promoting Your Book on the Internet
If you're an author, you want readers. More to the point, you want people to buy your books. The good news is that the Internet offers a host of promotional opportunities that are absolutely free; the key is knowing how to exploit them effectively. This chapter will discuss how to attract readers and turn them into buyers (and even marketers) of your work:

- How to use your Web site to promote your books and attract readers/customers
- How to promote your book (and site) through links, networking, and other connections
- How to take full advantage of online bookstores (and how to profit from them)
- How to promote a self-published book
- How to network with other authors
- How to work with your publisher to promote your book
- Other book promotion tools (including e-mail signature blocks)
- Pros and cons of electronic "self-publishing"

Chapter 10: Other Online Opportunities for Writers
In addition to expanding a writer's "traditional" markets and opportunities, the Internet offers new opportunities for writers to earn money from their skills. This chapter will discuss:

- How to start an e-zine or e-mail newsletter
- How to finance and promote a publication and develop a subscription base
- How to use autoresponders, majordomo software, and other response software
- How to develop and promote an online writing course
- How to become a paid "Web site guide"
- Other online opportunities

Appendixes:
- How to cite Internet sources in footnotes and bibliographies
- Useful sites for writers (listed by category)

PROPOSAL FOR *NEW CHOICES IN NATURAL HEALING FOR DOGS AND CATS* (BY AMY SHOJAI)

New Choices in Natural Healing for Dogs & Cats: Over 1,000 At-Home Remedies for Your Pet's Problems was published in 1999 by Rodale Press. The pitch title for this book was "Healing at Home *Naturally:* Alternative Pet Therapies That Work!"

HEALING AT HOME *NATURALLY*

Alternative Pet Therapies That Work!

by

Amy D. Shojai
A Book Proposal

Meredith Bernstein Literary Agency
2112 Broadway, Suite 503A
New York, NY 10023

HEALING AT HOME *NATURALLY*:
Alternative Pet Therapies That Work!

Overview

More Americans than ever before share their lives with pets. Consequently, the national obsession with health and fitness has spilled into the pet arena. Owners seek the best possible care for their four-legged friends, yet many of the pet generation have lost faith in traditional medicine. They yearn for a simpler, more natural method of promoting good health for themselves—and for their pets. HEALING AT HOME *NATURALLY* examines the world of nontraditional medicine for dogs and cats and offers real-world applications to the many health conditions affecting our pets.

There is a wall dividing conventional from alternative medicine, when, in fact, pets—and people—benefit most from complementary therapies of both. HEALING AT HOME *NATURALLY* will open a window in that wall to find common ground between the two, debunk the myths, and explore the possibilities.

There are a wide variety of alternative therapies available to pet owners; however, many remain investigational at this time, and some may seek only to profit from the "natural revolution" rather than promote the health of the pet. The therapies covered in HEALING AT HOME *NATURALLY*: Alternative Pet Therapies That Work! have been carefully chosen for their track record and proven benefits. My book is a no-nonsense look at which alternative therapies really work and how to use them safely and effectively at home. Not only cure, but prevention will be addressed. Information will be supported by direct quotes from expert veterinarians and others in the field. Readers can follow the advice set forth with confidence, knowing that years of study and practical experience—and the positive response of pets—supports the text. Further, the text offers concrete advice on when and where to seek qualified veterinary care—both alternative and traditional—when an expert's help may be required.

66.2 million cats and 58 million dogs are kept by Americans, and most welcome pets into their hearts and homes as full members of the family. This pet generation is eager to provide quality care for their furry families, but the appropriate tools are needed to make informed decisions. HEALING AT HOME *NATURALLY*: Alternative Pet Therapies That Work! is the first book to offer how-to advice on applying alternative cures to specific health conditions. My book empowers owners to make the best alternative choices for their cherished pets.

COMPETITION

<u>HEALING AT HOME *NATURALLY:* Alternative Pet Therapies That Work!</u> could not be more timely. More than 40 percent of U.S. households keep dogs, 38 percent keep cats, and all are seeking answers to pet health questions that conventional therapy seems unable to answer.

Several books address the pet owners' growing interest in alternative therapies. Most, like <u>THE NEW NATURAL CAT</u> by Anitra Frazier and Norma Eckroate (Nal-Dutton, 1990) and <u>THE NATURAL DOG</u> by Mary L. Brennan and Norma Eckroate (Nal-Dutton, 1994), deal with behavior problems, nutrition, and specific nursing care using a holistic approach. Other books, like <u>THE HEALING TOUCH: The Proven Massage Program for Cats and Dogs</u> by Michael W. Fox (Newmarket, 1991) and <u>COMPLETE HERBAL HANDBOOK FOR THE DOG AND CAT</u> by Juliette D. Levy (Faber & Faber, 1991), provide in-depth coverage of a single alternative therapy.

Nearly all "natural" pet titles address dogs and cats in separate texts and promote a single alternative approach to good health. My book stands out as featuring only the best scientifically proven safe and drug-free healing methods available for both dogs and cats. No book to date offers the comprehensive balance, positive approach, and step-by-step advice of <u>HEALING AT HOME *NATURALLY:* Alternative Pet Therapies That Work!</u>

BOOK FORMAT

HEALING AT HOME *NATURALLY:* Alternative Pet Therapies That Work! will be a 125,000-word (about 500-page) book. The proposed work examines the best alternative health care protocols as they relate to pets and suggests how best to benefit from these non-traditional therapies.

The book is organized in two parts. The first half explores the world of alternative medicine, describing the meaning of the term "natural" and touching on the difference between safe and effective protocols compared to investigational, "trendy" modalities.

Following this overview, the specific protocols advocated by the book are addressed. The traditions and principles behind each alternative treatment are explored in individual chapters. A poignant example of a pet helped by a given therapy introduces each of these chapters to illustrate how the protocol works and the potential benefits.

The second half of the book is the "THERAPY THESAURUS" section, similar in format to the highly successful THE DOCTOR'S BOOK OF HOME REMEDIES FOR DOGS AND CATS (Rodale, 1996). A comprehensive *A*-to-*Z* listing of (about) one hundred of the most common dog and cat illnesses and conditions is presented, followed by the alternative therapies that may be best applied to each to effect a cure. Where appropriate, sections as they apply to dogs or cats—"For Dogs Only" or "For Cats Only"—will be included.

The author incorporates the expertise of recognized alternative and conventional pet health care professionals, gleaned from personal correspondence, interviews, and other technical sources. Each illness, condition, or symptom is first described, followed by easily digested tips and advice presented in direct quotes from these experts, who describe home-care application for cures. Each entry will be summed up in a "Prevention" section.

Sidebars offer more detailed information where appropriate. Boxes of information, such as "The Homeopathic Medicine Chest" and "Medicating Your Pet," offer succinct information necessary for applying the book's recommendations. A "When To See The Expert" box offers advice on when an illness or condition requires attention beyond the scope of home care. In these instances, readers will be advised to seek the help of their alternative or traditional veterinary specialist as needed.

The text is written in an engaging, entertaining style that educates and informs without resorting to dry jargon. Checklists, charts, and tables, along with striking line drawings, are included to clarify or illustrate information and demonstrate treatments.

An Appendix offers: 1) "GLOSSARY," a list of alternative medicine terms and their meanings; 2) "DIRECTORY," with contact information for alternative pet care resources; and 3) "RESOURCES," a further reading list on the subject of alternative health care. Finally, a detailed index will be included to more easily access information.

TARGET AUDIENCE

HEALING AT HOME _NATURALLY:_ Alternative Pet Therapies That Work! will appeal to those members of the pet generation who yearn for a simpler, more natural method of promoting good health for themselves—and for their cats and dogs.

SUGGESTED MARKETING

- Direct mail
- Print advertisements placed in pet and health magazines:
    - ☐ "Natural" publications; e.g., _Natural Health, Natural Pet, Natural Remedies,_ and _The Natural Way_
    - ☐ _Animals_ (MSPCA), circ. 100,000
    - ☐ _Cat Fancy,_ circ. 303,000
    - ☐ _CATS,_ circ. 127,000
    - ☐ _Dog Fancy,_ circ. 276,000
    - ☐ _I Love Cats,_ circ. 200,000
    - ☐ _Parade,_ circ. 37,000,000
    - ☐ _USA Weekend,_ circ. 17,500,000
- Submit the book for review
- Place in bookstores, pet superstores like Petco, and "natural" product stores
- Press releases, including to cat and dog organizations, e.g.:
    - ☐ Cat Writers' Association and Dog Writer's Association (writers, editors, publishers, broadcasters, etc.)
    - ☐ Cat Fancier's Association, American Kennel Club, and others (umbrella organizations for cat and dog clubs)
    - ☐ ASPCA and other animal welfare organizations
    - ☐ American Holistic Veterinary Medical Association
    - ☐ International Veterinary Acupuncture Society
    - ☐ National Center for Homeopathy
- Subsidiary rights potential:
    - ☐ Selected chapters excerpted in magazines or through newspaper syndicates
    - ☐ Library sales/book club deals

To coincide with the book's publication, book signings should be scheduled at bookstores, cat and dog shows, and animal welfare and natural health organization meetings and events. The subject matter lends itself well to the popular issues of many television and radio talk shows, such as the _Today Show_ and others. The author frequently appears on television and radio in connection with her writing and is willing to vigorously promote the book in these venues and in person.

AUTHOR BIOGRAPHY

Amy D. Shojai is a nationally known authority on pet care and behavior who began her career as a veterinary technician. She is the author of ten nonfiction pet books and more than 250 published articles and columns, and is the spokesperson for Purina brand pet foods (an Author's Resume is attached).

Most recently, she contributed sixteen chapters to the Rodale Press book THE DOCTOR'S BOOK OF HOME REMEDIES FOR DOGS AND CATS, which is approaching 500,000 copies sold. She has three forthcoming pet books: THE PURINA ENCYCLOPEDIA OF CAT CARE and THE PURINA ENCYCLOPEDIA OF DOG CARE will be published by Ballantine, and COMPETABILITY: BUILDING A PEACEABLE KINGDOM WITH CATS AND DOGS by Crown. Her work also appears online with the Time Warner "PetPath" and with Purina's "Tidy Cat" Web sites.

Ms. Shojai has written widely in the pet field on training, behavior, health care, and the health benefits of keeping cats and dogs. She is the founder and president of the international Cat Writers' Association, a member of the Dog Writer's Association, and has won numerous awards for her books and articles.

Ms. Shojai frequently speaks to groups on a variety of pet-related issues and has often been interviewed on radio and television in connection with her pet writing. Most recently, she represented the "cat side" and won a nationally televised tongue-in-cheek debate (NBC *Today Show,* Fox, CNN, and others) arguing whether cats or dogs are the more appropriate White House pets.

PROPOSED OUTLINE

HEALING AT HOME *NATURALLY*:

Alternative Pet Therapies That Work!

INTRODUCTION:
Conventional versus Alternative, and What's "Natural"

PART I: OVERVIEW—PRINCIPLES THAT WORK AND WHY
Chapter 1   Acupuncture and Acupressure: Getting the "Point"
Chapter 2   Chiropractic: Major and Minor Adjustments
Chapter 3   Holistic Therapy: The Mind/Body Connection
Chapter 4   Homeopathy: When Less Is More
Chapter 5   Massage Therapy: Need to Be Kneaded
Chapter 6   Nutrition: Eating the Cure
             (Includes "cancer" diets, vitamin/mineral supplements, fasting)
Chapter 7   Water Therapy: It's All Wet—and Works!

PART II: THERAPY THESAURUS
A-to-*Z* directory of (about) one hundred common dog and cat illnesses/conditions with recommended alternative care—brief one- to five-paragraph introductions, followed by succinct tips on home treatment/care from the experts; topics including but not limited to:

ACNE	CANCER
AGGRESSION	CAR SICKNESS
ALLERGIES	CAT FLU
ANAL GLAND PROBLEMS	CLAW PROBLEMS
ANEMIA	CONSTIPATION
APPETITE, INCREASED	COUGHING
APPETITE, LOSS OF	DANDRUFF
ARTHRITIS	DEAFNESS
ASTHMA	DEHYDRATION
BACK AND DISK PROBLEMS	DENTAL PROBLEMS
BAD BREATH	DEPRESSION
BATHROOM "ACCIDENTS"	DIABETES
BLADDER STONES	DIARRHEA
BLEEDING	DISTEMPER (CAT)
BLINDNESS	DISTEMPER (DOG)
BODY ODOR	DRINKING, INCREASED THIRST
BOREDOM	DROOLING
BREATHING PROBLEMS	DRY COAT

EAR INFECTION
EAR MITES
EYE PROBLEMS
FELINE IMMUNODEFICIENCY VIRUS
FELINE INFECTIOUS PERITONITIS
FELINE LEUKEMIA VIRUS
FEVER
FLATULENCE
FLEAS
FOOD ALLERGY/SENSITIVITY
FROSTBITE AND HYPOTHERMIA
FUSSY EATING
HAIR BALLS
HEART PROBLEMS
HEARTWORMS
HEATSTROKE AND HYPERTHERMIA
HIP DYSPLASIA
HIVES
HOT SPOTS
HYPERACTIVITY
HYPERTHYROIDISM
HYPOTHYROIDISM
INFLAMMATORY BOWEL DISEASE
INSECT BITES AND STINGS
ITCHING
KENNEL COUGH
KIDNEY DISEASE
LAMENESS
LETHARGY

LICE
LICKING
LIVER DISEASE
LUMPS AND BUMPS
MANGE
NOSE PROBLEMS
OVERWEIGHT
OILY COAT
PANCREATITIS
PARALYSIS
PARVOVIRUS
POISONING
PROSTATE PROBLEMS
RINGWORM
SHEDDING/HAIR LOSS
SINUS PROBLEMS
SPRAYING
SUNBURN
TAIL PROBLEMS
TEETHING
TICKS
ULCERS
URINARY TRACT DISORDERS
VOMITING
WEIGHT LOSS
WOOL SUCKING
WORMS
WOUNDS

APPENDIX A
"GLOSSARY"—alternative medicine terms and definitions

APPENDIX B
"DIRECTORY"—contact information of alternative pet care resources, e.g., veterinary holistic practitioners, acupuncturist, chiropractors, etc.

APPENDIX C
"RESOURCES"—further reading list

INDEX

12

PITCHING TO INTERNATIONAL BOOK PUBLISHERS

by Huw Francis

You have a great idea for a nonfiction book. You're also an international writer—or you believe that your book would have international appeal. Globalization trends have made readers around the world more open to reading about international subjects. How can you turn this to your advantage and make your book stand out from the thousands of ideas editors and publishers see every year?

As the world becomes increasingly global, it is now practical and common for raw material to come from one country, be processed in a second, and sold in a third. In the publishing world the infrastructure exists to allow text to be moved quickly around the world to print books close to their distribution market—or somewhere with low overhead. My own forthcoming book was written in Turkey, requires the input of people worldwide, will be published in the United Kingdom, and will be distributed on four continents.

WHERE IN THE WORLD SHOULD YOU LOOK FOR A PUBLISHER?

Whatever your nationality and no matter where you live, you should look for the most suitable publisher in the world for your book, not just the best one in your home country or country of residence. Finding the perfect match between publisher and proposal is more important than proximity, and working with the best publisher for your book benefits both of you. The publisher gets a product that enhances its catalogue and suits its existing target market, and you will see bigger returns through higher sales.

TARGET MARKETS

Publishers concentrate on specific markets. Even global publishing houses have imprints and subsidiaries that specialize in individual markets or countries not targeted by other imprints within the same company. Consequently, it is important to identify the target market (both demographically and geographically) for your book before you start approaching publishers. By doing this, you can target your submissions to publishers who already produce books for that market.

The determining factor is not simply the type of book you want to write. A more important question is, Where will people buy that book? Most of the likely readers of a book on adopting a Chinese baby will be outside of China. A book on adopting a baby in the United Kingdom, however, will be of most interest to U.K. residents. The first step toward deciding whether to target an international publisher, therefore, is to determine where your target market lives.

This selection of publishers is important, because you not only have to demonstrate that there is a market for the book, but also that the target market is accessible to that particular publisher. For example, while there might be a large market for an English-language book on day trips from Paris, not all American publishers are going to be able to reach it. A French publisher, or a U.S. or European publisher with a French office, would probably be a better choice, because many tourists will buy the book once in Paris. A French-based publisher of English-language books is also likely to have a distribution agreement with companies in the United States and the United Kingdom, so your book can still be bought by people before they travel.

It is essential to research the distribution network of a publisher you are considering. Distribution networks vary enormously, from local to international, and cannot be determined just by looking at the country in which the publisher is headquartered. In addition, once you find a publisher with, say, a French office, you must then determine whether that office or another international office actually makes acquisitions. Some regional offices operate purely for distribution, while others operate as local imprints.

MARKETING

When you are marketing a book to a publisher in a country where you do not live, or are not a national, you will face some special obstacles that most local writers have no concept of. Finding a way past these obstacles can also help you develop your book to enhance its international appeal and make a publisher more likely to accept your proposal.

In general, the publishing industry has standard formats and procedures that are designed with domestic submissions in mind, and which all authors are expected to follow, even if they are submitting from abroad. As an international writer, you need to follow this process as closely as you can. However, you will need to adapt and bend the rules to suit your unusual circumstances.

For instance, you must show a publisher why *you* should write the book, rather than someone local. This means that you not only have to show that you can do it as well as a local, but that you are better placed to do so. The credentials you offer to make this point should be reflected in the content of your book (or proposal). For example, if you are pitching a book on the premise that you are an American living in Paris and writing a guidebook for U.S. and U.K. tourists, your book should include destinations and restaurants that American tourists will want to see, not destinations that would appeal to Japanese tourists.

Being in a different country or of a different nationality complicates the task of demonstrating your credibility to a publisher. From the start, a publisher is likely to be concerned that you may be remote, difficult to contact and communicate with, and also more expensive to deal with (telephone calls, faxes, mail, etc.). They may also (unfairly) associate all the worst stereotypes of your country of residence or nationality with you.

Establishing your credibility is a multileveled task and involves the following.

YOUR IMAGE

First impressions count for a lot in publishing. No matter where you live, you wish to project a professional image. Other chapters in this book explain what publishers expect to see in terms of professional style and presentation.

WRITING ABILITY

When trying to sell a book proposal internationally, it is important to show not only that you can write well, but that you can write for the target audience of your book. If you have not written and published articles or other books on the subject or for the target audience, then the best way to prove your ability is to write two or three chapters of your book and include them when you approach the publisher. At least one of these chapters needs to be a completed product, not an early draft. The other chapters, even if not finished, will support the primary chapter and demonstrate your dedication to the task of completing the book. This will help improve your image as well as demonstrate your writing ability.

When writing the sample chapters, it is important to make sure your grammar, spelling, and word usage are those in use in the country of the publisher. U.S. English should not be used in a submission to a British publisher (unless your book is aimed at Americans living in, or visiting, the United Kingdom), and British English should not be used for an American publisher.

Word usage can be very important, and getting it wrong can mean not getting a contract. Some perfectly acceptable U.S. words are rude in the United Kingdom (fanny definitely does not mean backside in the United Kingdom) and some words have different meanings ("quite good" means "very good" in the United States, but if someone in the United Kingdom said your book was "quite good," they are actually saying that it was nothing special).

SUBJECT QUALIFICATION

Why should a reader believe what you write? Would you buy a travel guidebook written by someone who had never been to the country? The publisher needs to be convinced that you are qualified to write on the subject.

If you already know your subject well, all you have to do is state, in some detail, how you obtained your knowledge. For a book on adopting a child from China, you might be able to say, "Over the last three years, my partner and I have been through the complicated and drawn-out process of adopting a child from a Chinese orphanage, and we now have a wonderful Chinese daughter."

If you have no experience or knowledge on the subject you want to write about, state how you will gain it. For a book on buying property in Belize, you could say, "I have been planning to buy property in Belize for some time, and in a few months I will be moving to Belize with the sole purpose of doing so." You should also outline why you believe it is possible to buy property in Belize and how you plan to do so.

THE MARKETABILITY OF YOUR BOOK

Who is going to buy the book, where will they buy the book, and why? Though the publisher will take responsibility for selling the book, you need to prove that there are enough people who are sufficiently interested in the subject to spend up to $15 on a book about it.

Publishers want to see more than a bald statement of, "I know there are lots of tourists and many expatriates in France who would love this book." Facts and figures are essential. How many expatriates live in France? How many of them speak English as a first language? How many speak English as a second language? How many U.S. tourists go to Paris every year? How many tourists are returnees? Where do expatriates in France buy their books? Where do U.S. tourists buy their guidebooks (U.S. bookshops, airports, or French bookshops)? How many books does each expatriate and tourist buy per year or trip? In what other countries is there a market where subsidiary rights can be sold?

SUBMITTING YOUR PROPOSAL

Identifying suitable publishers takes time and effort. *Writer's Market* can give you information on North American publishers, while *The Writer's Handbook* offers information for U.K., European, and British Commonwealth countries. *The Writer's Handbook* also includes comments from writers who have worked with specific publishers.

Such reference directories should only be the start of your research, however. Many publishers, even smaller ones, have Web sites that include their catalog, philosophy, details of their target market, and submission guidelines.

Despite the common perception that there are standard ways of writing to all U.S. publishers and standard ways of writing to all U.K. publishers, every publishing house is made up of different people with different ideas. The best way to determine the style your cover letter should take is to thoroughly review the publisher's Web site. This will give you a good understanding of house style and allow you to incorporate buzzwords and key phrases into your cover letter and proposal. If the Web site is written in a pedantic and technical style, follow that. If it is written in an easygoing style, relax your own style, but still maintain a professional and serious tone; flippancy is unlikely to endear you to a publisher, even if they do publish joke books.

An increasing number of publishers are including online submission forms on their Web sites or accept e-mailed submissions. These can be particularly useful for international writers, as they speed up submission times, improve communications, and demonstrate to the publisher that you are technically capable of supplying the text of your book electronically.

Your research will also give you an idea of whether you need to send your proposal directly to an editor or to a centralized submissions office. If in doubt, call the editorial assistant of the editor of a book similar to yours and ask how to proceed.

SURFACE MAIL SUBMISSIONS

When you send a surface mail submission, always send an SASE. Be sure that it either has the correct return postage in the stamps of the country *of the publisher* (not your own country's postage), or that you include an appropriate number of International Reply Coupons (IRCs) for a response. Two IRCs are usually enough to send a regular letter from one country to another; more will be needed if you actually want your proposal or manuscript returned.

Make sure that you include your full name and contact details. When submitting a book proposal internationally, an e-mail address is very important. Most of the publishers who expressed interest in my own proposal and asked for further information did so via e-mail.

E-MAIL SUBMISSIONS

E-mail submissions allow you to avoid the vagaries of the international mail system and deliver your proposal quickly. Because of the rise in e-mail viruses, it is a good idea to send the text of your proposal in the body of the e-mail, just after your cover letter. However, the drawbacks of e-mail submission are that the layout and format of your proposal may be altered or lost, and you may not be able to send artwork and sample articles. If you have a personal Web site with samples of your published work, some publishers are happy to refer to it, so be sure to mention it.

If you feel that you really need to send your proposal as an attachment, check with the publisher first to ensure your formats are acceptable and they are willing to risk opening your file on their computer.

ONLINE SUBMISSIONS

Online submission usually entails filling in a form designed by the publisher, which means that you *won't* be able to submit your carefully crafted proposal. To avoid spelling errors and to make sure that all the important information in your proposal is included, print off the forms to use as a guide. Then, type your responses in your word-processing program, proof them, polish them—and then cut-and-paste them back into the online forms.

Electronic submission works! That's how I sold my proposal.

As an international writer, don't downplay your international status; play it up. Highlight the positive aspects of why a non-national or nonresident should be writing this particular book.

Actively raise the publisher's interest by demonstrating why you should be writing the book from your perspective and location. Expressing confidence in your abilities and knowledge, without boasting, is the best way to make a publisher believe in you.

SECTION 3 RESOURCES

BOOK PUBLISHERS
Midwest Book Review: Book Lover Resources
www.execpc.com/~mbr/bookwatch/booklove/
In addition to other links for book lovers, this page offers a huge array of publisher links, including children's book publishers, trade publishers, scholarly/academic publishers, computer/software book publishers, e-book publishers and dealers, and more. It will keep you busy.

BookWire: Book Publisher Index
www.bookwire.com/index/publishers/publishers.html
In addition to a general listing of book publishers, this site offers both general and genre- or topic-specific listings.

Publishers' Catalogues Home Page
www.lights.com/publisher
A search tool enabling one to look up publishers by name, location, subject, or type of material published.

Publishers on the Internet
www.faxon.com/title/pl_am.htm
Though focusing primarily on academic and technical publishers, this list offers many links to mainstream publishers as well.

World Publishing Industry
http://publishing-industry.net/Publishers/
A directory/search engine for the publishing industry, offering extensive listings in various publishing categories.

WriteLinks: Commercial Book Publishers
www.writelinks.com/Creative/Links/BookPublishers/crea06_02.htm
A comprehensive listing of book publishers in every category, including genre, address, Web site, and e-mail.

The Writer's Mind
www.thewritersmind.com
A site that allows agents and publishers to post listings. Well-categorized.

Yahoo!
http://dir.yahoo.com/Business_and_Economy/Shopping_and_Services/Publishers/

ELECTRONIC PUBLISHERS
Association of Electronic Publishers
http://members.tripod.com/~BestBooksCom/AEP/aep.html

Electronically Published Internet Connection (EPIC)
www.eclectics.com/epic/
A clearinghouse for electronically published authors and information on electronic publishing.

Lida Quillen's List of Epublishers
www.sff.net/people/Lida.Quillen/epub.html

Mary Wolf's Guide to Electronic Publishers
www.coredcs.com/~mermaid/epub.html

MARKET REFERENCE BOOKS
United States/North America
Writer's Market (Writer's Digest Books)
Annual. Available through most bookstores and online booksellers in the United States.

Australia
The Australian Writer's Marketplace, by Rhonda Whitton (Bookman)
Annual. Most easily obtained from publisher's Web site at *www.bookman.com.au/awm/home.html.*

Canada
The Canadian Writer's Market, by Jem Bates (McClelland & Stewart Inc.)
Available from most major online booksellers.

United Kingdom
The Writer's Handbook, Barry Turner, ed. (MacMillan Publishers, London)
Annual. Available from most major online booksellers.

The Writers' and Artists' Yearbook (A.C. Black, London).
Annual. Available from most major online booksellers.

Section 4

THE FICTION PROPOSAL

13

A NOVEL PROPOSAL

It's not hard to find ghastly statistics about the number of novels that are rejected by "New York Publishers." Vanity/subsidy presses (both print and electronic) trumpet the fact that thousands, if not hundreds of thousands, of first-time novels are passed over by the commercial press every year. But why?

One very simple reason so many novels fail is that the vast majority of first-time novelists are unfamiliar with the submission process. Most new novelists simply wrap up their book and mail it off—only to have it languish for months, unread, in a stack of similarly ill-prepared manuscripts. Worse, more and more publishers are refusing to even consider unsolicited manuscripts, which means that such submissions will either be returned unread or, if the writer has failed to include proper postage, be consigned to the dumpster.

Given the volume of submissions generated by hopeful writers every year, editors and agents simply have no time (or patience) to deal with those who don't follow standard submission procedures. While a good proposal is no substitute for a good novel, it *can* make the difference between having your novel reviewed by an editor—and having it become landfill.

SUBMITTING YOUR NOVEL: A STEP-BY-STEP GUIDE

So what, exactly, is standard procedure? Fortunately, it is virtually the same whether you are submitting your novel to a print publisher, an electronic publisher, or an agent. Here are the basic steps you'll need to take:

1) **Finish your novel.** This is the most important step in the process. Gone are the days when an editor or agent might accept an author's work-in-progress, based on an outline and a few sample chapters. In today's publish-

ing market, if you haven't finished your book, no editor or agent will be willing to work with you. All too often, new writers never make it to the finish line—so, no matter what your potential may be, you must first prove that you can deliver the goods.

2) **Search for potential publishers.** Who might be an appropriate publisher for your novel? What publishers might make good second and third choices? Don't try to answer these questions by reaching for *Writer's Market* and looking up every publisher who produces books in your genre. For this kind of market research, you need to go to the market itself.

- **Check your bookshelves.** Presumably, you own a number of books in the same genre in which you're writing. If you write romance, you should be reading romance; if you write mysteries, you should be reading mysteries. Chances are, you've also saved your favorites—books that you'd be willing to read again. Who publishes those books? Scan your shelves to see what imprints appear most frequently: These are the publishers who produce the types of books you like to read. Would your book fit among their titles?

- **Check your local bookstore.** Browse the sections where your book would be most likely to appear. Again, what imprints do you see? Take a look at the actual books produced by different publishers. Do you like the quality of the production? Are the covers attractive, or do they look cheap? Do you recognize any of the authors? Do the cover blurbs appeal to you and entice you to read further? Jot down the names of publishers that produce the types of books you might be willing to buy.

3) **Look for publishers' guidelines.** *Writer's Market* and other market guides can help you here, but don't stop at their listings. Go online, and see if you can locate the Web sites for the publishers you've chosen. (See the "Resources" section for Web sites that can help you locate book publishers.) Search the site for "author guidelines" (which may also be labeled "submission guidelines" or "for authors"). Also, check the publisher's online catalog. Do you see a mix of known authors and newcomers? If a publisher offers only big names, you may have difficulty breaking in; if, however, a publisher features only unknowns, you may not be able to expect much in the way of an advance or promotion.

Pay careful attention to the "wants" specified in the publisher's guidelines. Make sure your novel fits within those guidelines. For example, does a publisher purchase horror novels "but no vampire stories," which yours just happens to be? Does your novel fit within the specified word limits? There's no point in submitting a 200,000-word novel to a publisher that won't accept manuscripts of more than 100,000 words. Never assume that you can be the exception; submitting a novel that falls outside a publisher's guidelines simply sends the message that you haven't done your homework.

Finally, determine exactly what procedure must be followed to submit to that publisher. Most publishers fit into one of the following three categories:

- **Accepts unsolicited manuscripts.** This means that you don't need an agent to approach the publisher, and you don't need an invitation (usually based on a query). It does not necessarily mean that you can submit a complete manuscript; the publisher may prefer to start with a synopsis and sample chapters.

- **Does not accept unsolicited submissions.** This does not mean that you need an agent; however, it does mean that you must query the publisher before submitting even a synopsis and sample chapters. If the guidelines don't make clear exactly what you can and cannot send, contact the publisher to find out, because if you send the wrong materials, they will be returned unread. (See chapter 15 for more information on developing a query letter for your novel.)

- **Accepts only agented submissions.** In this case, your only hope of selling to this publisher is through an agent. Don't even bother with a query, as it won't be considered. This publisher will only accept material that has been prescreened by a reputable agent.

4) **Prepare your package.** While some publishers do accept entire manuscripts, most prefer a proposal package that usually includes a cover or query letter, an outline or synopsis of your novel, and three sample chapters (the first three chapters of your book). Agents generally require the same materials; in fact, the procedure for approaching an agent is almost identical to that for approaching a publisher. Be sure you know exactly what the publisher (or agent) expects, including any limitations on page count, word count, etc. The rest of this section will discuss the specifics of preparing that all-important package.

THE QUERY

There is no specific formula for a winning novel query. Some writers like to start off with a dramatic hook: "What if a nuclear explosion leveled New York, and you were one of a handful of survivors?" Others prefer a more straightforward approach: "I am seeking representation for my 75,000-word mystery novel, *Death Dines Out* . . . " Whatever your approach, however, a book query often addresses many of the same questions as a periodical query, including:

1) **Your reason for choosing this agent or publisher.** Make sure the recipient of your proposal knows that you selected them with care. If you

chose a publisher based on certain book titles, or an agent based on authors that agent already represents, say so. This will demonstrate that you've done some market research—which is the mark of a professional. But don't "suck up" by telling a publisher how much you love their books, or that you've named your firstborn child after the lead character in their most popular series.

2) **The basics about your book.** Make sure your query specifies the type of book you've written (i.e., its genre), its length (word count), and a working title. If you're writing in a genre that has several subcategories (e.g., "cozy" mystery, "paranormal" romance), be sure to specify the appropriate category. Be sure that your book actually fits the publisher's guidelines: If the publisher only handles hard-boiled detective novels, don't bother submitting a "cozy" mystery. If your book defies categorization, do your best to categorize it anyway: Being able to place a book within a particular genre is a key selling point. You may wish to describe your book as "a cozy mystery with romantic elements," but don't try to pitch "a genre-busting blend of mystery, romance, time travel, and technothriller." If an agent can't determine how to best market the book you've written, he or she will be much less interested in reviewing it.

As mentioned above, your book should be completed—and you should indicate this in your query. But what if your book is part of a series? There's no hard-and-fast rule about this one; some editors and agents like the idea that you have more than one book to offer (presuming they like the first one), while others prefer to take a "wait and see" approach before offering to handle more than one book.

3) **A brief synopsis.** Your query letter should include a short overview of the book's plot and major themes. Don't attempt to summarize your entire novel in two paragraphs; this is a pitch, not an outline. Consider approaching this section as if you were writing the copy for the back cover of your published book: What elements would be most likely to attract a reader's attention? These might include:

- **The primary characters.** In your query letter, you'll only have space to introduce two, or at most three, major players in your novel—usually the key protagonists and, possibly, the antagonist. Here's how Lynn Flewelling introduces her protagonists in her query for *Luck in the Shadows* (see chapter 15):

> Seregil is an experienced spy for hire with a murky past and noble connections; Alec is the talented but unworldly boy he rescues and takes on as apprentice.

- **The basic plot.** Most stories answer a "what if" question: What if an exiled Russian countess falls in love with a rugged American frontiersman? What if a nuclear blast destroys New York in 2050, leaving only a handful of survivors? What if a local busybody is murdered, and the key suspect is the detective's own father? Identify the basic "what if" question that drives your plot. (Remember that "plot" isn't just the sequence of events that occurs in your novel; it's the *reason* for those events.)

- **The setting.** Where and when does your story occur? How important is that setting to the story? If your setting is essential to the plot—e.g., your protagonists are exploring a strange planet that confronts them with a series of perils and obstacles—say so. If, however, your setting is merely background, don't spend too much space describing it. Remember, too, that many settings can be conveyed in a few words: If your story takes place in a medieval fantasy universe, you won't have to explain that this world includes castles and serfs and bad plumbing.

- **The primary source of conflict.** What are the key obstacles your characters face? Where does the conflict come from? With whom (or with what) do your characters struggle? Is the conflict primarily internal or external? Is it with another character, with society, or with the forces of nature? Focus on the conflict that is central to the plot as a whole—e.g., your aristocratic heroine's struggle to escape the duties of her position so that she can be with the man she loves—rather than specific details, such as the arguments she has with her family and friends.

- **The theme.** Does your story have an underlying message? What is it about, beyond the actual plot? What issues does it explore or reveal? What questions does it raise? Don't confuse theme with preachiness; your novel doesn't have to be a sermon in order to raise intriguing questions or ideas in the mind of the reader.

4) **The market (readership) for your book.** Who would be most likely to buy your novel? Try to define a specific audience. No novel will appeal to everyone, and the writer who thinks otherwise will only appear naïve.

A good way to describe the potential market for your book is to mention comparable titles or authors. You might suggest, for example, that your book is likely to appeal to "fans of mystery writers such as P.D. James or Patricia Cornwall." Never suggest, however, that your book is just like that of another author, or is "just as good as" some other popular title. You don't want to give the impression that you're trying to imitate, or compete with, what's already on the market. Your book should stand on its own merits.

Should you link your book to a trend? Only if it is an enduring trend with a long-standing, established audience. For example, there may never be a shortage of fantasy novels about dragons, but the interest in fantasy novels about vampires tends to wax and wane. Be especially cautious about linking your book to hot new trends; you can be sure that publishers have already been flooded with Harry Potter knockoffs. Remember that your book isn't likely to appear on the market for at least two years after acceptance, by which time today's hot trends may be yesterday's cold news.

5) **Your credentials.** If you have relevant credentials, list them. If, for example, you have sold several short stories to reputable markets within your genre, list those credits. Don't, however, list sales to low-paying or nonpaying markets, or Internet sites where you can post your own work and call yourself "published." Mention any experience or expertise you have that relates to your novel—for example, mention your degree in history if your novel has a historical element. If your novel is set in Greece and you spent three years in that country, say so.

Sadly, nonfiction writing credentials rarely carry much weight in the fiction community. They are worth a brief mention, simply because they demonstrate that you can write professionally—but they won't sell your story. Even if you've been writing nonfiction for years, your novel will still be treated as the work of a new author.

Never discuss (or apologize for) your *lack* of credentials. Never mention, for example, that this is the first thing you've ever written, or that you've never been published before, or that you have no relevant background. If these happen to be true, say nothing.

6) **What to avoid.** As with any query, there are certain things you should never include in a novel proposal, including:

- **Hype.** Never tell an editor or agent how good you think your book is. Don't describe it as "exciting" or "a sure-fire success." Hyping your own book is a sure sign of inexperience; editors and agents prefer to make those judgments for themselves.

- **Flattery.** Don't try to convince an editor that you've read every book the publishing house has published. The editor doesn't care what you think of other books; he or she is only interested in the quality of *your* material.

- **Negative information.** If your book has already been rejected twenty times, don't say so. It is true that many books are rejected repeatedly before becoming "overnight best-sellers." Editors and agents, however, tend to respect the judgment of their peers, and there is no point in telling them that those peers have already passed judgment against your novel.

- **Irrelevant personal information.** Don't mention how old you are, your marital status, or how many children you have, unless this somehow relates to your novel. An editor doesn't need to know that you are a housewife who has written her first novel at the kitchen table. Don't explain *why* you wrote the book (e.g., as therapy, or because everyone told you that you ought to write down the story of your life).

- **Testimonies.** If your mother loved the book, or your spouse has been urging you to send it to a publisher for years, or your writing group thinks you're brilliant, or your writing instructor gave you an "A," that's great. Explaining any of this to a publisher or agent, however, is like scrawling "newbie!" across your manuscript in big red letters. Don't do it.

See chapter 15 for more information on crafting a query.

THE NOVEL SYNOPSIS

Sooner or later, you will need to provide a synopsis of your novel to an editor or agent. In some cases, you'll be expected to send it with your initial query; in others, you'll be asked to send it only on request.

Few things terrify the first-time novelist (or even experienced novelists) so much as the demand for "the dreaded synopsis." Condensing the salient points of a 100,000-word novel into a five- to ten-page summary is no easy task. But it can be done.

The first step is to understand the purpose of the synopsis. While it is a selling *tool* for your novel, it is not a *sales pitch* (like the overview in your query letter). The primary goal of your synopsis is to demonstrate that your story is coherent, logical, well thought out, and well organized. It should show that your characters act and interact in a realistic, consistent fashion; that the plot unfolds logically and at an appropriate pace; that plot twists don't seem contrived or coincidental; that the story will hold the reader's attention from beginning to end; and that the ending (the "resolution") is believable and satisfying.

While some publishers still ask for a chapter-by-chapter synopsis, most now prefer a narrative synopsis that follows the flow of the story as a whole. This format enables you to focus on the key points of the story, without having to say something about each individual chapter. This enables you to focus on the primary plot and major characters, without confusing the issue with subplots and secondary characters.

SYNOPSIS FORMAT

A synopsis should generally be formatted like a regular manuscript. Some writers double-space; some single-space. Some use a cover page that includes the book title, author's name (or pen name), author's contact information, and the word count of the book as a whole. Others include this information on the first page of the synopsis itself, as with an article or story.

How long should it be? If the agent or publisher doesn't give any guidelines on maximum length, a good rule is to allow one page of synopsis per ten thousand words of novel—up to a maximum of ten pages. Shorter is better; if you can say it in five pages, don't stretch it to ten.

A synopsis is written in the present tense: "Andrea returns to her home town for the holidays, to find . . . " Try to avoid long blocks of text; break it up into shorter paragraphs.

Put character names in CAPS or **boldface** the first time they appear. Try to limit the number of characters you actually name in your synopsis; too many names become confusing. (Thus, instead of saying, "Andrea shares her concerns with her best friend, Ginny," it would be better to leave the friend unnamed unless she plays a major role in the action.)

CONTENT

What should your synopsis cover? What should you leave out? If you ask ten different writers this question, you're likely to get ten different answers. Here's what one novelist has to say about "the basics" of a synopsis:

The Basic Elements of a Synopsis
by Rebecca Vinyard

The Setup. This is the starting point of your story: premise, location, time frame, and main characters' backgrounds. Just as you want to hook your readers with the first page of your book, you also want to hook the editor on the first page of your synopsis. In Sharon Ihle's synopsis for *Maggie's Wish* [see chapter 16], she accomplishes several of these elements in her first paragraph. The sooner you can establish your setup, the better. Choose your words with care to get the background information presented in a concise *and* entertaining way.

Why? I'm listing this second, but this is something you should consider throughout your synopsis. If you pose a question, answer it. A synopsis is *not* the time to tease a reader. Suppose your story begins with the heroine quitting her job. You should explain *why* she quit it. Reactions, decisions . . . whatever your character does within the framework of your synopsis, the reasons behind the actions must be clear.

For example, you can't just say, "Something happens to make the heroine change her mind." Instead, you need to explain what that something is and *why* it made her change her mind. Clarity, clarity . . . make that your synopsis mantra.

Characterization. This includes background, personality, occupation—everything that makes up your character. It is *not,* however, a physical description of your hero and heroine. Usually, the less said about that, the better, unless the character's physique affects her/him emotionally. Example: She's extremely short and feels self-conscious about it.

Bear in mind that you want the reader of your synopsis to feel a connection with your characters. Focus on the emotional elements: "A deeply religious woman," "A savvy businesswoman," "An introverted professor," "An agitated accountant." Phrases like these can be your friends because they give emotional and background information in just a few words.

You should name only characters that play major roles in your story. Often, writers feel the need to include mention of secondary characters (maybe because they fall in love with them). Unless those characters' actions affect the main plot throughout the story, you shouldn't include them, because then you'll need to provide characterization and background for them as well (and in the process, inflate your synopsis!). If a necessary reference pops up once or twice, you can simply say something like "her best friend," "his sister," etc.

Plot Points. These occur whenever your story departs from all that has gone before. Your character is forced to make a decision, or something unexpected and outside the experience of the character happens. You should include *all* the major plot points in your synopsis. However, do *not* include plot points for subplots. If it doesn't have anything to do with the main plot, forget it. Always concentrate on theme.

Conflict. Quick conflict lesson: Internal conflict comes from within the character; e.g., she has poor self-esteem. External conflict comes from without the character; e.g., a villain is blackmailing the hero.

For the purpose of synopsis writing, you need to present your conflict clearly. Which brings us back to the *why* element again: *why* is your heroine afraid of dogs? This is important if she refuses to go to the hero's house because he has a Doberman named Rex lurking about. Or perhaps your heroine refuses to go because she fears involvement, and she uses the dog as an excuse. Why does she fear involvement? By the same token, how does your hero feel about being rejected like this? Is she rejecting Rex or him? Perhaps rejection makes him defensive because he seeks to be accepted. He resolves never to have anything to do with her again.

In other words, conflicts are the obstacles the main characters must overcome in order to achieve their goals. In a romance, the main goal is for the hero and heroine to fall in love and stay together. In a science fiction story, maybe the goal is to overthrow an evil corporation dominating the planet. Whatever the goal, it can't be easy to achieve, or else you have no story. We need to know there's a problem and *why* this is a problem.

Emotion. This element is of utmost concern for romance writers, because for romance the magic is in the emotion, although I feel any synopsis should include it. Actions cause reactions. He kisses her . . . how does she feel about it? How does he feel? Whenever you have the chance to put emotion into your synopsis, do it. It makes the difference between a dull summary and a lively recounting of your story.

Action. Action drives most stories and is probably the story element used the most. However, in your synopsis, you should only include those actions that have consequences. If your heroine takes a trip to the store for some eggs, don't include that unless something happens to her along the way. This is fairly obvious, I know. But as a contest judge, I've read many synopses that included unnecessary action descriptions. If in doubt, leave it out.

Dialogue. Two schools of thought here. Some folks say you should *never* include dialogue in a synopsis. Some feel a sprinkling of it here and there helps. My personal preference is the latter. If a specific line has more impact than a description of the same conversation, why not use it? However, I wouldn't advise more than a few lines of dialogue. Don't go crazy and start quoting all over the place.

Black Moment. When all is lost, when it appears your characters will never reach their goals . . . The odds are on the opposing forces' side, and this is the moment when your characters realize it. In a romance, perhaps it's a conflict so overwhelming, it would appear that the hero and heroine will never be together. Whatever the genre, this moment of reckoning should not only be in your story, but also in your synopsis.

Climax. Your story has been thundering along to this point. Everything that has gone before should lead up to it. Whether it's the bad guy getting what's coming to him, the hero finally getting over his lack of self-esteem, or the heroine riding to the rescue, this is the moment when it all happens. Naturally, this element must also be included in your synopsis.

Resolution. All your loose ends get tied up here. Any questions posed in your synopsis should be answered by the time you reach this point. And yes, as we all know, the goal is for the hero and heroine to live happily ever after. Or not, depending on your genre. Whatever the case, include the resolution to your story. This is not the time to play guess-the-ending!

The Essential Basics. The number one essential is to write your synopsis in present tense. Think of it as telling a friend about your book. Avoid passive word usage. You want those words to flow evenly and keep the reader involved. Perhaps you've heard the saying that a writer's best work should be the query letter and synopsis. That puts the pressure on, doesn't it? Well, I'm not sure it's true; a better saying might be that a writer's clearest work should be the query and synopsis. Focus on the main story and avoid extraneous information.

Formatting. From my experience, most houses prefer a double-spaced format. However, there are exceptions, so *check the publisher's submission guidelines.* Or contest guidelines, whichever is the case. The majority of publishers prefer you to give your contact information and word count on the upper left corner of the first page. On subsequent pages, include the title, your last name, and the page number in your headers.

Submissions. Check the guidelines. Am I making this point clearly enough? And for heaven's sake, make sure you have the editor's name spelled right. Always include an SASE with every submission. If you want to make sure your submission is received, include a stamped, self-addressed postcard that can be sent back to you.

(See chapter 16 for a sample synopsis and chapter 17 for an evaluation of that synopsis.)

THE PROPOSAL PACKAGE

Once you've written a synopsis for your novel, you've accomplished the most difficult—and most important—part of the proposal process. You may have to edit that synopsis for different publishers, but you have the basics.

The final thing that most publishers and agents will request from you is "three sample chapters." These must be *the first three chapters of your book*—not three chapters that you choose at random. Need I say, therefore, that it is in your best interest to polish those three chapters to the best of your ability? Review them. Edit them. Run them by a critique group. Ask someone to help you proofread them. Make sure that they are the best example of your work that you could possibly send. Format them according to basic manuscript format principles (double-spaced, ample margins, indented paragraphs, no extra spaces between paragraphs, numbered pages, etc.).[1]

Do not send any of the following items with your proposal:

---

[1] If you have any doubts about proper manuscript format, see my article, "A Quick Guide to Manuscript Format," at *www.writing-world.com/basics/manuscript.html.*

- A personal (or publicity) photo
- An expanded bio, resume, or curriculum vitae (in some cases, it might be appropriate to include a list of relevant publications)
- Samples of other published (or unpublished) writings
- Letters of reference or recommendation

Now it's time to assemble your package. Be sure to include an SASE. If you would like confirmation that an editor or agent received your query or proposal, include a self-addressed, stamped postcard for an immediate response. Just type a line on the back that reads something like:

Dear Author,

We have received your manuscript, "title," on (Date): _____.

We hope to be able to respond to your manuscript by (Date): _____.

(Signed): _____

The second line is optional, but useful if you'd like an estimate of when you can expect to hear from the editor or agent.

If you have a professional business card, add one of those as well, as it will make it easier for the recipient to keep track of your contact information.

If your total proposal is more than twenty pages, sandwich it between two 8½″ × 11″ pieces of cardboard (e.g., cardboard from the back of a notepad), and secure it with a rubber band. This will prevent the pages from being damaged in shipping. Choose a sturdy manila or Tyvek envelope that will hold your proposal snugly. (Too large an envelope will allow your proposal to slide around and become battered; too small an envelope will cause it to bend and crimp the pages.) If your proposal is too large for an envelope, use a thin stationery box instead.

After you've assembled your package (but before you seal it), weigh it. If it weighs less than a pound, you might wish to include an SASE of sufficient size, and with sufficient postage, to allow the return of your entire proposal. If, however, the proposal weighs more than a pound, it's better to include a letter-size SASE for a response only, and allow the editor or agent to discard the proposal itself (assuming it isn't wanted!).

Now that your proposal is out the door, there is one more thing for you to do: *Wait.* Response times for publishers and agents are notoriously slow, especially if your work is unsolicited. Agents may take from two to four months to respond; publishers may take between six months and a year. (Electronic publishers tend to respond more quickly—usually within less than two months.) Check the response times listed in the publisher's (or agent's) guidelines, and assume that in many cases, these may be underestimates.

If the specified response time has elapsed and you have heard nothing, follow up with a polite letter or e-mail inquiring as to the status of your proposal. Wait two weeks, then follow up again. If you still receive no reply, you may wish to send a final letter withdrawing your proposal from consideration (it's important to do this to avoid confusion or accusations of "simultaneous submission"), and send it to the next agent or editor on your list. Don't be surprised if you have to repeat this several times.

The key at this point is persistence. Your goal is to find an editor or agent who will believe in your book as much as you do. That person may not be the first on your list, or even the fifteenth or twentieth. But if you're willing to persevere in the belief that such an editor or agent is out there, you're a thousand times more likely to achieve publication than the writer who despairs after the first or second rejection.

14

SEEKING AN AGENT

Many writers assume that finding an agent is a necessary first step toward getting published, or that it may be impossible to get published without an agent. This is not necessarily true. One of the first steps you should take is not necessarily to *find* an agent, but to determine whether you actually *need* one.

A good way to answer this question is by reviewing the guidelines of publishers in your genre or interest area. If most of the publishers in your genre (and especially the top publishers) accept only agented submissions, then you would be well-advised to seek an agent before attempting to market your manuscript.

If, however, most of the publishers in your field or genre accept unagented submissions (including unsolicited submissions and submissions by invitation only—e.g., based on an initial query), then you may wish to proceed without an agent. You could, for example, hunt for an agent and a publisher simultaneously, or seek an agent *after* you've received an offer from a publisher. (At that point, it's wise to ask the publisher for a recommendation, as you may want to find an agent who can help you negotiate that particular contract.)

In making this decision, it's also important to know what an agent will do for you and what an agent will expect from you.

WHAT AN AGENT OFFERS A WRITER

The primary function of an agent is to find a publisher for your work. Agents work almost exclusively with book-length manuscripts (fiction and nonfiction); they rarely handle short fiction or articles. There are occasional exceptions, but generally speaking, if you are trying to market short stories or articles, you should be handling this on your own.

An agent will also help you negotiate a book contract. This is a key advantage, as an agent is *your* representative in the industry. The agent works for *you* and will strive to get you the best deal possible in terms of money, rights, etc.

An agent will also market the subsidiary rights to your book, which can be a lucrative field that you might have great difficulty tapping on your own. An agent is the best person to sell translation rights, international rights, audiobook rights, electronic rights, movie rights, etc. Your publisher will generally not make much effort to sell these rights (even if the publisher owns them). Often, an author can reap an even greater income from subsidiary rights sales than from the original book sale.

In the processing of handling these transactions, your agent will serve as an "escrow" account for your funds. Generally, your advance and royalties, and any other monies, will be sent directly to your agent, who will subtract his or her commission and pass the rest to you. (Your agent is not an accountant, however; don't expect help with writing expenses and taxes.)

It's important to realize that an agent is *not* an editor. While some agents will offer suggestions on how a book can be polished into a more marketable form, many agents will work only with books that are already market-ready. An agent will *not* line-edit your work, correct your spelling and grammar, or do any other basic editorial tasks.

In some cases, an agent will provide you with a contract that spells out what is expected on both sides. Many agents, however, do not work with contracts. Don't assume that having a contract is good or that not having one is bad. What matters is being able to work well with the agent; if you can't, a contract can sometimes lock you into an unwanted long-term relationship. One thing to determine before you even enter a relationship with an agent is how to end it, if it isn't proceeding as you hoped.

WHAT AN AGENT EXPECTS OF YOU

The first criteria an agent uses in determining whether to represent an author is the quality of that author's work. While you don't have to be published to find an agent, you do have to have publishable-quality material.

Agents also seek career authors, rather than one-book writers. Agents want to work with writers who will provide an ongoing source of income (which means writers who plan to produce more than one book). When seeking an agent, therefore, it's wise to present yourself as an author with long-term plans, rather than someone who simply wants to find a publisher for the "book of a lifetime."

Finally, an agent expects a fee. The standard fee at this time is 15 percent of all domestic sales made by that agent, and (in some cases) 20 percent of international sales. A few agents also charge for unusual expenses, but most do not charge for the basic expenses of copying and mailing manuscripts.

Note that this fee is assessed on *sales* of your work. Until your work is actually sold, the agent will collect no commission.

What to Watch Out for When Seeking an Agent

While there are hundreds of reputable literary agents, there are also hundreds of predatory sharks swimming in the publishing pool, hunting for inexperienced writers who are willing to do (and pay) anything to get published.

Experienced writers warn authors to stay away from any agent who:

- **Asks for a reading fee.** If an agent charges a fee (no matter how small) to read and review your manuscript, that agent is earning his or her income from writers—*not* by selling work to publishers. Charging reading fees is not illegal, but agents who do so are avoided by professionals.

- **Asks for an up-front fee (e.g., "to pay expenses") to market your work.** A reputable agent won't accept a manuscript that he or she doesn't believe can be sold—so such an agent doesn't regard the basic expenses of submitting manuscripts to be a risk. While some agents may charge for unusual expenses, the basics of copying and mailing manuscripts are considered to be covered by an agent's commission.

- **Offers to edit your manuscript for a fee.** Again, reputable agents only accept material that is market-ready. If an agent is making money from writers by providing editorial services, that agent has little incentive to try to *market* your work.

- **Suggests that you submit your manuscript to a specific editor or book doctor for editing.** While an agent *may* recommend that you seek editing for your manuscript, be wary of any who (a) suggests that you go to a specific service, and (b) implies that he or she will "accept" your manuscript after you do so.

- **Refuses to disclose information about his or her client list or sales history.**

- **Has a large percentage of sales to smaller or less reputable publishers.** Don't waste time with an agent who is likely to submit your work to small presses, electronic publishers, or (worst of all) subsidy publishers. You don't need an agent to approach those markets; what you want is an agent who can open doors that would otherwise be closed to you.

- **Asks for a higher commission.** Don't accept any excuses. Don't let an agent convince you that because you are a new writer, or don't have a track record in the industry, or have an unusual or "difficult" book, that you should pay a higher fee. If a reputable agent thinks he or she can place your work (even if it may take some effort), that agent will charge the usual fee; otherwise, he or she will simply refuse to represent you.

- **Is not a member of the Association of Author's Representatives (AAR).** While membership is not a sure sign of a reputable agent, it does mean that the agent has agreed to a certain standard of ethics.

HOW TO LOCATE AN AGENT

Knowing what to look for in an agent is one thing; knowing where to look is another. Many sources of information on agents exist, but it can be difficult to track down just the *right* agent for your work.

Ideally, you want an agent who appreciates and understands the type of material you write. If you write science fiction, you want to find an agent who regularly sells science fiction, who is familiar with all the major science fiction publishing houses, who knows what an alternate universe is, and who would never, ever accept a book by a new writer who uses terms like "warp drive" and "phaser."[1] Since science fiction comes in many flavors, you should also look for someone who appreciates the type of novel you have written.

Two general sources of agent listings include *The Literary Marketplace* and *Literary Agents of North America* (both of which can be found in most libraries' reference sections). Writer's Digest Books offers an annual *Guide to Literary Agents* (which includes lists of fee-charging agents). Several Web sites (including the AAR) post lists of agents online (see section 4 resources).

Be cautious about agent listings in writers' magazines. Reputable agents generally don't want to attract submissions from amateur and inexperienced writers and so are less likely to place advertisements in publications that have a high percentage of such writers in their readership.

Another way to find an agent is to ask another writer. This doesn't mean, however, that you should go online, hunt down a writer's Web site, and send an e-mail out of the blue asking that writer to tell you the name of his or her agent. Most writers won't share that information unless they are familiar with you and the quality of your work.

A good way to establish that type of relationship is to join a high-quality online discussion list or newsgroup for writers, one that includes several published authors in its membership. Contribute to discussions, and share your material in critique groups. Once you become known to and respected by the other members of the group, you are more likely to be able to ask those members for information about their agents.

APPROACHING AN AGENT

Approach an agent just as you would approach a publisher, and with the same types of materials. Start, for example, by researching the agent's Web site to determine:

---

[1] An experienced agent will know that (a) these terms are common to the trademarked Star Trek universe, and (b) only a rank amateur in the science fiction genre (and someone who has not read widely in the field or read any books about *writing* science fiction) would use such terms in a serious science fiction novel.

- What types of material the agent handles
- Whether the agent is accepting new clients
- What type of client the agent is looking for (e.g., how much experience or publishing background a client should have)
- What clients the agent currently represents and/or what titles the agent has sold
- Exactly what the agent wants you to send (e.g., a query letter, a query and synopsis, a nonfiction proposal, a complete manuscript, etc.).

Once you have determined the answers to these questions, follow the instructions in the relevant chapter of this book to prepare the requested materials.

The good news is that agents usually respond more quickly than publishers. Many will respond to a query within three to six weeks, and to a larger proposal (such as a synopsis and sample chapters) within two to three months. As always, observe an agent's posted response times before following up—and always remain courteous and professional.

What should your query include? Here's some advice from best-selling science fiction author Tara K. Harper:

WRITING THE AGENT QUERY
by Tara K. Harper

What advice would I give to others who are trying to write queries? I have heard many, many stories about query failures, even more stories about odd or offensive queries, and many rhetorical pleadings for proper query letters—all of these from agents, authors, and editors who have had to write or read queries over the years. My automatic response to a question about a query is to say, "Be polite!" My second response is to list the following seven points that address the basic and most common mistakes made in queries.

I'll address this advice to those who are querying agents, not publishers. (If you are querying a publisher, not an agent, consider the points following the agent-query advice.) The general advice is, for the most part, applicable to any business correspondence. For a professional writer, good communication means understanding your audience, addressing the needs of your audience, and communicating your points effectively.

BASICS OF QUERYING AN AGENT
- Fit the query to the agent. If the agent says he handles horror but not science fiction, don't query him about science fiction.

- Make your points quickly and succinctly. Don't flog a dead horse; if you do, it will only prove that you can't write well for a market (in this case, your agent).
- Restrict yourself to one page if possible, two if necessary. More than that, and you should start thinking about taking an ax to your query.
- Be professional. Make sure your writing tone is confident and informative without being arrogant or obsequious.
- Don't try to be witty unless you really are witty. There's little that's worse than a flat joke—it just demonstrates that your readers will probably be as unimpressed as this prospective agent.
- Don't try to tell the agent how much he will love your work. It's up to him to decide how he feels about what he reads.
- Proof your letter carefully! Good grammar and spelling are extremely important in this first-impression query. Remember, the agent will think this: If you don't care enough about your writing to proofread your one-page query letter, your four-hundred-page manuscript will probably be in horrible (translation: slush pile) shape.

HOW TO WRITE QUERY LETTERS

Before you can write your query letter, you need to know some things about your work and yourself. First, you'll need to know how to describe your story in one or two paragraphs. You will want to be able to touch on the important points, identify any new/interesting technology, and introduce the characters and areas without putting in too many unknown terms. You will have to give the agent reason to believe that 1) you are a good enough writer to write a salable story, and 2) you have enough self-discipline or dedication to complete the manuscript when it's sold.

Do all query letters follow the format recommended here? Of course not. Queries are as varied as the people who write them. But I do think good query letters answer these questions:

What Kind of Story Are You Trying to Sell?

What kind of story is it? If it's science fiction, what category is it: hard-SF? Cyberpunk? SF-adventure? Space opera? Military SF? . . . There are many publishing houses that handle science fiction, but some really like hack-'em-slash-'em-big-booms-in-space stuff. Some houses seem to handle more space opera, some handle SF with a more scientifically technical theme, etc. Immediately upon opening your letter, a prospective agent will want to know the genre for which you've written and how your story will fit into that genre.

For example, if you have written a cyberpunk science fiction story, in the first paragraph of your letter, you could include a statement like this: "Readers who enjoy cyberpunk/suspense in a near-future setting will also enjoy this story." That statement gives a prospective agent an idea of where he can try to sell your work.

Almost all stories fit into an existing category of fiction (or nonfiction). If your story truly doesn't fit into any category, you may or may not want to address that immediately in your query. Such a story may be hard to sell, thus putting you and your agent in a difficult position. For such a novel, there will be no existing readership to address, so not only will your name and the book be new, but an entire market must be developed.

For example, it took Northwest author Jean Auel years (and something like forty-two rejections) to sell her first novel, *Clan of the Cave Bear.* This was partly because, although the story is considered romantic, there was no prehistory-romance category already in place. No one knew how the book would fit into the market or what kind of (or how many) readers would buy it. Since then, an entire category of fiction has developed. Now, you can go to any bookstand and see titles like *Daughter of the Forest, The Animal Wife, Reindeer Moon,* and so on.

Is Your Topic Popular or Gaining Popularity in the Market?

This is more difficult. The entertainment market is notoriously fickle. What is popular this month may be disdained the next. And even if you sell a story with a popular idea, it can take two to six years to get that story on the retail shelves—even if it sells quickly to the publisher.

However, if readers love dragon stories, and you've written a dragon story, you have a better chance of selling that story than if the current market hated dragons. If refugee memoirs are "in" and look like they will be "in" for a while, your leaving-your-country manuscript may be just what an agent is looking for.

Unless the ideas in your manuscript are particularly timely or farsighted, don't talk specifically about markets and topics in your manuscript. The book description should give the agent all the information he needs to determine what kind of ideas you have.

Is Your Work Similar to the Work of Any Other Published Authors?

Something that can help you attract an agent is a similarity in style to another, popular author. I'm not saying you should write like other authors—you should, of course, develop your own style. However, in some cases, your own style may be reminiscent of or similar to the style of another published author. Even if you write in a genre other than that of the published author, being able to make a comparison will give an agent some idea of which editors enjoy that style of writing. For example, perhaps you can say that readers who love Mary Higgins Clark will enjoy your work. If the agent is interested in the market for readers of M. H. Clark, he might be interested in you, too.

For example, if your SF/fantasy has a beauty of prose but is technically detailed, perhaps you could say: "This book combines the emotional depth of prose similar to the achievements of Orson Scott Card with the technical detail of work such as that seen from Greg Bear." If your work has the detail and depth of David Poyer's novels (military action/suspense), then you could give your agent a good idea of market placement with a statement like this: " Readers who like the realistic, gritty detail of military engagements in the style of David Poyer will also enjoy this book."

There are two things to be careful of here. The first is attaching yourself to an already-saturated market. If there is no more room for books similar to Anne Rice's vampire work, then saying that your work is similar to that work means a quick ticket to the slush pile. (Of course, as my publisher says, there's always room for another good book.) If the market is saturated by a single author's extensive number of releases, you're going to have to come up with a very good reason why the agent should try to sell a publisher on yet another unknown who writes in the same style as the author(s) already saturating the market.

The second thing to be careful of is attaching yourself to an author who writes in the same genre but whose style really isn't at all like yours, or whose style is so varied that your statement of similarity is ineffective. For example, Piers Anthony (SF/Fantasy author) writes books that are dark (such as *Chthon*), but also writes very light, facetious stories (such as the Xanth series). To say simply that you write in the style of Piers Anthony can be misleading. Better to say that readers who enjoy Piers Anthony's darker, more serious work will enjoy your novel, or that readers who enjoy Piers Anthony's Xanth series will enjoy your new novel.

Think of it this way: You're not really trying to attach yourself to someone else's coattails. What you're trying to do is give a prospective agent an idea of the style in which you write. Mentioning an already-known writing style that is similar to yours can give an agent an idea of what kind of readers will like your work. That then tells him whether or not he has the contacts to be able to work effectively to place your manuscript. The more specific the information you can give a prospective agent, the better he can determine whether or not he is able to or will be interested in representing you.

What Is Compelling or Interesting About This Story?

Include a synopsis of your story—why it is compelling, poignant, exciting, terrifying, whatever. Don't tell your agent that he will love the poignancy or excitement of the story. Just tell him about the story. Let him make his own judgment about how he reacts to your work once he sees it.

One way to write the synopsis is as though you were writing a blurb for the back cover of your book. For one thing, this helps keep the description short. For another, it concentrates the plot into a few major points. If you can't figure out how to describe your story in one or two paragraphs, you may need to take a closer look at what you're trying to say in the book.

Another point to keep in mind when writing a synopsis: Keep new terms and names to a minimum. In most genres, new terminology won't be a problem. However, in SF/fantasy, it is important to make sure you do not introduce more than two or three new terms, including character names (unless they are already common names). Otherwise, there are too many items floating around without any context.

Some people advise including a blow-by-blow plot description with your query. If you really feel you must include an outline, try it, but I think it's premature at this stage. It's an editor, not a prospective agent, who will want a detailed description of your book. Remember, the agent is looking at your work for only three things:

- Is there a market for this kind of story?
- Do I know a publisher/editor who is interested in trying new authors who have written this kind of story?
- Do I think this story is written well enough to sell?

He doesn't need an outline to tell him these things. He needs a quick summary of how your work answers those questions. (Of course, he'll probably forgive you for including that four-page outline if it's really that fantastic.) Later, when he has agreed to represent you, then he will want details—and a copy of the manuscript, of course.

Do You Have Any Name Recognition?

If you have built name recognition for your novel-length fiction through the publishing of short stories, you are in good shape. It will be important for you to point out that you have a solid history of readership. For example, perhaps, in two years, you have had nine short stories published in professional magazines and one story published in an anthology. In that case, you should include a statement like this:

> "In the past two years, I've had nine short stories published in professional magazines, such as *Asimov's* and *Omni*. In 1996, one of my stories, "XXX-title," was included in the *XX Anthology* as one of the featured stories."

Such a statement tells the agent that your work was either popular enough or interesting enough to be included in top-of-the-field magazines, and that you have developed a readership within two years. That will be useful information in getting a publisher to look at your book-length fiction.

If you are bringing name recognition in from another field, you might mention that also. This is not necessarily a strong selling point, but it can help. If your name recognition is not in the genre in which you are now writing, mention the name recognition last.

What Are Your Qualifications for Writing Fiction?

Everyone has one good story in them—that's what the old adage says. But that doesn't mean everyone is qualified to write that one good story. In general, I would put my professional qualifications last in a query letter. In fiction, they are the least likely to sell the manuscript, when compared to the type of story, the current market demand, and how similar your work is to others. For example, if you write action/suspense novels, and you have experience in many action sports or events, you might include a line like this: "The author's personal experience in scuba diving, shooting, and racing has helped to bring both excitement and realistic suspense to the action in this novel."

If I did include my qualifications (which, yes, I did in my query letter), I would not use more than a single paragraph to describe them. If you have other published work, you might include a listing of those titles on an attached sheet, but I wouldn't include them in the body of the letter unless those titles were well-known. Remember that you want your basic query letter to be short and easy to read. Putting a long list of other titles or a writing resume in an attachment allows the agent the choice of reading additional details without missing anything important.

Should You Include a Synopsis or Outline?

Not unless your initial information about the agent (such as the agency description in the writer's guide) indicates that he wants a synopsis or outline submitted along with the query.

The query letter is just that—a query about whether the agent is interested in representing a client who has written a work in a particular field, genre, or category. If the agent is interested in your work, he will tell you what he wants from you. For example, he will let you know whether he prefers the information about your work in an outline, as a synopsis, as sample chapters, or as the entire novel.

If you feel you must include an outline with your query, make sure the outline is on a separate page (or pages) from the one-page query letter. This allows the agent to read the entire query at a glance and determine after that whether he wants to read on to the outline.

If you want to act professionally, then send the agent what he wants to receive—not what you want to show off. He wants only the information he needs in order to 1) determine whether or not he wants to represent your work, and 2) sell the book to an editor/publisher.

How Long Should You Wait for a Response from an Agent?

I'm tempted to say, "As long as it takes."

In general, agents say that they respond within three months to queries. However, remember that agents, like editors, are deluged with queries and manuscripts. It is not uncommon to see responses after six or even nine months. Some agents never respond to a query.

Should you follow up your query with a phone call? I'd say no. Follow up with another letter, and make sure the second letter is polite. Don't make accusations about the agent not bothering to respond, throwing out your query, etc. Instead, simply say something like this: "This is a follow-up query regarding my completed manuscript, *Diseases of Little-Known Nematodes.* My previous query was sent to you on XX date, and I have not yet received a reply from you regarding the possibility of your agenting the manuscript." Then continue with the query as if it was a standard query letter, including the blurb, the brief description of why this novel is interesting, and so on. Most legitimate agents respond as soon as they can—they don't like piled-up paperwork any more than the rest of us.

If two queries have not elicited a response, it's time to make the phone call or try a different agent. However, if you make a phone call, make sure you continue to be courteous. Treat the call as if it is your first contact with the agent. The reality is that this call *is* your first contact. Be professional; be polite. You still have a chance to make an impression, and you want to make sure it's a good one.

How Not to Write Query Letters and Responses

Here's the actual text of part of a letter from someone who had just had a manuscript refused: "YOU F—ING LIAR, STAY OUT OF MY LIFE."

For shock value, that was an effective letter. As far as getting published goes, this person just got blacklisted. If you think editors won't remember you when you are rude, you're mistaken. There are too many decent writers who will behave professionally—or at least somewhat courteously to the editor's face—for an editor to waste time on an intentionally offensive idiot. If the idiot is that difficult to work with when he wants something (for an agent or editor to read the manuscript), imagine how horrid he will be when contracts are being negotiated, when changes are requested, and during any other normal business or publicity activities.

Regardless of how disappointed, humiliated, or otherwise unhappy you are about having your work rejected, do not take it out on the agent, editor, or publisher. If you want other professionals to respect you—in any field—you must create and maintain a reputation for behaving in a professional manner. Curses, gratuitous insults, angry sarcasm—these things might be overlooked in a junior-high student, but not in a professional. If you must, write out how you feel, but then burn that paper. Get it out of your system before trying to communicate again with the agent or editor. Don't sacrifice your future for a chance to prove how crass, immature, or offensive you really are.

PITCHING YOUR NOVEL AT A CONFERENCE

Another way to locate an agent is to pitch your book directly at a writing conference. Many conferences now offer opportunities for writers and agents (and editors) to meet face-to-face. Usually, this means signing up for a ten-minute "pitch" session. You have to register for the conference to be able to gain such an appointment (which means you may pay anywhere from $100 to $500 in registration fees), and you must generally book your appointment well in advance, as "pitch sessions" fill up quickly. You will have no more than ten minutes to present your idea, and sometimes less.

Will it work? If you have a good idea, you have a good chance—provided, of course, that you have selected an appropriate agent for your pitch. If you are able to impress the agent, you may even be able to sell a different book, if the agent doesn't want your original concept.

How should you approach an agent? Author Robin Catesby writes:

Enthusiasm for your own work goes a long way. By that I don't mean saying "this is the best book you will read"—agents don't want to hear that—but rather, launch into your pitch with a great level of positive energy. Do what you need to do beforehand to get into this state of mind, whether it's a brisk energizing walk around the conference, or a relaxing cup of herb tea. You want to make sure your mind and body are ready and not all jittered out on caffeine or anything. I've seen people blow pitches simply because they haven't given any attention to being in the right state of mind. Also, don't schedule two pitches back to back. I did that once and discovered that I'd used up much of my energy on the first pitch, so the second wasn't nearly as good.

Another important point: You're not just presenting the agent with a verbal synopsis of your book, you are selling it to them, so you've got to think about what is going to make your book jump out from all the others they've heard about that day. Before even launching into the outline, have a hook—one or two sentences that sum up the theme, the lead character's dilemma, the tone . . . everything that makes your book a must-read. If it's a funny novel, don't be afraid to give them a funny pitch. If it's a mystery, build a little suspense. You don't need to turn it into a dramatic monologue, but a little of this kind of energy can be a huge help, especially if the agent has just gone through five monotone pitches in a row. Practice the pitch in front of a friend or two if you need to—it is, in a way, a theatrical experience, so a little rehearsal can't hurt.

The most you'll need to bring with you is a one-page synopsis. Very few agents are going to ask for sample chapters right then and there. If they are interested, they'll give you their card and ask you to mail them. Last time I pitched, I didn't have anything with me, and to be honest, I think it worked much better. If you have your synopsis in front of you, it can become a crutch, as with an actor who wants to glance at his script during performance. That reads as nerves to the agent, so if you bring one at all, keep it in a folder until the agent asks to see it.

Finally, remember that agents come to conferences to find clients, so unless they are just naturally grumpy, they aren't going to be brusque with you. The only exception would be if you didn't have an agent in mind already and you were to schedule an appointment with an agent who is entirely inappropriate for your novel. Do your homework. Get the conference brochure and study that guest list. Don't just grab the first agent's name out of a hat; make sure the agent actually represents your type of book!

Pitching can be scary, but if you're prepared, relaxed, and proud of what you've written, it can also be pretty great.

Several agents also shared tips on this process:

Before pitching to an agent, put together a zippy, two-sentence description "a la *TV Guide*" about the book. Tell why it's different and new and better. Know what you're talking about—and don't be nervous. We're only human.

—Elizabeth Pomada
Michael Larsen/Elizabeth Pomada Literary Agents

When pitching to an agent or an editor at a writer's conference, don't read off of cue cards. This gives the impression that the writer doesn't know his/her own work. Don't exaggerate about your credentials and experience. Keep the pitch short and to the point. Answer any questions quickly and honestly. If they request your material, don't wait to send it out to them.

—Ginger Norton, Senior Editor
Sedgeband Literary Associates

Be succinct. Be able to sum up your book in a single sentence. Be professional, polished, and interesting—the agent looks at the writer the way an editor does: Is the writer him/herself promotable? Would she play well on camera, in radio interviews? etc.

—Jeff Kleinman
Graybill & English

If you're going to pitch a book to agents/editors at a conference, you should be prepared to state concisely exactly what your book is about and who its audience is. And, be aware that most agents and editors are going to ask that you formally submit your material rather than giving it to them on the spot.

—Michael Psaltis
Ethan Ellenberg Literary Agency

A FINAL WORD: ON SIMULTANEOUS QUERIES

Given that it can take months to receive a response to a query, is it acceptable to query several editors simultaneously? The answer used to be no—despite the fact that publishers might take as long as six months to respond to a submission. However, that seems to be changing toward a more realistic understanding of the writer's dilemma.

Author A.C. Crispin conducted a survey of agents and publishers on this topic, and reported the results in the Fall 2000 *Science Fiction & Fantasy Writers of America Bulletin*. She found that the agents and editors agreed that simultaneous *queries* were acceptable. Two of the four agents queried were also willing to review partial works (e.g., synopsis and sample chapters) or even complete manuscripts submitted simultaneously to other agents; the other two would not. Similarly, two of the publishers were willing to review multiple submissions; one was not, and one accepted only agented submissions.

The bottom line, then, would seem to be this:

- It is generally considered acceptable to send simultaneous queries to multiple agents and/or editors.

- If you do send out multiple queries, inform the agents/editors that you are doing so. This is basic courtesy, and if you omit this step, you're likely to alienate an editor or agent who might otherwise have been willing to review your package.

- Though some agents and editors are willing to review simultaneously submitted packages or even complete manuscripts, this is not yet a widely accepted practice. Agents and editors are more likely to respond to your query by requesting an exclusive review of your submission package.

15

THE FICTION QUERY LETTER

by Lynn Flewelling

Whether I'm giving a bookstore reading or teaching a writer's workshop, one of the most frequently asked questions is always, "How do I get my first novel published? What's the trick, the secret?"

The secret is that there is no trick, just skillful, focused effort. The first step is to write a really good book. The next, equally important, step is to attract the notice of someone in a position to get it into print. Some people do this by networking at conventions, or striking up a relationship with a published author who recommends them to her publisher, both of which are viable routes. For most of us, however, it's a "market by mail" venture. Whether you decide to seek an agent or go straight to publishers, you need a letter of introduction—the query.

Dissected and examined critically, the query letter is an elegantly concise piece of promotional writing. You have exactly one page to introduce yourself and your novel—just four or five clean, tight paragraphs, each with its own specific purpose. That doesn't sound so hard. We are writers, after all, right? But the devil is in the details, especially for a newcomer with no track record or flashy credentials.

That's where I found myself a few years back, when it came time to market my first fantasy novel, *Luck in the Shadows*. I hadn't published any short fiction; I'd never been to a convention to network; the few published authors I knew were literary sorts with no connections in the genre world. According to the prevailing collective wisdom that persists among the unpublished, I didn't have much of a chance.

Happily, the prevailing wisdom is wrong. It's certainly a plus to have a few fiction credits or an influential mentor, but it's not an absolute necessity. If it were, I wouldn't be writing this article.

THE WRITER'S CALLING CARD

There I was, back in 1994, with a book I was burning to sell and no idea how to go about it. As I chewed my way through various "how-to" books, it quickly became clear that the most important tool I needed was a great query letter. It's a writer's introduction, our calling card, and, hopefully, our foot in the door.

For us nobodies, it's basically a cold sales job; we've got one page to engage an agent or editor's interest, to make him want to flip the page to scan our carefully chosen sample chapters. Some agents and editors glance at the letter but read the chapters first. Others read the query and reject the chapters unseen if the letter doesn't sing. You never know, so write the letter like it's the one thing standing between you and success. It just might be.

Here's the query letter that sold several agents on *Luck* and ultimately led to a two-book contract with Bantam:

Dear (Agent/Editor's Name):

I am seeking representation for my fantasy/adventure novel, *Luck In The Shadows,* complete at 170,000 words. I am enclosing a synopsis and a sample chapter. The sequel, *Stalking Darkness,* is nearing completion, and another freestanding book featuring the same characters is in outline form.

I love thieves and spies—those sneaky people who live by intuition, skill, and inside knowledge. In fantasy, however, they are often portrayed as dark, ruthless characters or relegated to second-string roles, a la Falstaff, as useful or amusing foils for more conventional heroic types. *Luck in the Shadows* gives the rogues center stage.

Seregil is an experienced spy for hire with a murky past and noble connections; Alec is the talented but unworldly boy he rescues and takes on as apprentice. "I admit I've cut a purse or two in my time," Seregil tells Alec soon after they meet, "and some of what I do could be called stealing, depending on who you ask. But try to imagine the challenge of overcoming incredible obstacles to accomplish a noble purpose. Think of traveling to lands where legends walk the streets in daylight, and even the color of the sea is like nothing you've ever seen! I ask you again, would you be plain Alec of Kerry all your life, or would you see what lies beyond?" Alec goes, of course, and quickly plunges into danger, intrigue, and adventure as their relationship deepens into friendship. The interaction between these two forms the core of this character-driven series.

I've been writing professionally for ten years and am currently a freelance journalist. My articles appear regularly in the *Bangor Daily News, Preview! Magazine,* and *Maine In Print.* I've covered everything from software to psychics; my interview credits include Stephen King, Anne Rice, and William Kotzwinkle.

Thank you for your consideration of this proposal. I look forward to hearing from you soon.

Sincerely,

Lynn Flewelling

First things first. When approaching any market, make certain you're writing to the right person. If you're using a reference book—the *Writer's Market,* for instance—make sure it's the latest edition. Addressing your query to someone who left the agency three years ago shows a lack of research on your part and can prejudice some readers against you before you've even begun your pitch. The same goes for spelling their names wrong or addressing them by the wrong titles or genders. (Any mail I get addressed to "Mr. Lynn Flewelling" is immediately suspect.) Such errors may not automatically land your query in the round file, but they aren't going to win you any points, either.

Reading the market news in trade journals like *Writer's Market* can help keep you up to date on who's where. Most agents and editors I've talked to say that a brief call to their office to verify the information is also acceptable.

Now, on with our dissection:

Paragraph 1: The Opening

This brief opening accomplishes a number of things. It states what you're selling, how long it is, and that it's complete. (Some agents and editors will consider a few chapters and an outline from an unknown; most won't. A finished novel proves that you can go the distance.) The "synopsis and sample chapter" mentioned in this paragraph are the exact items this particular agent's listing asked for. Giving them what they want—no more, no less—demonstrates that you've done your homework and are approaching them as a professional. If you send out multiple queries, be sure to tailor each query package and letter accordingly. No one likes a form letter.

If you have other related works underway, it's a good idea to mention them here, showing that you're not a one-shot wonder. If you don't, however, don't worry about it, and don't bother mentioning other works in a genre the agent or editor does not handle.

Paragraph 2: The "Why I Wrote This Book" 'Graph

Those of you who are basing your science fiction epic on your Nobel Prize–winning research in human genome mapping won't have much trouble with this one. For those of us "nobodies" with less stunning credentials, it can be a bit daunting. Most of the sample letters I found while researching queries were written by people who were, as stated above, basing their latest novel on their own research or some life-changing personal experience. In every case the author had an impressive publishing background of some sort, and none of them were first-timers.

I, on the other hand, had simply written a book I really liked, so I said that and let the enthusiasm carry it. Keep it simple and direct. Don't go on at length about your literary influences or what book first turned you on to the genre; they've seen that a million times. Just be sincere.

Paragraph 3: Give 'Em a Glimpse of the Goods

You can't tell the whole story; that's what the outline or synopsis is for. Just give them the flavor, introduce the protagonist, and, above all, demonstrate that you can write well. How you present your book here is just as important as the story itself. Make your thumbnail description concise but lively. Try to capture what or who the book is about. In short, consider this paragraph your book's audition scene, and know that this paragraph is the one most likely to get you rejected for the right reasons.

Right reasons? you ask.

Absolutely. Most editors and agents are book lovers just like the rest of us, with the same subjectivity of taste. If an agent doesn't like books about dragons and that's your main focus, then they aren't going to want your book, and you don't want them representing it. What you want from an agent is an enthusiastic representative for your work. With editors, you want someone who's excited by the prospect of polishing your manuscript into a salable book and getting it on the shelves.

A wise friend once observed that the ratio between rejections and acceptances is about 12:1. What happens generally is this: Agent One reads your carefully crafted query and thinks he's seen your idea a hundred times before. Agent Three thinks it's the freshest treatment he's seen of that idea in ages. Agent Seven just plain hates that sort of plot. Agent Eleven can't get enough of it.

Simple persistence and faith are required to run this gauntlet, and rejection letters do have their uses. We'll return to this shortly.

Paragraph 4: Experience and Background

Got it? Flaunt it! Don't got it? Keep quiet.

While the freelance writing I mentioned in my query by no means guarantees that I'm a good novelist, it does suggest that I probably know how to string words together. I also tried to be creative in my spin on the subject. I've written dozens of feature articles for local papers and interviewed lots of interesting people; the ones I chose to mention in the query were selected to highlight my interest in the fantasy field, and in literature and authors in general. Whether or not it impressed anyone is debatable, but it did relate to the book I was selling.

A caveat: If your background has no bearing on the novel in question in some readily apparent way, it's best to just leave this paragraph out, or keep it brief.

Paragraph 5: Your Standard Polite Good-Bye

Don't press them for response times, hand down ultimatums ("You've got two months, then I'm sending it somewhere else"), or offer to call. The market listing that provided their mailing address should also include an estimated turnaround time. Be patient, and don't expect them to meet their own deadlines to the day. However, if you don't hear back for a month after the listed time, a polite phone inquiry is usually appropriate.

A Few Additional Basics

- **Stationery.** Queries should be neatly typed on high-quality, unadorned, 8½" × 11" business stationery. While white is your safest bet colorwise, you can probably get away with ivory, buff, or a light gray. Avoid brightly colored paper and ink at all costs. The same goes for cute border prints, patterns, and dot-matrix printing unless you want your query to scream, "Amateur!"

- **Letterhead.** A plain, businesslike letterhead looks sharp and conveys your address information in a professional-looking manner. If you have access to a good laser printer, you can design your own, avoiding pretentiously ornate or hard-to-read fonts, as well as illustrations. If you are gainfully employed, do not use your company stationery, no matter how classy it is. A letterhead from "Joe Bloe, Attorney at Law" will only cause undue confusion. And resist the temptation to style yourself "Jane Doe, Novelist." That should be self-evident.

- **The query package.** As stated above, do your homework. Research each market and send them only what they ask to see. This usually doesn't include "return reply" coupons (first class postage is your best bet), photos of yourself, photocopies of writing samples, your resume, or manuscripts other than the one you're currently offering.

- **Proofreading.** Do I even have to address this? According to my agent and editor friends, the answer is a world-weary *Yes!* A query (or manuscript) marred by typos, blotches of correction fluid, erasure marks, or coffee stains is a red flag to publishing professionals. If you're sloppy with something as important as a query, what will you be like to work with on a manuscript? Chances are, they'll spare themselves the trouble of finding out. Proofread your letter carefully for errors, then show it to some other trustworthy soul. Our own mistakes are often the hardest to spot, since we know what's supposed to be there on the page and tend to see it whether it's really there or not. Finally, retype or print out a crisp, blameless copy of the corrected letter.

While the purpose of this article is to help you make that wonderful first novel sale, I'd like to finish up with a few thoughts on rejections. Fear of rejection is a reality for most of us. Many a good manuscript has languished in a drawer because the author just couldn't face the possibility. Let's face it, rejection sucks. But it's also a normal part of the game. Sit around with any group of writers, and sooner or later, the war stories start flying. One-upping about who's gotten slammed with the nastiest rejection letter is practically a sport. Rejections are our battle scars, and only those with the guts to strive earn them.

Take comfort in the fact that all writers deal with rejection time and again throughout their careers. I keep a copy of Andre Bernard's *Rotten Rejections* (Pushcart Press, 1990) close at hand. It's an inspirational collection of rejection letters received by the likes of Ernest Hemingway, James Joyce, and Jane Austen for books that now grace university required-reading lists.

So, when that first rejection shows up in your mailbox, toast yourself with a tall glass of something very nice. It's proof that you're off the porch and running with the big dogs now.

Later, as those dozen or so rejections pile up on the way (we hope) to that first, glorious "yes," study them carefully. They can be a useful guide. It was an agent's thoughtful rejection letter that ultimately led to revisions that sold my first book.

The most valuable rejection letter gives reasons. Many will be contradictory. One letter will praise what the last one damned as trite, then go on to nail you for something completely different. Some will be valid criticisms, others are purely subjective. If a certain comment strikes an "ah ha!" chord, then take a second look at your work, but realize, too, that you can't and shouldn't rewrite the book to please every critic.

What you do need to watch for, however, are patterns. If five out of seven agents mention that they did not understand your main character's motivation, or that your opening chapter did not engage their interest, then you need to take a hard look at what you're sending out.

I began by saying that there is no secret trick to getting published. You can, however, think of the process as a game. Games have steps, rules, and strategy. The better you become at these, the better you can use them to your advantage. The good query letter is one of your most valuable assets.

16

SAMPLE NOVEL SYNOPSIS

MAGGIE'S WISH
by Sharon Ihle

The sluggish days of summer are giving way to the crisper fall evenings of 1881 in Prescott, Arizona Territory, as MAGGIE THORNE glances out the kitchen window and sees her six-year-old daughter hoeing the pumpkin patch. Halloween is just two months away, which means that soon, Christmas will be upon them—again.

Just the mere thought of that most revered of holidays is enough to sink Maggie's spirits. Not that she has anything against Christmas itself. She has a lot to be thankful for when the sun rises each December 25. Her daughter HOLLY, whom she adores without reservation, came into the world at twenty minutes past eight on Christmas morning. A deeply religious woman, Maggie also thinks of the holiday as Christ's birthday, never failing to recognize it as such in a respectful manner.

As she is the bread baker and pastry chef in a small restaurant owned by her Aunt Lorna, the holiday season also keeps Maggie happily productive and fills her coffers well enough to see her and Holly though the winter. But something supersedes all the good the holiday brings, a dark and dreary cloud that obscures the yuletide lights and dulls the sparkle in Maggie's wide brown eyes. Lord help her, how much longer can she go on this way?

Maggie's first inkling that Christmas would become a time for sorrow struck nearly seven years ago on the very day Holly was born. Although the baby's father promised to show up in Prescott before the birth, he hadn't so much as written by the time their daughter pushed her way into the world. Maggie had an idea that he never would. So far, and nearly seven years later, she is right.

She was a tall, plain-faced spinster of twenty-two, with little hope of landing a man of her own, the first time Maggie laid eyes on RAFE HOLLISTER. At the time, a hard Utah winter had settled over the family farm, bringing with it the kind of cold that bites hollows in the chubbiest cheeks and freezes nose hairs stiff as pokers—and that was if a body stayed indoors. Rafe was close to dead the morning Maggie found him huddled in a corner of her father's barn. He'd been shot clean through the shoulder, and while the wound itself isn't life-threatening, the loss of blood made him pitifully weak. When Maggie comes across him, he's also nearly frozen clear through. She should have run and got her pa the minute she saw him lying there. She should have taken the gun from Rafe's stiff fingers and finished him off right there on the spot, saving them all a ton of grief. Maggie could have done a lot of things, anything but what she settled on once Rafe turned those big calf eyes on her and grinned that devil grin. If she had, she wouldn't be sitting at her kitchen table now wondering how in hell she was going to explain one more time why Santa Claus hadn't brought Holly the only thing she'd ever asked for; her very own daddy.

It wasn't as if her first—and only—true love hadn't known the trouble Maggie was in. Spring thaw was late in coming that year. By the time Rafe had healed and Maggie had nursed him to his former robust self, she had a pretty good idea there would be a baby come winter. She told him, of course, sure he'd do right and take her away with him, but excuses why not spilled out of his mouth faster than the teardrops from her eyes. He was on the run from the law, a thing she'd pretty well guessed on her own, and although he hadn't done a blasted thing wrong according to him, he had to get it set right before he could settle down and raise a family.

Maggie can hardly remember flying into hysterics that day, but she recalls flinging enough of a fit over what her future held once her father got wind of her "little" problem for Rafe to decide he ought to help her figure out what to do. After slapping her around a little, making damn sure she wouldn't alert her entire family to the fact that he was living in their barn, Rafe dipped into his overstuffed saddlebags, pulled out a wad of bills, and told Maggie to use the money to buy a train ticket. She chose the destination, Prescott, because her mother's sister lived there and would take her in until Rafe could join her.

On the morning Maggie runs away from home, Rafe tells her he loves her, shows her one more time exactly how much, and then promises to get square with the law and meet her in Prescott well before Christmas day. Six long years and six longer Christmases have gone by since then. And at each of the last four, a little red-haired girl cries fat teardrops all over her birthday cake at the close of that most celebrated day. This year, God willing, things will be different.

This year, Maggie has hired a retired Texas Ranger, a man just a few years older than she, who has given up the badge and hard chases because of a bum leg. Her friend, the sheriff of Prescott, is also a friend of the ranger, a man he believes is perfect for the job because he's very, very good at tracking people who don't know they need tracking. People like Rafe Hollister who have lost their way.

Once she meets Ranger MATT WESTON, Maggie is suddenly at a loss to explain her circumstances and finds herself making up excuses for Rafe, not just for Holly's sake, but also for her own. After all, she'd once loved Rafe enough to bear him a child born in shame—how could she show herself as a woman who'd allowed that love to die? Wouldn't that make her time of sinning with Rafe somehow more depraved? Matt Weston would definitely think so—Maggie senses that in the man after one look in his silvery, no-nonsense eyes. For reasons she can't imagine, this near-stranger's opinion of her is extremely important. Evading the truth rather than lying to Matt, Maggie simply explains that her man ran out on his responsibilities and that she wants him brought back to her—alive and well. She believes that explanation will give the former lawman the impression that Rafe is her husband, and why shouldn't it? Her Prescott neighbors have long believed the very same thing.

At thirty-two years of age, Matt Weston hates his early retirement with a passion, and for what he sees as two good reasons: The first, and hardest to take, is his exclusion from the manhunts, the feel of his own blood thundering in his veins as he runs his quarry down. The second, and somehow more threatening than a cornered outlaw with blazing guns, is his sudden vulnerability to the single ladies in town. For over thirty years Matt has easily avoided the perils and, he has to admit, the responsibilities of turning his life over to a member of the fairer sex. Now that he is almost deskbound, he's practically tripping over available women, and even more alarming, rapidly running out of excuses for remaining a bachelor.

Funny how that final excuse—not to mention a man's mind—can vanish with the blink of a warm, brown eye. A pair of them, to be exact, each rimmed by a lush bank of lashes the color of pitch. He has no business looking into those eyes or thinking thoughts that don't include ways of catching up to Maggie's wandering husband, but Matt can't seem to stop himself. He is an honorable, professional man, one who never lets his personal life get in the way of business, so why in hell can't he keep his mind on his work whenever she is around?

He supposes this lapse of ethics has something to do with Maggie's gentle ways and honest charms, the kind of beauty that fairly radiates the goodness in her heart. Not that he believes any of those things can excuse his utter fascination with the lady. He has a job to do, and sets out to do it with an almost personal vengeance.

It doesn't take Matt but two weeks to locate the bastard—the precise opinion he forms of Rafe Hollister within minutes of locating the man. The meeting takes place at a run-down saloon in El Paso, when Matt stumbles over a drunken Rafe, who is passed out on the floor. When Rafe finally comes to, Matt decides that Miss Maggie is in for a rude shock—and "Miss" Maggie is the way Matt thinks of her, no matter how hard she hints that she's actually married to this stinking outlaw.

While Rafe is still unconscious, Matt takes him into his custody and discovers that he has been wounded—most of his left ear is blown to smithereens, and a bullet fragment is lodged in his right wrist. Although Matt wishes whoever wounded the man had been a better shot, he tends to the injuries Miss Maggie's "lost" husband has suffered, then binds him hand and foot and tosses him in the back of his wagon.

When Rafe sobers up and awakens to find himself traveling west toward Arizona Territory, Matt informs the miserable bastard that his wife and child are looking for him, and that he's been hired to take him to Prescott. Far from being grateful, Rafe begins cursing Maggie, calling her a horse-faced spinster, among other things, and declaring that she was lucky to have gotten as much as she did from him—a good time and the only piece of "loving" she'd ever get from a sane man. He tries to go on raving about Maggie, assuring his captor that he wouldn't have touched her at all had he not been weak and crazy in the head from loss of blood.

When the ranger pulls the wagon to a halt and climbs down from the driver's seat, Rafe is certain that he is about to be set free. Instead, he receives the worst beating of his miserable life. When he comes to again, Rafe quickly discovers that both of his eyes are swollen shut, his lips are split and caked with blood, and he is hanging by his wrists, including the injured one, from a rafter inside a darkened barn. Then, through what is left of his ear, he hears the voice of the former ranger as he explains the terms of Rafe's "pardon."

You will submit yourself to a month of intensive training as a decent law-abiding citizen and loving husband and father, he is told. This will take place in Prescott, where Miss Maggie Thorne can follow your progress and make a final decision about whether she should or should not accept your marriage proposal—and yes, you will ask her to be your wife. You will then abide by Maggie's decision and do your level best to uphold it for the rest of your natural life.

If you choose not to do those few things, Matt informs Rafe, there's another option for you to consider: You can continue to hang by the wrists here in this abandoned barn, which happens to be situated on the Mexican side of the Rio Grande. This will undoubtedly bring your life to a very unnatural end.

Rafe quickly accepts the original terms and keeps his complaints to himself during the rest of the journey to Prescott. Once they settle into Matt's cabin, Rafe is shackled to a chain hanging from an overhead beam, but otherwise free to move about the perimeters of the room. He also proves to be a surprisingly apt pupil, learning how to speak and behave like a gentleman in just a few weeks, and actually asks to see Maggie again in the hopes of meeting his young daughter.

For Matt, it is a time of raging conflict. Although he works hard to turn the outlaw into someone worthy of Maggie and Holly, from the basest part of his soul, Matt is praying that Rafe will fail. His visits to Maggie each day to report on Rafe's progress are taking a toll on his sanity, not to mention his body. He awakes in a sweat night after night, his dreams filled with images of the woman he has fallen in love with. Even worse, he has convinced himself that he sees his own frustrations and needs each time he looks into her expressive eyes.

It is as Thanksgiving draws near that Matt slips into the darkened coffee shop late one night to discuss Rafe's progress and finds Maggie awash in tears. He takes her in his arms, comforting her, and asks her what is wrong. There is no way she can explain how much her feelings for Matt have grown or to let him know how badly she wants him—not after he's been working so hard to make her "almost" husband presentable enough for her to marry. Even Maggie can't understand how she can have such deep feelings for Matt when the man she thought she wanted is just up the street. In spite of her less-than-high opinion of her lustful nature, Maggie's desire for Matt continues to build, turning her tears into sobs. When Matt's attempts to comfort her become passionate, Maggie does nothing to cool his ardor, allowing herself instead to linger over his forbidden touch. Unable to deny herself the man she so desperately yearns for, Maggie succumbs to temptation.

Although he wouldn't trade the night spent with Maggie for his own life, Matt is plagued with guilt and self-loathing the next day, taking the entire blame for what happened between them upon himself. He avoids Maggie as best he can while continuing to encourage perfection in this less-than-perfect clump of humanity known as Rafe Hollister, but it isn't easy. He punishes himself with thoughts of turning Maggie's perfect husband over to her once his job is done, and polishes the outlaw to perfection if for no other reason than just to see her smile, to witness for himself a sparkle of happiness in those sad brown eyes.

On December 15 and according to plan, Matt arranges the long-awaited reunion between Maggie and Rafe. She feels awkward in Matt's presence, certain that the coolness he exhibits toward her is due to her immoral behavior, but remains composed as he leads her into his cabin to visit her lost love. Although it's been almost seven years, Maggie notices immediately that Rafe still has those calf eyes and a devilish grin to match them. When he turns those considerable charms on her, for a fleeting moment Maggie becomes that lonely, vulnerable farm girl again, grateful and smitten by what she'd once mistaken as true love.

Witnessing Maggie's rebirth, glimpsing the sweet hot luminance in her painfully honest eyes, is more than Matt can tolerate. Without a word, he takes his broken heart and slips out of the room, leaving the pair of lovers with the only thing he has left to offer them—their privacy.

The click of the latch snaps Maggie out of yesterday and brings her back to the independent, self-reliant woman she is today, but by then, Matt is gone. Feeling in control of herself again and of Rafe for the first time ever, she sits him down, chews him up one side and down the other for his sins of the past, then queries him about his plans for the future. Where and how, she wants to know, will those plans affect Holly? What kind of a father does he expect to be, and how long will he be there for her physically, emotionally, and financially? Exactly what does he expect in return?

This interrogation continues for nine days, with Matt just outside the door of the cabin most times and generally listening in. No matter how far Maggie corners Rafe or how tough the questions, he always comes up smelling like a rose. All he wants out of this life, he swears, is to have Maggie as his wife and to be a father to his daughter at long last.

Throughout this period, Matt continues to instruct Rafe on the ways of gentlemen, even though he hasn't behaved like one himself, fulfilling the task he was hired to do. When Christmas morning finally arrives, Maggie pleads with Matt to visit her home at sunup and share in the spoils of a job well done. Although he is reluctant, his heart heavy, the ex-lawman arrives just moments before Rafe does.

As Maggie carefully positions her former lover near the Christmas tree, then calls Holly to come downstairs and see what Santa has left for her, Matt can barely watch when the sleepy-eyed youngster drags into the room. Once she sees a stranger by the tree, and that stranger identifies himself as her father, Holly lets out a strangled cry and vaults into his arms. In moments the rest of them—Maggie, Matt, and even Rafe—are awash in tears.

Giving her daughter a few minutes alone with her father, not to mention time to pull herself together, Maggie tugs Matt into the kitchen and closes the door behind them. Remarking that she ought to be celebrating with the joyous pair under the tree, Matt thanks her for inviting him, then heads for the door, intending to let the newly reunited family enjoy their holiday in private. Maggie softly asks him to stay, even through Christmas dinner if he likes, but Matt can't understand why she'd want a used-up lawman hanging around on Christmas day, especially since his job is done. Maggie gently kisses Matt's weathered cheek and thanks him again for making Holly's wish come true. She then thanks him for the changes he made in Rafe Hollister, in particular the way Matt convinced Rafe to humble himself by begging her to marry him during each of the past nine days. It's done her heart good, she confesses, and also freed her enough to realize that she doesn't love Rafe and probably never did. Her answer for the past nine days, she says, has been an unequivocal no, thanks to Matt Weston. With that, Maggie again kisses the man she really loves, this time square on the mouth.

Overwhelmed by her confession, unable to keep from touching her a minute longer, Matt takes Maggie into his arms, then asks her what she would do if he were to have an unfulfilled wish the way Holly did. Who could I hire to help me make my wish come true? he wonders aloud.

Maggie swears if there's anything she can do to help, she'll do it. Anything. Vowing to hold her to that promise, Matt pulls her even tighter into his embrace and whispers, "See if you can help me with this—I wish I could find a beautiful woman to marry who has laughing brown eyes, kissable lips, and is tall enough for me to kiss back without bending myself in half."

As tears of joy roll down Maggie's cheeks, Matt loosens her hair from the coil at her neck and fans it between his fingers. "Make sure the lady also has golden brown hair that smells of cinnamon and apples, and that she loves me at least half as much as I love her. When you find her, make sure to tell her that I promise to make her wishes come true for the rest of her life."

And so, as Christmas of 1881 comes to a close, a daughter's wish for her very own father is fulfilled; an outlaw who thought he never wanted fatherhood or to know the true miracle of Christmas finds both, along with more joy than he's ever known; and a man and a woman find themselves free to love one another with everything they have to give, joining together as one to wish for a lifetime of happiness together.

17

ANATOMY OF A SYNOPSIS

by Rebecca Vinyard
(with the help of Sharon Ihle)

I've attended many workshops on this topic in the desperate hope that I'd learn enough to compose a coherent synopsis. Sometimes, a speaker will attempt to whip up the audience's enthusiasm by saying things like, "Repeat after me, the synopsis is your *friend.*"

With friends like these, I don't need enemies.

Okay, enough with the dissing. Let's roll up our sleeves and get to work. First, you should check out Sharon Ihle's synop for *Maggie's Wish* [in chapter 16]. This will be our sample synopsis. Finished? Good. Now, let's get to work.

THE SETUP

The first part of a synopsis is the setup. Here's how Sharon's setup begins:

> The sluggish days of summer are giving way to the crisper fall evenings of 1881 in Prescott, Arizona Territory, as MAGGIE THORNE glances out the kitchen window and sees her six-year-old daughter hoeing the pumpkin patch. Halloween is just two months away, which means that soon, Christmas will be upon them—again.

Sharon packs a lot of information in two simple sentences. In the first sentence, she establishes setting, a home in Prescott, Arizona Territory, in 1881. She establishes the heroine, Maggie Thorne, and lets us know Maggie has a six-year-old daughter. We know the time of year, two months before Halloween. She also gives us an inkling to Maggie's mood: anxiety over Christmas. We read on, because we wonder, *why* is Maggie worried about Christmas?

That's what your setup should do: establish location, character, and mood. But most of all, it should pique the reader's interest. Just as your novel should hook the reader on the first page, so should your synopsis. One of the best workshops I've ever attended on synopsis writing was done by Christina Dodd. She said you should be able to get the initial setup information across in one page or less.

To continue with Sharon's setup:

> Just the mere thought of that most revered of holidays is enough to sink Maggie's spirits. Not that she has anything against Christmas itself. She has a lot to be thankful for when the sun rises each December 25. Her daughter HOLLY, whom she adores without reservation, came into the world at twenty minutes past eight on Christmas morning. A deeply religious woman, Maggie also thinks of the holiday as Christ's birthday, never failing to recognize it as such in a respectful manner.

> As she is the bread baker and pastry chef in a small restaurant owned by her Aunt Lorna, the holiday season also keeps Maggie happily productive and fills her coffers well enough to see her and Holly though the winter. But something supersedes all the good the holiday brings, a dark and dreary cloud that obscures the yuletide lights and dulls the sparkle in Maggie's wide brown eyes. Lord help her, how much longer can she go on this way?

Here Sharon establishes *characterization*. We know now that Maggie adores her daughter and is a spiritual person, and we know her occupation. We also now know that Maggie is more than just anxious about Christmas; she dreads it. We can feel her emotions, and again we ask, *why?*

In the next section of her synopsis, Sharon tells us why by providing Maggie's background:

> Maggie's first inkling that Christmas would become a time for sorrow struck nearly seven years ago on the very day Holly was born. Although the baby's father promised to show up in Prescott before the birth, he hadn't so much as written by the time their daughter pushed her way into the world. Maggie had an idea that he never would. So far, and nearly seven years later, she is right.

> She was a tall, plain-faced spinster of twenty-two, with little hope of landing a man of her own, the first time Maggie laid eyes on RAFE HOLLISTER . . .

> . . . On the morning Maggie runs away from home, Rafe tells her he loves her, shows her one more time exactly how much, and then promises to get square with the law and meet her in Prescott well before Christmas day. Six long years and six longer Christmases have gone by since then. And at each of the last four, a little red-haired girl cries fat teardrops all over her birthday cake at the close of that most celebrated day. This year, God willing, things will be different.

This is only a few paragraphs from this section. All of the information Sharon included is important, though. We learn much about Maggie's character and Rafe's. We know how they met and how they parted. We know this relationship was the turning point of Maggie's life, causing her to move away from home to Prescott. Most importantly, we now know *why* Maggie dreads Christmas. It is because it is also her daughter Holly's birthday, and her daughter wishes for her Daddy to come home every year.

This ends the setup and brings us to the first plot point.

PLOT POINTS AND CONFLICT

This year, Maggie has hired a retired Texas Ranger, a man just a few years older than she, who has given up the badge and hard chases because of a bum leg. Her friend, the sheriff of Prescott, is also a friend of the ranger, a man he believes is perfect for the job because he's very, very good at tracking people who don't know they need tracking. People like Rafe Hollister who have lost their way.

Maggie has decided to do something about her daughter's unhappiness. This is the first plot point: the departure from all that has gone before. We understand her motivation for doing this because of the background information Sharon provided. It is also our first introduction to the hero. We know that he's a good tracker. In the next paragraph, Sharon tells us about Maggie's reaction to him and sets up the conflict between them.

Once she meets Ranger MATT WESTON, Maggie is suddenly at a loss to explain her circumstances and finds herself making up excuses for Rafe, not just for Holly's sake, but also for her own. After all, she'd once loved Rafe enough to bear him a child born in shame—how could she show herself as a woman who'd allowed that love to die? Wouldn't that make her time of sinning with Rafe somehow more depraved? Matt Weston would definitely think so—Maggie senses that in the man after one look in his silvery, no-nonsense eyes. For reasons she can't imagine, this near-stranger's opinion of her is extremely important. Evading the truth rather than lying to Matt, Maggie simply explains that her man ran out on his responsibilities and that she wants him brought back to her—alive and well. She believes that explanation will give the former lawman the impression that Rafe is her husband, and why shouldn't it? Her Prescott neighbors have long believed the very same thing.

Maggie doesn't tell the whole truth about her relationship with Rafe, because she's afraid that if Matt knows she's an unwed mother, he won't help her—and because *his* opinion of her is extremely important. We can already sense that she is attracted to him. We understand her motivation and why she chooses not to reveal the truth.

In the next paragraph we are introduced to Matt's character from his point of view. You might call this the second setup. We get Matt's background and his current motivation:

At thirty-two years of age, Matt Weston hates his early retirement with a passion, and for what he sees as two good reasons: The first, and hardest to take, is his exclusion from the manhunts, the feel of his own blood thundering in his veins as he runs his quarry down. The second, and somehow more threatening than a cornered outlaw with blazing guns, is his sudden vulnerability to the single ladies in town. For over thirty years Matt has easily avoided the perils and, he has to admit, the responsibilities of turning his life over to a member of the fairer sex. Now that he is almost deskbound, he's practically tripping over available women, and even more alarming, rapidly running out of excuses for remaining a bachelor.

We know he's a man of action, forced into retirement. We also know he's not looking for a woman, that he prefers the bachelor life. Until . . .

Funny how that final excuse—not to mention a man's mind—can vanish with the blink of a warm, brown eye. A pair of them, to be exact, each rimmed by a lush bank of lashes the color of pitch. He has no business looking into those eyes or thinking thoughts that don't include ways of catching up to Maggie's wandering husband, but Matt can't seem to stop himself. He is an honorable, professional man, one who never lets his personal life get in the way of business, so why in hell can't he keep his mind on his work whenever she is around?

He supposes this lapse of ethics has something to do with Maggie's gentle ways and honest charms, the kind of beauty that fairly radiates the goodness in her heart. Not that he believes any of those things can excuse his utter fascination with the lady. He has a job to do, and sets out to do it with an almost personal vengeance.

Here we have Matt's initial conflict. He's determined to do his job, but his attraction to Maggie is getting in the way. And since he is an honorable man, he's disgusted with himself for having feelings for the "married" Maggie.

THE ACTION

In the next section, we leave the second setup and begin the action of the story:

It doesn't take Matt but two weeks to locate the bastard—the precise opinion he forms of Rafe Hollister within minutes of locating the man. The meeting takes place at a rundown saloon in El Paso, when Matt stumbles over a drunken Rafe, who is passed out on the floor. When Rafe finally comes to, Matt decides that Miss Maggie is in for a rude shock— and "Miss" Maggie is the way Matt thinks of her, no matter how hard she hints that she's actually married to this stinking outlaw.

Again, we are shown Matt's conflict. He can't bear to think of Maggie as a married woman. His feelings for her affect his dealings with Rafe. He always keeps Maggie's best interests in mind. In a romance synopsis, *emotion* is the most important element. You should convey what the characters are feeling as often as possible. A synopsis is *not* simply a summation of the story's action. If you just do that, you aren't doing enough.

> When Rafe sobers up and awakens to find himself traveling west toward Arizona Territory, Matt informs the miserable bastard that his wife and child are looking for him, and that he's been hired to take him to Prescott. Far from being grateful, Rafe begins cursing Maggie, calling her a horse-faced spinster, among other things, and declaring that she was lucky to have gotten as much as she did from him—a good time and the only piece of "loving" she'd ever get from a sane man. He tries to go on raving about Maggie, assuring his captor that he wouldn't have touched her at all had he not been weak and crazy in the head from loss of blood.

Here, we are introduced to the secondary character of Rafe. As a rule, the less secondary characters appear in a synopsis, the better, *unless* they are essential to the story. Rafe is. In the first plot point paragraph, where Sharon mentions Maggie and Matt's mutual friend, the sheriff of Prescott, we aren't given his name or background because his only major function is to get Maggie in touch with Matt. Rafe, on the other hand, is an important character. We want to know *why* this man would abandon his "wife" and child.

> When the ranger pulls the wagon to a halt and climbs down from the driver's seat, Rafe is certain that he is about to be set free. Instead, he receives the worst beating of his miserable life. When he comes to again, Rafe quickly discovers that both of his eyes are swollen shut, his lips are split and caked with blood, and he is hanging by his wrists, including the injured one, from a rafter inside a darkened barn. Then, through what is left of his ear, he hears the voice of the former ranger as he explains the terms of Rafe's "pardon."

This section brings us to the second plot point. Matt has decided to depart from the simple plan of bringing Rafe to Prescott. He now wants to reform him for Maggie's sake. Plot points are turning points in the story, and here is Matt's first turning point. He gives Rafe an ultimatum, and Rafe, seeing little choice, agrees to be reformed.

> For Matt, it is a time of raging conflict. Although he works hard to turn the outlaw into someone worthy of Maggie and Holly, from the basest part of his soul, Matt is praying that Rafe will fail. His visits to Maggie each day to report on Rafe's progress are taking a toll on his sanity, not to mention his body. He awakes in a sweat night after night, his dreams filled with images of the woman he has fallen in love with. Even worse, he has convinced himself that he sees his own frustrations and needs each time he looks into her expressive eyes.

This paragraph describes the emotional consequences of Matt's decision. For every decision you describe in a synopsis, you should also show the consequence, not only in the action, but in the *emotion*. We see here the internal conflict Matt is suffering. And notice the words Sharon uses here to convey this: *raging, basest, praying, frustration*—all emotional adjectives. This is often the element new writers leave out of their synopsis . . . how the action makes the characters *feel*.

> It is as Thanksgiving draws near that Matt slips into the darkened coffee shop late one night to discuss Rafe's progress and finds Maggie awash in tears. He takes her in his arms, comforting her, and asks her what is wrong. There is no way she can explain how much her feelings for Matt have grown or to let him know how badly she wants him—not after he's been working so hard to make her "almost" husband presentable enough for her to marry. Even Maggie can't understand how she can have such deep feelings for Matt when the man she thought she wanted is just up the street. In spite of her less-than-high opinion of her lustful nature, Maggie's desire for Matt continues to build, turning her tears into sobs. When Matt's attempts to comfort her become passionate, Maggie does nothing to cool his ardor, allowing herself instead to linger over his forbidden touch. Unable to deny herself the man she so desperately yearns for, Maggie succumbs to temptation.

Hallelujah, we're at plot point number three. (I say hallelujah, because I always enjoy the part of the story where the heroine and hero succumb to temptation.) Ahem . . . anyway. This is plot point number three, because here Maggie and Matt allow their feelings for each other to reach the physical level. It is another turning point, an *emotional* turning point, and as such will have consequences, which are described in the next paragraph. Cause and effect, folks. Show the reaction to every action. Am I stressing this enough?

> Although he wouldn't trade the night spent with Maggie for his own life, Matt is plagued with guilt and self-loathing the next day, taking the entire blame for what happened between them upon himself. He avoids Maggie as best he can while continuing to encourage perfection in this less-than-perfect clump of humanity known as Rafe Hollister, but it isn't easy. He punishes himself with thoughts of turning Maggie's perfect husband over to her once his job is done, and polishes the outlaw to perfection if for no other reason than just to see her smile, to witness for himself a sparkle of happiness in those sad brown eyes.

Poor Matt. Being the honorable man he is, he blames himself completely for what happened. His guilt leads him to avoid Maggie and work harder on making Rafe a better man for her. This is the consequence of their succumbing to temptation.

> On December 15 and according to plan, Matt arranges the long-awaited reunion between Maggie and Rafe. She feels awkward in Matt's presence, certain that the coolness he exhibits toward her is due to her immoral behavior, but remains composed as he leads her into his cabin to visit her lost love. Although it's been almost seven years, Maggie notices immediately that Rafe still has those calf eyes and a devilish grin to match them. When

he turns those considerable charms on her, for a fleeting moment Maggie becomes that lonely, vulnerable farm girl again, grateful and smitten by what she'd once mistaken as true love.

And, as we see in the next paragraph, their tryst also had consequences for Maggie. She feels guilt over her behavior. But this doesn't stop her from being vulnerable to Rafe's charm.

> Witnessing Maggie's rebirth, glimpsing the sweet, hot luminance in her painfully honest eyes, is more than Matt can tolerate. Without a word, he takes his broken heart and slips out of the room, leaving the pair of lovers with the only thing he has left to offer them— their privacy.

My heart just aches for Matt, doesn't yours? Again, as another consequence of his actions, he made Rafe into the perfect man, and now he has to live with how Rafe makes Maggie feel. Notice the emotional level of this simple paragraph. It has action, but it also makes the reader feel for Matt's pain. This is Matt's black moment. The *black moment* is when the character realizes he will not achieve his goal.

CLIMAX AND RESOLUTION

Of course, Maggie is nobody's fool. She immediately gets hold of her emotions and, for nine days, questions Rafe about his intentions. Then, Christmas day arrives and we have the climax of the story.

> As Maggie carefully positions her former lover near the Christmas tree, then calls Holly to come downstairs and see what Santa has left for her, Matt can barely watch when the sleepy-eyed youngster drags into the room. Once she sees a stranger by the tree, and that stranger identifies himself as her father, Holly lets out a strangled cry and vaults into his arms. In moments the rest of them—Maggie, Matt, and even Rafe—are awash in tears.

This is the climax, the moment Sharon has been building towards since the first word. A happy Christmas morning. After the climax comes the resolution:

> Giving her daughter a few minutes alone with her father, not to mention time to pull herself together, Maggie tugs Matt into the kitchen and closes the door behind them. Remarking that she ought to be celebrating with the joyous pair under the tree, Matt thanks her for inviting him, then heads for the door, intending to let the newly reunited family enjoy their holiday in private. Maggie softly asks him to stay, even through Christmas dinner if he likes, but Matt can't understand why she'd want a used-up lawman hanging around on Christmas day, especially since his job is done. Maggie gently kisses Matt's weathered cheek and thanks him again for making Holly's wish come true. She then thanks him for the changes he made in Rafe Hollister, in particular the way Matt

convinced Rafe to humble himself by begging her to marry him during each of the past nine days. It's done her heart good, she confesses, and also freed her enough to realize that she doesn't love Rafe and probably never did. Her answer for the past nine days, she says, has been an unequivocal no, thanks to Matt Weston. With that, Maggie again kisses the man she really loves, this time square on the mouth.

The resolution: Maggie's actions and emotions are resolved when she realizes Matt is the man she always wanted, not Rafe. This also resolves Matt's conflict, when he realizes he is now free to love Maggie. The moment carries the most emotion, and Sharon emphasizes this by using dialogue in the next two paragraphs.

Maggie swears if there's anything she can do to help, she'll do it. Anything. Vowing to hold her to that promise, Matt pulls her even tighter into his embrace and whispers, "See if you can help me with this—I wish I could find a beautiful woman to marry who has laughing brown eyes, kissable lips, and is tall enough for me to kiss back without bending myself in half."

As tears of joy roll down Maggie's cheeks, Matt loosens her hair from the coil at her neck and fans it between his fingers. "Make sure the lady also has golden brown hair that smells of cinnamon and apples, and that she loves me at least half as much as I love her. When you find her, make sure to tell her that I promise to make her wishes come true for the rest of her life."

The dialogue and the action here precisely describe this emotional moment. Some folks say never to use dialogue in a synopsis, but when it can convey the feeling better than a summary, I'm all for it.

And so, as Christmas of 1881 comes to a close, a daughter's wish for her very own father is fulfilled; an outlaw who thought he never wanted fatherhood or to know the true miracle of Christmas finds both, along with more joy than he's ever known; and a man and a woman find themselves free to love one another with everything they have to give, joining together as one to wish for a lifetime of happiness together.

This is a final paragraph. It ties everything together, describing the changes this story has brought to each of the main characters' lives.

My deepest thanks to Sharon Ihle for sharing her synopsis of *Maggie's Wish*.

18

Display Sites: An Alternative to the Query/Synopsis Process?

by A.C. Crispin and Victoria Strauss

Every aspiring writer knows how hard it is to attract the attention of a top agent or editor. They have the rejections to prove it, often just form letters. Did the agent or editor even read the submission before returning it? No way to tell. It takes time to research markets and track submissions. And then there's the cost: photocopying, postage, envelopes . . . adds up.

What if there were an easier way? What if you could make not dozens of submissions, but just *one*—and make it electronically? What if agents and editors came to *you,* rather than the other way around, sparing you all that tedious research and manuscript tracking—and guaranteeing that your submission would actually be read? What if the power of the Internet could be harnessed to replace stuffing manuscripts into mailers, then enduring months of waiting?

That's the promise of the manuscript display Web site, a growing phenomenon on the Internet. Display sites undertake to showcase your writing (usually in the form of a query, synopsis, and a chapter or two), in order to attract the attention of agents and editors. These sites claim that publishing professionals are eager to visit a venue where manuscripts have been presorted into easily surfed categories and genres. Some of these sites even screen submissions in order to weed out the really awful slush. Editors, agents—come one, come all! Read our samples, and you can avoid putting another unwanted stack of paper on your already crowded desk!

What Display Sites Offer

Right now, there are close to fifty display sites online, with another one springing up every couple of months (they disappear quickly, too: In the two months we spent researching this article, four display sites vanished from the Web). While most display sites provide the same basics—a query, synopsis, and excerpt of your manuscript placed on display for agent, editor, and public access—they vary widely in how these are formatted and made available and in the "extras" that go with them. You may be limited to 2,500 words, or you may be able to post several chapters; sometimes you can even post your whole book. (Not a good idea, incidentally: Many professional editors would regard that as publication, thus making any subsequent sale a reprint.) To dress up your display area, you may be able to include a cover letter, a bio, a photo, and custom graphics.

Display sites vary widely in other respects as well. Some are very large, with several hundred manuscript listings, but others list less than fifty, and many less than ten. A surprising number are free, though most do charge fees. Costs are calculated in any number of ways, from a flat rate to a per-page charge, and can run anywhere from a few dollars to several hundred.

Most will accept any submission. Some claim to screen the agents and publishers who use them (though when we went undercover to test this claim, we found that in many cases that isn't done). Some protect submissions with a password system that only registered members can use; most provide free access to their listings. Most have simple navigation systems, with manuscripts sorted into clickable lists of subject categories, but a few have sophisticated search engines or special software designed to make it easy for agents and editors to surf the site.

DO THEY WORK?

So, how successful are manuscript display sites? It's hard to tell from the sites themselves; not many post success stories. Also, few display sites seem to do any kind of real marketing. Some just sit there in cyberspace, hoping someone will drop by. Others confine their publicity efforts to search engine listings or to sending mass e-mail (aka "spam"). Publishing professionals don't appreciate being spammed any more than you do, so this is a dubious way of advertising products. Other sites target their marketing efforts mainly to writers (not surprisingly, since all of these charge fees). Only a very few reach beyond the Internet or make the face-to-face contact that's so essential in publishing: placing ads in trade journals, attending writers' conferences and book fairs, scheduling personal meetings with agents and editors.

We spoke with three of the biggest display site owners: Doris Booth of Authorlink, Gaylene Givens of Writer's Showplace, and Anthony Jacobson of Goodstory.com. In addition, we sent out inquiries to a score of other display sites, asking about their successes. Besides the big three, only a few, such as Manuscript Depot and Rosedog.com, even bothered to respond; neither of these sites formally tracks sales resulting from postings on their sites.

"It's important that writers understand that agents and editors do not surf the Net looking for talent," says Gaylene Givens of Writer's Showplace. Accordingly, Writer's Showplace doesn't rely solely on the display site to draw interest, but uses it as part of an integrated approach. Givens and her partner, Francesca Vrattos, contact agents and editors directly to discuss their needs and interests. When an appropriate manuscript reaches them, the agent or editor is alerted via e-mail and given a link where they can view the writer's query letter and excerpt. In its nineteen months in business, Writer's Showplace claims two book contracts (both with small presses) and twenty-four agent contracts, some with well-known agents.

Anthony Jacobson, president of Goodstory, thinks that agents and others will use a display site if it's functional and offers enough value. Goodstory believes its very large reservoir of authors and screenwriters (over one thousand so far, nearly twice as many as its next-largest competitor) and its powerful, flexible search function will make the site appealing to publishing and film professionals eager to be free of the burden of paper. Unlike most display site proprietors, Jacobson has worked within the industry—he's formerly of the William Morris Agency's motion picture department—and plans to use his experience and connections, and those of his advisory board, to mount a strong marketing campaign for Goodstory. He plans to focus on direct contact with agents, editors, and producers. Because Goodstory is a brand-new site, still in beta testing, only time will tell whether Jacobson's approach will work.

Authorlink is one of the oldest and most established display sites. The site itself is worth cruising (as is the Writer's Showplace site) because of the news and articles of interest to writers. Owner Doris Booth explains that Authorlink does not limit its marketing approach to online advertising. "We aggressively market our writers to editors and agents through personal visits to New York two to three times per year. There, we promote both the site in general, as well as specific titles to senior editors and agents . . . I personally speak to about ten to twelve writers' conferences per year, where I meet with editors and agents to discuss both the site in general, as well as individual writers' projects." Authorlink claims to have been responsible, either directly (hooking a writer up with a publisher) or indirectly (by bringing together an author and an agent) for sixty-one sales. It must be noted that, while many of these sales are to advance- and royalty-paying commercial publishers, some we noted were to vanity publishers or e-book publishers, which traditionally do not pay advances.

PERILS AND PITFALLS

During our research, we noted that some questionable, fee-charging literary agencies now have display sites as part of their services. We advise against such sites, for the simple reason that, if a literary agent can manage nothing more than to display a writer's work and then hope an editor comes along and sees it, that agent isn't doing his job. Real agents evaluate manuscripts, then send them to the editors that they know might be interested in purchasing the work.

If you're considering a display site, our research indicates you're better off with one of the larger ones, which means you'll have to pay. Writer's Showplace charges $50 for an eight-week listing. Authorlink prices vary from a maximum of about $130 for a twelve-month listing to a minimum of $56 for a three-month listing. Still in beta-testing phase, Goodstory's price structure is not yet listed.

As we researched this article, we concluded that a display site could well be one facet of an effective campaign to market your work. But, like anything else, the sites do have potential pitfalls, and prospective clients should be aware of them. They include:

- **Offers from questionable, fee-charging agents.** Most fee-charging agents have few or no verified sales to paying publishers, and many are outright scammers. They "market" their clients' work to their own subsidy presses, or worse, to scam "co-op" publishers the likes of Northwest or Commonwealth. It's been our experience that agents who charge reading fees to writers do so because they're making their primary income off charging *writers—not* from selling manuscripts.

- **Offers from questionable publishing houses.** Some of the new publishers springing up offer display site authors print-on-demand, e-publishing, or subsidy print deals. Such publishers offer little to nothing in the way of marketing, and their touted "big royalties" seldom earn the writers' investment back. Others offer non-negotiable contracts that no sane writer would sign (but plenty of clueless aspiring authors *do* sign them—and live to regret it), contracts fraught with nightmare option clauses, rights grabs, and other fine-print traps.

- **If you put up an entire manuscript, you may well use up first rights to your work.** Some publishers would regard such a posting as a first printing. Also . . . e-piracy is becoming ever more prevalent. If you put up an entire manuscript, what's to prevent someone from downloading it, printing it out, then submitting it in the traditional fashion under their name? True plagiarism is, admittedly, rare. But why take chances?

Do Agents and Publishers Visit?

We contacted eight top agents and eight top editors in our field (editors from science fiction and fantasy imprints such as Berkley/Putnam, Penguin/Putnam, DAW, Tor, Del Rey, and Bantam) and asked them the following questions:

- Are you familiar with the manuscript display site concept?
- Have you ever seen or received advertising for a manuscript display site?
- Have you ever visited a manuscript display site (and why, if you don't mind telling us)?
- Have you ever purchased a manuscript/acquired a client as a result of something you saw on a manuscript display site?

Their responses were illuminating, and rather discouraging to those who are considering using such sites. *None* of the editors or top agents we queried had ever acquired a manuscript or signed a client as a result of visiting such a site. Most of the editors and agents were vaguely aware that such sites existed—the site they recalled having heard of was Authorlink. A few had cruised the sites out of curiosity, just once, and had never returned. One editor from Tor commented, when questioned about the usefulness of manuscript sites, that: "A writer would probably have a greater chance of having her work bought if she left her boxed manuscript on the seats of the subways in the publishing district in Manhattan." Several editors voiced the same sentiment. "Why would I go there? I have enough slush to read already."

Two top-selling agents gave us comments for the record. Ashley Grayson said: "On average, the manuscripts I saw [at the display site he'd visited] were embarrassing for the author in their mundanity, poor use of English, and unimaginative content." Don Maass said: "I'm skeptical of the usefulness of these sites."

One agent told us he'd acquired twelve clients as a result of cruising display sites. Just one problem—this agent charges writers up-front fees for "submission expenses" and, in two years of being in business, hasn't managed to make a single sale. Hardly what you'd consider a top-selling professional.

With this in mind, it seems clear to us that, while a manuscript display site may indeed help a writer to find representation or a publisher, in many cases that agent or publisher won't be top of the line. We advise writers who use these sites to check references of agents or companies very carefully (this is always good advice!), especially if they've never heard of them before. Keep in mind that newer, second- and third-tier agents who have few or no sales are easy to approach, and you could probably get their attention without paying to display your work.

Our recommendation to anyone considering a manuscript display site is "buyer beware." Also . . . make your displayed manuscript just one facet of a multipronged approach to selling your work. Even when your sample is up there, keep querying and submitting in the traditional fashion. Network. Learn about the field, who the players are, and who is publishing what. Selling your writing is truly a field in which knowledge is power.

QUESTIONS TO ASK BEFORE USING A DISPLAY SITE

- **What does it cost?** Free sites don't market themselves, so forget them. But don't make too big an investment. Spending $50 for three months or $100 for six is probably enough to tell you if it's working for you.

- **How big is it?** The bigger, the better. Sites with less than fifty offerings aren't worth an agent's time, or yours.

- **Does its marketing reach beyond the Internet?** Search engine registration and bulk e-mail aren't effective marketing tools. A good site should maintain direct, personal contact with publishing professionals.

- **Are the agents and editors screened?** There are lots of scam sharks out there, and an open display site is like blood in the water. Even if the site screens, be wary, and check references. Scam agents tend to lie, as well as rip off writers.

- **Is it easy to search?** Busy agents and editors want to go directly to their area of interest. At a minimum, a good site should offer detailed category headings; preferably, it should be searchable.

- **Does it disclose its successes?** A good site should track and list its achievements. If it doesn't have any, why are you considering it?

- **Do the proprietors have industry experience?** That's a big plus. Knowing how publishing works from the inside is invaluable.

- **Do they limit the size of excerpts?** Posting entire manuscripts may compromise your rights. A good site shouldn't allow more than 2,500–5,000 words. *Never* post your entire story or manuscript.

These things are irrelevant:

- **A snazzy Web site.** Good looks don't spell success.

- **Photos, bios, and graphics** posted along with your synopsis or excerpt. These are considered extraneous with traditional hardcopy submission, and online is no different.

Last, but not least:

- **Even the most careful display site can't guarantee that the agent or editor who contacts you is reputable.** Carefully check any offer you receive. Check references, read contracts, and verify sales. If in doubt, contact the Science Fiction Writer's Association's "Writer Beware" Web site (*www.sfwa.org*). Writer Beware maintains an extensive database of questionable agents and publishers and can help you determine legitimacy.

19

E-PUBLISHING, SUBSIDY PUBLISHING, AND SELF-PUBLISHING: VIABLE ALTERNATIVES?

Trying to sell a novel can be a confusing and frustrating task. While some authors have been successful with their very first submission, others find themselves sending off packages to publisher after publisher, and waiting months after each submission only to receive another disappointment.

What can you do if the procedure outlined in the preceding chapter doesn't work? Should you try something different, such as approaching an electronic publisher (assuming this wasn't your first choice to begin with) or paying to have your novel produced, either by publishing it yourself or having it published through a subsidy house?

All of these options deserve careful study and consideration. Never make a decision like this in haste—each of these approaches has a number of important pros and cons.

ELECTRONIC PUBLISHING

Of all the alternatives to traditional (i.e., print) publishing, electronic publishing is rapidly becoming the most respected. Commercial electronic publishers—those who screen manuscripts for quality, just as print publishers do—are establishing a foothold in the market and carving out respect in a field that was originally considered nothing more than a catchall for novelists who couldn't achieve "real" publication. The fact that big-name authors, such as Stephen King, Dean Koontz, and John Grisham, have all chosen to offer titles in electronic form has helped this medium achieve a greater aura of respectability.

Electronic publishers offer a wide range of genres, and many are open to books that fall into subgenres (e.g., paranormal romance) that are less popular with print publishers. Electronic publishers are also less concerned about book length: They can be ideal markets for shorter works, such as novellas, that are rarely acceptable to print publishers, and they are also ideal for longer books that would be too expensive to print without an established market.

Electronic publishing offers a variety of advantages and disadvantages:

ADVANTAGES OF E-PUBLISHING

- **More control over the process.** Writers generally have more freedom to dictate plot, characterization, etc. Editors are less likely to ask writers to make substantive changes to their work or cut out huge sections of the novel simply to meet page limitations.

- **Higher royalties.** Because the costs of e-publishing are significantly lower than those of print publishing, authors receive a far higher percentage of revenues. Royalties range between 20 and 40 percent, with 30 percent being fairly typical. Most e-publishers also pay royalties more frequently than print publishers, offering quarterly statements rather than annual or semiannual payments.

- **Author-friendly contracts.** Most e-publishers ask only for electronic rights, leaving the author free to market print rights and subsidiary rights elsewhere. In addition, most e-publishing contracts are renewable rather than indefinite. Thus, instead of tying up an author's work until it "goes out of print" (a meaningless term in e-publishing!), either party usually has the option to renew or terminate the contract at the end of a specified time (usually a year).

- **Shorter response times.** Most e-publishers attempt to respond to submissions within two to four months. Response times at the most well-known houses are lengthening, however, as the number of submissions increases.

- **Faster publication.** In theory, a book can become available to readers within weeks of acceptance. In reality, most e-publishers try to space out their offerings, so that they can generate more advance reviews and publicity. Also, many e-publishers are developing backlogs of material, and closing their doors temporarily to new or unsolicited submissions.

- **Longer "shelf life."** Since it costs very little to keep an e-book in stock, a book does not have to sell thousands of copies to remain in print. As long as sales remain good (by e-book standards), most e-publishers are willing to keep a title in their inventory, rather than dropping it for a more profitable title.

DISADVANTAGES OF E-PUBLISHING

- **Lower sales.** Sales figures of five hundred copies are still considered high in this industry. It's also important for the writer to become heavily involved in promoting the book, as e-publishers generally have small promotion budgets and rely on their authors to spread the word.

- **Lack of availability in bookstores.** Though e-books are available through many online bookstores, such as Amazon.com and Barnes & Noble, they are rarely available in physical bookstores.

- **No advance.** Besides the obvious financial disadvantage, the lack of an advance can create other problems for authors. Several genre organizations consider a book "commercially published" only if an advance is paid, which means e-books may not qualify as part of an author's membership prerequisites or for certain industry awards.

- **Fewer reviews.** While some publications (especially online) review e-books, most traditional book review sources have been slow to accept e-books. E-books are not likely to be reviewed in major book and library trade publications, such as *Kirkus Reviews* or *Editor and Publisher*.

- **Limited formats.** Not all e-publishers offer books that can be read by any user with any computer platform. Some offer Windows-only formats. Very few offer formats that can be read by handhelds or e-readers, such as the RocketBook. Adobe Acrobat PDF files are becoming more widespread, however, which enables more computer users to access e-books.

- **High prices.** E-books often cost as much as a comparable print book. Major publishers who offer e-book editions of their print titles (e.g., for the RocketBook) generally charge the same amount for an electronic version as for the hardback. This tends to discourage readers, who don't feel that they are getting the same product for the price.

- **Consumer reluctance to read online.** While the popularity of e-books is growing steadily, many consumers are still reluctant to read a novel onscreen—or to add the cost of printing a book on one's own paper and with one's own toner to the cost of the book itself. Sales of handheld e-readers are still slow; many readers aren't willing to pay $200 for a piece of equipment that enables them to read a product that they only have to pay $7 for in the store. Consumers still complain that it's hard to curl up on the couch with an e-book.

SELF-PUBLISHING VERSUS SUBSIDY PUBLISHING: KNOW THE DIFFERENCE!

After you've spent six months to a year (or longer) shopping your manuscript to agents and editors with no success, subsidy or self-publishing begins to look like a very tempting option. After all, you'd be a "published" author, wouldn't you? Your book would be on the market, and you would have a chance to make a name for yourself.

If you're thinking along those lines, please think carefully. First, be sure you understand the difference between self-publishing and subsidy publishing. The success stories you may have heard about authors who "did it themselves" (e.g., *The Christmas Box*) are about authors who *self-published* their books.

Self-publishing has gained more respect in the publishing industry, but it still is an extremely difficult process. If you self-publish, you must be prepared to do *everything* yourself: obtain editing, obtain artwork for your cover, arrange for the internal design and typesetting of your book, pay for the actual printing and binding, find a place to store the printed copies of that book, and handle all the marketing and distribution.

As a self-publisher, your work just begins when the book rolls off the press: Now, you must find reviewers, mail out copies to those reviewers, and find some way to reach your target market. Your chances of getting that book into bookstores and libraries are minimal; most bookstores and libraries buy only from major distributors, who, in turn, buy only from major commercial publishers. Space advertising is expensive and often not productive—and you face the choice of paying an advertising agency to design and place ads for you, or attempting to do it yourself.

Self-publishing has still not proven viable for most novelists (though it can be effective for nonfiction). While a handful of fiction writers have been successful with this approach, most are not—simply because this means becoming a full-fledged publisher, not just a writer.

Subsidy publishing is an even less appealing choice. When you self-publish, you at least retain all rights to your work and all proceeds from your sales. This is not true of subsidy publishing. Here are ten reasons to be wary of paying someone else to "publish" your book:

- **No money.** If you want to earn a profit, subsidy publishing isn't the answer. The cost of print subsidy publishing can be thousands of dollars, while royalties range from 10 percent to (in rare cases) 40 percent. Let's do the math. You spend $10,000 for publication and receive 15 percent royalties on "net" sales (the amount received after discounts). Your book is priced at $10.95, but often sold at a 50 percent bookstore discount. This means you'll receive 15 percent of 50 percent of $10.95—or 82¢ per book. Thus, you must sell more than 12,000 copies (a staggering number even by commercial terms) just to regain your investment—before you see a penny of profit!

- **No bookstore distribution.** When was the last time you saw a subsidy imprint in a bookstore? Bookstores rarely carry subsidy titles. But if your book isn't in stores, it isn't reaching the vast majority of book-buying customers—for this is the one place people who have never heard of you can "discover" your title. Your book may be listed in online bookstores, such as Amazon.com and Barnes & Noble, because any book with an ISBN can be included in an electronic catalog. Unless customers know about your title in advance, how-ever (which means "unless you're an incredible self-promoter"), they'll have no reason to look for it.

- **No library distribution.** Like bookstores, libraries rarely invest in sub-sidy-published books. This cuts off another opportunity for readers to discover your work.

- **No reviews.** Most book reviewers ignore subsidy titles. In addition, subsidy publishers often send out only a limited number of review copies and expect you to pay for any additional copies. This greatly limits the opportunities for people to find out about your book.

- **No publicity.** Most subsidy publishers promise a certain amount of adver-tising. This is rarely in the place you need it most, however. For example, if your book covers women's health issues, don't expect it to be advertised in health magazines, women's magazines, or other publications that target prospective readers. The general rule about publicity for subsidy-published books is that if you want it, you must do it yourself—at your expense.

- **No editorial screening.** Most subsidy publishers do not accept books on the basis of quality or marketability, but simply on the author's willingness to pay. This is the primary reason that such books have such a poor reputa-tion with reviewers, genre organizations, bookstores, distributors, and con-sumers. In addition, many subsidy publishers offer little or no editorial assistance, publishing books "as delivered." While some authors relish the idea of no editorial interference with their vision, rare is the book that couldn't benefit from the suggestions of a good editor—not to mention copyediting and proofreading.

- **No industry acceptance.** Most writing guilds and associations won't accept a subsidy-published book as a qualification for membership, or for consideration for an industry or genre award. To qualify, a book must be commercially published (as defined by sales figures or an advance).

- **No ownership.** Do you simply want a book to distribute to family and friends? If so, subsidy publishing isn't the answer. You'll usually receive no more than ten free author copies; if you want more, you'll have to buy them. This means you pay for your book twice: once to publish it and again to obtain extra copies. Authors usually receive a 40 percent discount, but some subsidy publishers don't pay royalties on sales to the author.

- **No subsidiary rights sales.** This varies from publisher to publisher. Some subsidy presses openly acknowledge that they are in no position to exploit subsidiary rights (such as movie, audio, electronic, or translation rights). Others, however, issue a "standard industry contract" claiming those rights—or demand that the author pay them a percentage of any such rights that the author happens to sell.

- **No respect.** While many authors have been successful with self-published books, subsidy publishing is rarely a stepping-stone to fame. The reading, writing, book-buying, and publishing communities regard subsidy publishing as the last resort of the truly desperate—i.e., of authors who can't get their work published any other way. This means that no matter how good your book is, most consumers will assume that it is of poor quality and won't give it a chance to prove itself. If you're a serious author, therefore, keep in mind that subsidy publishing is more likely to damage your reputation than to enhance it.

The exception to the above is electronic subsidy publishing. A host of sites exist that allow you to post or otherwise "publish" your book electronically or in print-on-demand format (where a book is printed off and sent to the customer when ordered). Many of these sites charge very low start-up fees ($100 or less), and some charge no up-front fees at all, asking only for a percentage of royalties.

Many writers who would otherwise choose self-publishing are finding that electronic subsidy publishing is a viable alternative, as it offers the opportunity to produce and market a book at minimal expense. In many cases, a writer can choose to offer the same title, through the same "publisher," in either electronic or print-on-demand formats, depending on the customer's preference.

As with any other form of digital publishing, however, the writer should proceed with informed caution. Be sure to read all contracts carefully, and make sure that you aren't giving up any rights that (a) you might need to sell your book in other venues, and (b) aren't logically required by the publisher. (One such service, for example, demands the right to use portions of an author's work, without notice, in other materials published by the same company.) Be sure the royalties are reasonable; some electronic subsidy publishers try to offer what they call "standard" royalties, i.e., the level offered by commercial print publishers (usually 10 percent or less). And, finally, be sure that you are willing to take on all the tasks that would normally be handled by a commercial publisher, including marketing and promotion.

WHY NOT SELF-PUBLISH FIRST, THEN SEEK A PUBLISHER?

Many writers wonder whether it might not be best to self-publish a book first (or produce it through a print-on-demand publisher), and then submit the "published" book to commercial publishers. I believe this notion stems from the impression that something that "looks" like a book will carry more weight than a mere manuscript. Perhaps this is because, as authors, we yearn for the sight of our own work in "book" format—and we imagine that editors and publishers will be similarly impressed.

Unfortunately, nothing could be farther from the truth. Rightly or wrongly, this form of publication smacks of desperation. The message it sends to a publisher is not, "Wow, look, a real book!" but rather, "This person couldn't get published any other way." In other words, it makes a *negative* impression, not a positive one.

Commercial publishers generally do not view a self-published or subsidy-published book as "published" in any sense that counts. The only way that you would be able to impress a publisher with such a book is by actually demonstrating a track record of *sales*. If you can prove, for example, that your self-published novel has already sold ten thousand copies just through your marketing efforts alone, a publisher might be tempted to consider it (though many won't, just on general principles).

Though commercial publishers won't regard your book as "published" in a positive sense, they may regard it as "published" in a negative sense—i.e., they may regard it as a "previously published" work, even if you haven't sold a single copy. Since most publishers purchase only original manuscripts rather than reprints, the very act of self- or subsidy-publishing your book could automatically disqualify you from achieving commercial publication. In short, this option not only won't help you find a traditional print publisher, it is more likely to actually decrease your chances of ever doing so.

The bottom line is that while there *are* alternatives to the standard submission route, and many authors *have* used those alternatives successfully, you must know what you are doing if you decide to try another route. Otherwise, you may find yourself even more disappointed by the alternative than by your original course—and, possibly, out a considerable amount of money (and perhaps a share of rights) as well.

SECTION 4 RESOURCES

AGENTS

Association of Authors' Representatives Inc.

www.publishersweekly.com/aar/
Information on finding an agent, working with an agent, and what to look for (or look out for) in an agent, plus links.

LiteraryAgent.Com

www.literaryagent.com/
A searchable list; search by name, state, category, etc. (Hard to assess quality; anyone can "join" the list.) Also includes monthly columns on issues of writing and agents.

Literary Agents
http://mockingbird.creighton.edu/NCW/litag.htm
Sponsored by the Nebraska Center for Writers, this site offers links to agent lists and to a variety of articles on finding (and using) an agent.

Preditors and Editors: Agent Listings
www.sfwa.org/prededitors/peala.htm
This site is a good place to look for warnings against agents who are "not recommended."

SFF Net
www.sff.net/sff/agents.htp

WritersNet: Literary Agent Directory
www.writers.net/agents.html

The Writer's Mind
www.thewritersmind.com
A site that allows agents and publishers to post listings.

BOOK PUBLISHERS
Midwest Book Review: Book Lover Resources
www.execpc.com/~mbr/bookwatch/booklove/
In addition to other links for book lovers, this page offers a huge array of publisher links, including children's book publishers, trade publishers, scholarly/academic publishers, computer/software book publishers, e-book publishers and dealers, and more. It will keep you busy.

BookWire: Book Publisher Index
www.bookwire.com/index/publishers/Childrens-Publishers.html
In addition to a general listing of book publishers, this site offers both general and genre- or topic-specific listings.

Children's Publishers (BookWire Index)
www.bookwire.com/index/Childrens-Publishers.html

Children's Publishers' Submissions Guidelines Online
www.signaleader.com/childrens-writers/
Guidelines for children's book and periodical publishers.

The Mysterious Home Page: Publishers
www.webfic.com/mysthome/pub.htm

Mystery Publishers (BookWire Index)
www.bookwire.com/index/Mystery-Publishers.html

Publishers' Catalogues Home Page
www.lights.com/publisher
A search tool enabling one to look up publishers by name, location, subject, or type of material published.

Romance Publishers
www.rwanational.com/pub_links.stm
A list of publishers "recognized" by the Romance Writers of America.

Science Fiction, Fantasy, and Horror [Novel] Markets
www.paradoxconcepts.com/novel_markets.html
Frequently updated list of speculative fiction novel markets.

Science Fiction Publishers (BookWire Index)
www.bookwire.com/publishers/Sci-Fict-Publishers.html

World Publishing Industry
http://publishing-industry.net/Publishers/
A directory/search engine for the publishing industry; offers extensive listings in various publishing categories.

WriteLinks: Commercial Book Publishers
www.writelinks.com/Creative/Links/BookPublishers/Crea06_02.htm
A comprehensive listing of book publishers in every category, including genre, address, Web site, and e-mail.

The Writer's Mind
www.thewritersmind.com
A site that allows agents and publishers to post listings. Well-categorized.

Yahoo!
http://dir.yahoo.com/Business_and_Economy/Shopping_and_Services/Publishers/

DISPLAY SITES
Writer's Showplace
http://writersshowplace.com/

Authorlink
www.authorlink.com

Goodstory
www.goodstory.com

Rosedog.com
www.rosedog.com

ELECTRONIC PUBLISHERS
Association of Electronic Publishers
http://members.tripod.com/~BestBooksCom/AEP/aep.html

Electronically Published Internet Connection (EPIC)
www.eclectics.com/epic/
A clearinghouse for electronically published authors and information on electronic publishing.

Lida Quillen's List of E-publishers
www.sff.net/people/Lida.Quillen/epub.html

Mary Wolf's Guide to Electronic Publishers
www.coredcs.com/~mermaid/epub.html

SCAM WARNINGS
Before You Write That Check
www.writer.org/scamkit.htm
A good article on scams against writers.

How to Smell a Scam
www.scalar.com/mw/pages/myudkin.html
Six telltale signs of scams, by author Marcia Yudkin.

Writer Beware
www.sfwa.org/beware/
Victoria Strauss's excellent compilation of tips, warnings, and updates about a wide variety of hazards to writers.

Writer Beware! Protecting Yourself from Questionable Agents, by Marg Gilks
www.writing-world.com/rights/agents.html

Writing Scams: Advice from Those Who Know, by J.A. Hitchcock
www.writing-world.com/rights/scams.html
An overview of some of the major scams perpetrated against writers, with tips on how to avoid being scammed.

SUBSIDY, ELECTRONIC, AND SELF-PUBLISHING
Electronic Subsidy Publishing: An Inexpensive Alternative
www.writing-world.com/publish/esubsidy.html

The Price of Vanity
www.writing-world.com/publish/vanity/html

FAQs About Electronic Publishing
www.writing-world.com/epublish/FAQ.html

Subsidy Publishing versus Self-Publishing
www.writing-world.com/publish/subsidy.html

Should You Pay for Publication?
www.writing-world.com/publish/pay.html

OTHER USEFUL SITES
By Any Other Name: Writing Under a Pseudonym
www.writing-world.com/general/pseudonym.html

Promoting Your Book on the Internet
www.writing-world.com/promotion/promote.html

A Quick Guide to Manuscript Format
www.writing-world.com/basics/manuscript.html

MARKET REFERENCE BOOKS
United States/North America
Writer's Market (Writer's Digest Books)
Annual; available through most bookstores and online booksellers in the United States.

Australia
The Australian Writer's Marketplace, by Rhonda Whitton (Bookman)
Annual; most easily obtained from publisher's Web site at *www.bookman.com.au/awm/home.html*.

Canada
The Canadian Writer's Market, by Jem Bates (McClelland & Stewart Inc.)
Available from most major online booksellers.

United Kingdom
The Writer's Handbook, Barry Turner, ed. (MacMillan Publishers, London)
Annual; available from most major online booksellers.

The Writers' and Artists' Yearbook (A.C. Black, London)
Annual; available from most major online booksellers.

Section 5

OTHER OPPORTUNITIES

20

SPEAKING AND TEACHING

Whether or not you subscribe to the adage, "Write what you know," sooner or later you're probably going to know quite a lot about *writing*. At that point, you have a new option for marketing your writing skills: becoming a speaker and/or instructor on writing-related topics.

While public speaking is rarely high on a writer's list of favorite activities, it is often a wise step. If you've published a book, you may find that the best way to promote it (and yourself) is to offer talks and workshops. At the last two conferences where I've given talks, for example, my books have flown off the book table. This makes my publisher happy and adds a few dollars to my royalty check. Add to that the honorarium you're likely to receive just for talking about your favorite subject for an hour or two (and the fact that your travel expenses and hotel room are—or should be—paid for by the conference, which may well take place in an exotic locale, such as Maui), and you might just view the prospect of speaking in public in a new light.

Speaking opportunities abound for writers. Writing conferences and workshops are always looking for speakers. Local clubs and organizations (including bookstores and libraries) are delighted to "book" authors for talks and will generally let you set up a book table. (This enables you to buy copies of your book from your publisher at the typical author's discount of 40 percent and sell them at full price, or at a minor discount, to readers who come to the talk.) Local colleges welcome writers who can offer classes on their area of expertise. And finally, if the thought of speaking to a group is still too horrifying to contemplate, you can offer a class online and "speak" to your audience by e-mail.

WHY SPEAK?

Writers typically branch out into speaking and teaching for one (or all) of the following reasons:

- To earn additional income
- To promote their books (or themselves)
- To pass on what they have learned to others

SHOW ME THE MONEY

If income is your goal, you'll want to limit your engagements to those that actually pay. Not all conferences offer honorariums, and many do not cover travel expenses. Before pitching a talk, therefore, make sure you'll be paid for your trouble, and that the cost of getting there won't eat up your profits.

Smaller conferences usually can't pay much for speakers. Some offer as little as $100 per workshop and no travel expenses. High-end conferences, on the other hand, may offer $1,000 or more for a well-known speaker, and cover your expenses. Almost all conferences offer free registration to speakers, which enables you to attend all the other talks and events. As many conferences are in attractive locations (and nice hotels), getting a speaking engagement can be a way to get a paid vacation!

Most conferences will also order copies of your books—not only those that relate directly to your talk, but any other books that you've published. If your books are commercially published, this will add a few extra dollars to your royalty statement, but it won't make you rich. If, however, you're self-published, those book-table revenues can add up.

Local clubs and organizations rarely offer a large fee ($50 to $100 is typical), but most will let you set up a book table (again, ideal for self-published authors). Since you won't have travel costs, these engagements are well worth an hour or so of your time.

Payment for a continuing education course can vary widely. Some give instructors a percentage of registration fees—e.g., $25 per student. Others pay a flat rate, but insist on a minimum number of attendees (which means your class will be cancelled if not enough students sign up). Some schools also deduct taxes from your check.

When offering a class, be sure to consider all the hours involved: not just those in the classroom, but those you'll spend in preparation and reviewing student assignments. A fee of $300 may sound impressive, until you realize that it covers six nights of instruction at two hours per night, plus the time required to write lectures and read homework. Classes also offer fewer opportunities to sell books; while private continuing education programs (like The Learning Annex) don't mind if authors hawk their books, most colleges frown on this.

MAKE ME FAMOUS

If your goal is to become better known as a writer, conferences are a tremendous way to boost recognition. This is your opportunity not only to speak to fans but to hobnob with other writers, agents, and editors as a peer. Once you've been invited to one conference, you're likely to be invited to others, because you're now recognized as a speaker.

If you want to become better known in your community for your particular area of expertise, seek out speaking engagements with civic and community groups. Don't just offer yourself as a writer; consider other topics on which you're qualified to speak (such as the subject you write *about*). If you're a business writer, for example, consider giving talks on business; if you write about travel, consider offering talks about some of your favorite destinations. Don't limit yourself to adult audiences; you'll also find speaking opportunities with youth organizations and schools.

Internet chats are another way to gain publicity (and, perhaps, to sell more books). All you need to chat is the ability to type quickly and accurately; it's a great speaking venue for anyone who gets butterflies at the thought of facing a crowd. (For tips on how to "speak" online, see chapter 20.)

LET ME HELP

Finally, any of the opportunities described in this chapter will give you a chance to "give something back"—to pass on what you've learned as a writer, to help the next generation of writers, and to share tips on a subject you love. Sometimes, that by itself is ample reward!

WRITERS' CONFERENCES

Writers' conferences are always looking for interesting speakers who have a sufficient reputation to draw attendees. The first question to ask yourself, therefore, is whether you have the credentials to interest a conference—or its participants.

To win an invitation to speak at a conference, you will need to be a published writer. Having a published *book* is often helpful, but not absolutely necessary; my first conference invitation was offered on the basis of the articles I'd published online with Inkspot/*Inklings*. If you write fiction, having a few stories published with reputable publications may be all you need.

It also helps to have a certain amount of name recognition. If no one has ever heard of you, your name isn't going to be a draw—and conference organizers look for writers who will attract attendees. However, fame is difficult to define. Chances are, you won't have heard of half the speakers at any conference you attend, so don't assume you don't have a chance just because your publications have been limited to obscure literary magazines.

You also need to have something to say. If you're already known for a particular subject or write in a particular field or genre, this will probably be the best topic to pitch. For example, if you write mystery fiction, you should probably offer to talk about how to write mystery fiction. Such a topic offers many possibilities: Perhaps you could pitch a workshop about forensics, or police procedures, or incorporating "true crime" into one's stories. Or you could discuss how to create suspense, how to plant clues and red herrings, or—the perennial favorite—how to get published.

MAKING CONTACT

One of the best places to find writers' conferences online is The Guide to Writers Conferences and Workshops. This site lists conferences by date and by location—thus, if you only want to apply to conferences in your area, you can look for listings in your state (or nearby states).

Each listing gives you the date of the conference, the general subject matter, the location, and a contact person and address. Look for titles like "conference organizer," "conference coordinator," or "conference chair" (or "co-chair"). You'll find these names toward the bottom of the listing.

Conferences plan their schedules as much as a year in advance, so don't expect to get an engagement in the actual conferences listed in the Guide. Your goal is to find conferences that may be willing to add you to *next* year's speaker's list. (If you can attend the conference this year and get a better idea of its focus, so much the better!)

Make a list of conferences that interest you—e.g., conferences in your area, conferences that focus on your subject, etc. Make sure that the dates fit into your schedule and that you're actually willing to travel to wherever the conference is held.

Now it's time for the initial pitch. Your first contact with the conference organizer should be a basic query letter, stating your interest in offering a workshop, and your credentials. Offer two or three ideas for workshops, along with a brief (no more than one paragraph) outline of each. Include a copy of your resume or writer's bio, a publications list, and a few relevant clips. Be sure to include an SASE. And be prepared to wait; conferences are planned by committee, so you won't hear anything until the committee has met and reviewed your proposal.

MAKING YOUR PITCH

If the response to your initial query is favorable, you will be asked to submit a more complete workshop proposal. You may be asked to submit a proposal for just one of your topics or for all of them—or even for completely different topics.

These proposals should be far more detailed than your original query. A good proposal length is about half a page; anything longer, and you are either giving too much detail or your topic will be too long to cover adequately in the time available. Keep in mind that you will have somewhere between forty-five and ninety minutes to speak—and that you will be expected to leave time for questions at the end of your talk. Don't try to squeeze "Twenty Ways Writers Can Benefit from the Internet" into thirty minutes of speaking time!

Your proposal should include the following information:

- The title of the talk
- A general overview of what you plan to cover (giving an idea of what participants will learn from your workshop)
- Any interactive elements you'd like to include (such as exercises)

- Any special equipment you'll need (such as a slide projector, an overhead projector, or even an electrical outlet)
- The proposed length of the talk (you can often wangle a longer time slot, if you want it, by indicating the need for more time in your proposal; if you don't care, you can omit this section)
- Whether you are offering handouts or other materials (find out first whether the conference will copy handouts for you)

Following are two sample proposals. One offers considerable detail; the other is shorter and punchier. Both were successful.

HOW TO WRITE EFFECTIVE QUERY LETTERS

One question I often hear as a writing instructor is, "Why bother to write a query when I could write the complete article?" This seminar will offer the answer to that question, along with tips on how to develop effective, successful queries. Some of the topics addressed in the seminar will include:

Why query letters are so important
- Because many publications don't accept unsolicited articles
- Because queries can save a writer valuable time
- Because some publications pay more for assigned articles

How to develop an effective query letter
- How to write an attention-grabbing "hook" or lead paragraph
- How to demonstrate the topic's relevance to the audience
- How to summarize the article's content
- How to present your credentials (even if you have never been published)
- How to solicit a response

What happens next
- Understanding assignments versus "on-speculation"
- Understanding the editorial process (and mind-set)

E-mail queries and other "netiquette" issues
- When (and how) to submit an e-mail query
- When (and how) to follow up by e-mail

When to write a query—and when to write the article instead

Proposed length: 1 hour 15 minutes
Handouts to be provided

CONDUCTING RESEARCH ONLINE: BEYOND BASIC SEARCHING

When you're looking for the answer to a complex question, basic search techniques often aren't enough. This workshop offers tips on locating information quickly and effectively. It will cover advanced searching techniques, how to select effective keywords and phrases, how to use alternative search engines, and where to find information outside of search engines (including newsgroups, e-mail, experts, databases, and international information sources). Participants are invited to bring their own "challenging research questions" to the workshop so that we can explore how to find the answers online.

Once your proposal is accepted, you'll be asked to provide a bio and a photo. At this time, you might also want to write a condensed version of your proposal for use in the conference bulletin. Otherwise, you may be surprised by the way your workshop is actually described. For example, the bit about bringing "challenging research questions" in the second sample never made it into the final description, which meant that the interactive portion of the workshop had to be dropped.

Keep your presentation flexible. Rather than writing out a talk that you plan to deliver word-for-word, write an outline of the points you want to cover. This enables you to drop material if you run out of time (e.g., if you have to answer lots of questions or you find that your audience already knows the material and is starting to look bored), or to add in material if you find that your audience has less background in the subject than you expected (or no one asks any questions). Be sure to bring flyers for your book, business cards, and any other materials that you'd like to distribute; conference participants love handouts and "freebies."

Once you've completed your workshop, shaken hands with everyone, and gone home, sit down at your computer and work up a proposal for next year. Send it to the conference organizers while they're still basking in the success of the last conference, and you're that much more likely to get a new engagement!

SPEAKING LOCALLY

Conferences aren't the only place to give talks about writing—or about subjects related to your writing. Local organizations—clubs, associations, youth groups, writers' groups, libraries, and bookstores—are all in need of speakers and are delighted to work with local authors.

Your telephone directory is the best place to start your search for local speaking opportunities. Look in the yellow pages under listings like:

- Clubs
- Associations
- Foundations
- Organizations (in my local directory, this points me to listings for political organizations, religious organizations, social service organizations, and youth organizations and centers)

These headings will provide you with an ample list of local civic and community groups, local branches of national organizations, and a host of special interest groups (such as boater's clubs, gardening clubs, cooking clubs, etc.). Don't overlook the latter, especially if you happen to write about a specialized subject area!

Your local Chamber of Commerce is likely to have a list of local clubs and organizations as well. For groups that don't tend to be listed in the yellow pages (such as writers' groups and book clubs), check with your local libraries and bookstores. Barnes & Noble, for example, often offers a bulletin board (usually near the restrooms) where such groups can post meeting announcements. While you're there, be sure to ask the library or bookstore if *they* would be interested in a talk or book signing from a local author.

Before approaching a group, it's a good idea to find out something about them. Call and ask for an information packet. Find out if the group has a Web site. Once you know what the group is "about," you'll be better able to pitch a talk that matches their needs and interests.

Then, call the organization and ask to speak to the person who handles event scheduling. Explain that you are a local author and would be interested in speaking at a luncheon, dinner, or special event. Mention a few appropriate topics (based on your research). At libraries or book clubs, a "how I got started" or "how I got published" talk is often a good draw, especially if you're a well-known author. If you have any prior speaking experience, mention that as well.

With clubs and organizations, your telephone conversation may be the only pitch you need; you may not be asked to write up an actual proposal. In many cases, your talk may be scheduled and confirmed before you even hang up the phone. In others, you may be asked to send along some biographical information and clips. If you have a Web site, mention it— and, at an appropriate point in the conversation, ask if you can bring copies of your books to sell. Then, just show up, give a good talk, have a good time—and be sure to ask if you can use the organization as a reference for your next pitch!

TEACHING A CLASS

Adult education programs offer excellent opportunities for writers. These go by many names: community education, continuing education, etc. Some are managed by local colleges and universities; others are offered by private organizations, such as The Learning Annex. Civic centers sometimes offer classes; so do many parks and recreation departments.

Many offer classes in creative and professional writing (including business and technical writing). Since such classes are usually not offered for academic credit, you don't need the same credentials that are often required for regular courses (e.g., a specific degree). Instead, most programs are looking for instructors who have actual experience in the field. If you're going to pitch a course on writing a novel, for example, you should generally have actually written (and published) a novel. If you're going to talk about freelance writing, you should have some magazine sales under your belt. In short, if you can prove that you have *done* it, you can probably make a case for your ability to teach it.

MAKING CONTACT

The first place to search for teaching opportunities is your local yellow pages. Try looking under the following headings:

- Schools: Business and Secretarial
- Schools: Technical and Trade
- Schools: Universities and Colleges (Academic)

If you'd like to explore opportunities outside your immediate city or county, you can find listings of colleges and universities by state at several Web sites (see section 5 resources). To locate independent programs, look for flyers at your local library, bookstore, or community center.

Your directory may not actually list the number for a continuing education department. To find the right person to contact, simply call the college or university and ask for that department. (Usually, the operator will know what you mean, even if the department uses another name.) Be sure to ask for the actual extension and a contact name if you can get it, so that you can call back directly if you don't make a connection the first time.

Once you're connected with the right department, ask to talk to the person in charge of hiring instructors. Tell that person (often the director of the program) that you are interested in teaching a class through that program, and ask about the application procedure. Usually, you'll be asked to give a little information about yourself and the type of class you'd like to teach. If your initial telephone pitch interests the director, you'll be given more detailed instructions about how to actually apply. Sometimes, this involves filling out an application package; sometimes, it's as simple as submitting a class proposal and a cover letter. You'll also need to provide a curriculum vitae (a resume, to nonacademics!).

PROPOSING YOUR CLASS

Continuing education programs can be remarkably flexible about the structure of a course. Often, they'll leave it up to you to decide how many nights a week you wish to teach and how many hours per night. You may also have the option of offering daylong (or half-day) courses on weekends.

After you've decided *what* you want to teach, therefore, you'll need to decide how much time you need to teach it effectively. If you don't plan to offer any actual writing assignments, you might want to consider teaching a single-day course (usually six hours with a break for lunch). If you want to give homework, or give students a chance to review handouts between sessions, it's better to schedule several classes over a period of days or weeks. For evening classes, a schedule of four class sessions of two hours each usually works well (though some instructors opt for six or even eight classes).

You'll also want to find out in advance whether the department will pay for photocopying handouts. Some continuing education departments have very small budgets and expect you to pay for your own copying. Others may allow you to order a textbook, which students will pay for as part of the course. If you want to provide extra materials, be sure to discuss this with the program director. Similarly, make sure the director knows whether you'll need special equipment (such as a slide projector) or an electrical hookup.

Finally, you'll need to provide a detailed overview of the course you want to teach. Your overview should provide:

- A class title
- A description of the course (including the expected "outcome" of the course, i.e., what students will learn or achieve during the course)
- A schedule (e.g., the number of sessions and the topic of each session; for a one-day course, include topics for morning and afternoon).
- Special needs, such as photocopying, electrical outlet, projector, etc.
- A minimum/maximum number of students, if appropriate (if, for example, you're planning lots of one-on-one interaction or homework, you may want to limit enrollment)

Here's an example:

SUCCESSFUL FREELANCING:
WRITING FOR THE MAGAZINE ARTICLE MARKET

Instructor: Moira Anderson Allen, M.Ed.

Length: 8 weeks/3 hours per class

Participants who have basic writing skills and an interest in writing professionally will find this the perfect opportunity to develop their freelance potential. The instructor, who has worked as both a freelance writer and a magazine editor, will guide students through the process of developing articles tailored specifically for an appropriate market. Students will learn how to explore and familiarize themselves with markets, how to work with editors, and how to make their work stand out from the competition. By the end of the class, students will have written a complete, marketable article and will have begun the process of submitting that article to a magazine.

Session 1: You are an expert. Discover your area(s) of expertise and learn how to "mine" it for article topics. In this session, students will identify areas of interest and knowledge and develop potential article topics from those areas. The session will also include an introduction to the magazine market: its potential, how to break in, and what to expect from the market.

Session 2: Focus, focus. Students will learn how to turn an idea into a topic, a topic into an outline, and an outline into a rough draft. Exercises include "focusing" (narrowing down a subject) and "brainstorming" (building up a topic).

Session 3: Who's your audience? Before one begins to write an article, one must identify whom one is writing for. This session teaches students how to locate markets, how to identify the needs of a particular market (magazine) just by looking at it, and how to approach that market with an idea.

Session 4: Putting meat on the bones. Now that participants have defined a working topic and identified the audience for that topic, it's time to start building a rough draft. This session explores different approaches to articles, sources of information, interview techniques, and decisions that must be made before and during the development of the article.

Session 5: Playing editor. By now, students should have an actual working draft of an article. Guided by the instructor's editorial expertise, students will now learn to look at their article the way an editor would. In this session, participants will learn about expanding, cutting, slanting, using quotes and interviews effectively, and tailoring information to the target audience.

Session 6: Making it irresistible. As participants move closer to having a completed, salable article, they will learn how to add "bonuses" that save editors work—and enhance sales. Students will learn how to use artwork, photos, stylistic techniques, and other tools to "rejection-proof" their material.

Session 7: Taking the plunge. This session focuses on how to sell one's work. It will explore query letters, working with editors, and presenting manuscripts properly. Students will be asked to "query" the instructor and will receive feedback on how to target their queries to actual magazines.

Session 8: What next? The final class provides an in-depth exploration of the freelance marketplace. It discusses editorial procedures, building relationships with editors, understanding contracts, payment schedules, different types of magazines, rights and sales, and professional standards. It answers the questions, What happens to my article when it is submitted/accepted/published? The session will also explore book markets and contracts.

Each session will include approximately ten pages of handouts.

Include a separate proposal, on a separate piece of paper, for each class that you want to teach. Provide a cover letter that summarizes the classes you're offering (and keep in mind that those summaries may be used as the official catalog course descriptions).

TEACHING ONLINE
The process for obtaining online teaching jobs is much the same as for obtaining "real-world" positions. The difference is that you're no longer limited by geography: You can offer your ser-

vices to any of dozens of sites that offer online writing courses, no matter where you live. You also don't have to worry about scheduling "convenient" hours, hiking up lots of steps to a dingy classroom, or making your way through a dark parking lot when the class is over.

You'll find a number of sites that offer online writing courses in the resources listing at the end of this section. You can find more by typing appropriate search terms into your favorite search engine. Try several different terms, such as:

- Writing classes
- Online writing classes
- Writing courses
- Internet writing courses

Before pitching your class, visit the site first and determine whether (a) you like the presentation and content of the site, and (b) you have something to offer that isn't already being taught. If you're not sure about a site's reputation, run a search on the name of the site. Search newsgroups as well to see whether the site has been discussed (positively or negatively). Review the site thoroughly to determine whether it has received good reviews and whether it seems to be a "class act." (A site that purports to teach writing but is riddled with typos and grammatical errors, for example, would not give you much of a career boost.)

If the site doesn't offer an obvious link for potential instructors, search for contact information. Try to find something more personal than "info@"—but if that's the best you can do, use it. Send a basic e-mail query describing the type of course you'd like to teach and your credentials. If you receive no response after two to three weeks, follow up; if you still don't get a response, move on.

Internet courses can be a good alternative for a writer who isn't quite comfortable with the idea of "speaking" in public. Most courses are conducted primarily by e-mail, which means that you'll need to be able to write weekly lectures and respond to student questions. If you give assignments, those will also be submitted and reviewed by e-mail. What you won't have is the interaction of discussion and question-and-answer sessions (though some courses do include scheduled chat meetings). Instructors are usually paid a percentage of each enrollment.

Chances are that you became a writer because you felt that you had something to share. As you become more proficient in the writing field, you may discover that you have even more to share: your love of writing, your expertise as a writer, and your desire to "mentor" the next generation of writers. By stepping up to the podium—whether at a writing conference, a civic club meeting, or in a classroom—you can give back some of the lessons you've learned along the way, promote your career, and earn some extra income at the same time.

21

CHAT YOUR WAY TO SALES

by MaryJanice Davidson

One of the easiest, cheapest, and funnest (Funnest? Yeah, me write good!) ways to promote your book (or yourself) is to do a chat on the Web. Below are tips on finding a Web site to do your chat, as well as tips for a smooth chat and what comes afterward.

FINDING CHAT OPPORTUNITIES

Lots of Web sites are looking for guest speakers. You might feel like you're pestering them, but trust me, they want you. They need you. They have to have you! (I just read six romance novels in a row . . . does it show?) Web sites want traffic, and they know a great way to generate traffic is to host a chat.

I belong to several writers' lists on the Web, and they're always advertising author and writer-friendly Web sites looking for writers to chat about upcoming releases, writing techniques, favorite books, etc. Painted Rock and Inkspot are great places to start. Another good start is to go to Yahoo! or any search engine, type in "writers chats," and check out the opportunities that pop up. I tried that, and seventy-six Web sites came up.

PROPOSING A CHAT

Once you've decided where you'd like to do your chat, send the chat coordinator an e-mail explaining why you're so swell. Try to come up with a reason *besides* your upcoming release, because every writer is going to go down that road. For my chat, "Escaping the Slush Pile," I pitched not only my upcoming release (coincidentally titled *Escape the Slush Pile*), but the fact that I'm a wife, mother, have a grueling day job, write for several publishers, and sold eight manuscripts in less than three years. The chat coordinator was intrigued to receive an e-mail from someone who apparently never slept and wrote me back with a proposed chat date.

So, as above, try to find a reason besides your book (unless you've got a great nonfiction book with a timely topic) to do a chat: You're a neurologist who writes medical thrillers, and you'd like to chat with other writers in that genre. You're a private investigator who writes mysteries, and you can give chat participants a chance to find out how a real gumshoe thinks. You write romances (or wedding guides), and you've been married nine times. You're an ex-con who writes true crime. That sort of thing.

PREPARING FOR YOUR CHAT

Once you have a chat date, don't panic. Which is what I did. Once the date was set, I was tempted more than once to call the whole thing off. I, blabbermouth supreme, was overwhelmed by the burning question: What was I going to say to all those people? The way to get around that is to have friends e-mail you questions for practice. Or try to think up the questions you absolutely don't want to be asked, and formulate answers for them. With a little practice, and with answers for your worst-case questions, you'll be a lot less nervous.

In the week or two before the chat, promote it. Mention it on your listservs, and tell friends and family. If you've got an e-mail list you use to promote your releases, send everyone on your list an e-mail with the chat day, time, and location. Do it once or twice before the chat, so people can put it in their calendar, and again the day of the chat. It helps to go with a Web site that will promote your chat as well. I saw ads for my chat everywhere I looked, which, while great for the ego, was hell on my nerves. But looking back, I'm grateful they did so much publicity.

Karen Wiesner *(http://karenwiesner.hypermart.net),* author of *Electronic Publishing: The Definitive Guide,* had this to say about chats: "My advice is to know your topic. If you don't know your topic inside and out, well, outside of being embarrassing, you're creating a 'hard sell' for yourself, because no one wants to buy something when they're not sure the person who wrote it is knowledgeable about their topic. If you get nervous, write yourself a list of questions and answers, trying to anticipate the strange questions, print it out, and have it next to you so that you can refer to it if your brain decides to shut off. Go to the bathroom before you log on, and try not to drink too much before and during the chat. Mention your site URL more than once—at the very least, during your introduction paragraph and once in closing. Give them a place to go after the chat. Mention your book a couple of times, and use specific examples from it. Make connections with your audience by answering their questions personally. Say their name, wish them luck, tell them you're glad they came. Make them log off and go straight to your Web site or your publisher's."

Karen mentioned the introduction paragraph, and I can't urge you strongly enough to have one prepared. My chat coordinator suggested that, and I shrugged it off. The result was, after I was introduced, I was frantically typing a greeting, an introduction, and a general "thanks for having me" paragraph, while participants started peppering me with questions. I'm sure they thought I'd had a seizure or something, because it took me so long to say something. So, have your opening paragraph prepared—include your name, your URL, and a bit about your topic—and paste it right into the chat once you're introduced.

It also helps to be a fast typist. For me, the questions came hard and fast. While I was typing out one answer, three more people would have questions. Thus, my chat turned out to be the fastest hour of my life and loads of fun to boot. And remember, your chat coordinator is on your side. If she sees you're getting overwhelmed, she'll step in and help you. If you're having trouble keeping up, don't be afraid to type something like, "Bear with me, folks, I'm typing as fast as I can!" People will understand.

Speaking of people, don't fret about the number of participants . . . there's just no way to judge a successful chat based on who comes. My coordinator told me he'd seen anywhere from five to twenty people show up for a chat, and it had nothing to do with the author's name or topic (probably has more to do with TV reruns than anyone's name). If there are only two or three people in the chat room, you'll have plenty of time to be thorough and answer their questions.

If you can, offer giveaways (usually a copy of your latest release or something from your backlist). It increases interest and attendance. During my chat I had a brainwave and suggested that anyone who wanted a free sample chapter from my upcoming release should e-mail me. The result was a self-promoter's dream.

After the chat, the coordinator will often post a transcript of the chat at the Web site. This is wonderful for you, because it's more free promotion. I'm still getting private e-mails from people who either participated in the chat or saw the transcript and had questions about my upcoming release.

I would suggest you send a thank-you to the chat coordinator for their help and support. Don't forget to e-mail them a few months later and ask to do another chat. Now that you're a chat veteran, you know how simple and exciting this excellent promotional tool is.

In my case, the only thing the chat cost was an hour out of my life—which, given that I normally would have spent that hour gorging on coffee ice cream and watching *Simpsons* reruns, was time well spent indeed.

22

WRITING FOR THE BUSINESS WORLD

For a writer accustomed to the world of query letters and manuscript submissions, writing for the business world may seem like a huge leap. For many, this was the world we were trying to escape by becoming freelance writers; what could possibly induce us to return?

The answer might be "good pay and lots of opportunities." While business writing is rarely as glamorous as writing for magazines (you probably won't want to pass around copies of your latest sales letter to family and friends), it can offer a steady, reliable income. Often, it can fill the gaps left by more unreliable types of markets—and give you more freedom to write what you really want to write.

UNDERSTANDING THE MARKET

Business writing is often referred to as corporate freelancing, but don't be fooled by that term. There is more to the business world than corporations. You can find opportunities with big businesses, small businesses, nonprofit organizations, academic institutions, research centers, and even home-based and Mom-and-Pop companies. For example, I've edited research reports for a nonprofit "think tank," written computer documentation for a government office, developed an internal newsletter for a private corporation, and edited a book manuscript for a lawyer. All of these qualify as business writing.

Peter Bowerman, author of *The Well-Fed Writer,* divides business customers into two categories: "end users" and "middlemen." End users are those businesses that are the direct users of your product: the company for whom that brochure, report, or press release is written and distributed. "Middlemen" are agencies—such as graphic design firms, advertising agencies, PR firms, and writing brokers—that offer a range of services to end users. You can work directly for end users or market your services to and through middlemen agencies.

CHOOSING THE WORK

Business writing doesn't have to be boring (though some of it undeniably is). While you may want to take any work you can get in the beginning, you'll soon determine what types of projects interest you most. Some options include:

- Press releases
- Brochures and handouts
- Product documentation and literature
- Employee instructional materials
- Sales literature (including direct mail promotions)
- Speeches
- Annual, company, and sales reports
- Research reports
- Web site development and content
- Audiovisual materials (including promotional videos)
- Company newsletters (internal)
- Company newsletters/magazines for external distribution
- Grant/fundraising proposals
- Company biographies and "histories"
- Public relations material for publication in magazines and newspapers

Each of these categories offers a variety of opportunities for freelancing. You may offer your services as a writer (developing original material, often through interviews and research), or as a copyeditor or proofreader. If you have other skills, such as graphic design, desktop publishing, photography, Web site development, or translation abilities, you can make yourself even more marketable by offering a package deal—e.g., the ability to write, edit, design, and produce a company brochure from the ground up.

FINDING CLIENTS

If you're accustomed to hunting for traditional writing markets, the prospect of seeking corporate clients may seem intimidating. It doesn't have to be, however. Information on potential clients is everywhere; once you start looking, you'll be amazed at how many sources are available.

Start with the yellow pages. If you'd like to work for a particular type of company (e.g., law firms, nonprofit organizations, public relations agencies), check your telephone directory under that category. Make a list of likely prospects.

Next, review your local paper. The Writers-Editors Network suggests scanning the Sunday "help wanted" pages for ads for writers, editors, copyeditors/writers, advertising, public relations, proofreading, technical writing, and anything else that might relate to the type of services you offer.[1] A company that is seeking to hire a full- or part-time writer might be open to the suggestion of contracting out those same tasks to a freelancer—who can offer the same services as a regular employee without the added costs of benefits, insurance, vacation pay, etc. A scan of the want ads will also give you an idea of the types of businesses in your area.

Your town may have a business-related newspaper; check office-supply stores and business printers, or ask your local chamber of commerce (COC). Or check the yellow pages under "publishers: newspaper."

Your local COC is also a good place to look for potential clients. Many will have display racks that offer flyers and cards from local businesses. Ask for a list of businesses that are members of the COC. Find out whether the COC sponsors any sort of networking functions.

Do an online search on the name of your city. The official "city Web page" will usually pop up among the first ten results. Look for links such as "businesses" or "community" to find direct links to many local firms.

Visit online job sites. You may be able to find a site specific to your area; for example, "craigslist" focuses on freelance writing jobs in the San Jose/Silicon Valley area. You can also set search criteria to select companies in your area. You might also consider joining a writing or editing guild or organization that offers job listings to members.

Finally, corporate freelance writer Tina Miller notes that it's a good idea to spread the word that you're looking for this type of work. "I try to tell everyone I know—including people I'm interviewing for articles for the newspaper and for magazine and e-zine articles—that I also do business writing, ghostwriting, Web content, etc. I've got several irons in the fire right now as a result of that."

MAKING CONTACT

THE BUSINESS "QUERY"

There are two ways to approach a potential client: by mail or by phone. Tina Miller uses the first approach: "Believe it or not, I have never yet made a cold call," she says. She recommends that your mail package include a "brief, professional cover letter, a marketing brochure outlining your services, your business card, and possibly a list of your previous and existing clients. If desired, you may wish to include a few clips or samples of your work, depending on the type of projects you're trying to land."

---

[1]The Writers-Editors Network, *www.writers-editors.com/Writers/Free_Tips/Marketing/marketing.htm;* accessed 10/17/00.

Your cover letter should include a brief overview of the services you would like to offer—e.g., proofreading, newsletter development, ad copy, audiovisual scriptwriting, etc. Focus on two or three services at most; even if you can offer more, listing too many services can make you look like a "jack-of-all-trades, master of none." Emphasize any supporting skills you can offer, such as graphics or Web site design.

What if you have no previous business-writing background? One option is to determine how your other writing credentials may fit into the business world. "If you've written anything similar before, use that as a sample, and emphasize the parallels," says Miller. For example, if you've written magazine articles, you can apply those skills to writing corporate bios, profiles, and similar public-relations pieces for local and national publications.

Another option is to emphasize your subject background. "If you're familiar with the particular industry and its unique jargon, that may be a plus, even if you haven't actually written for that industry before," notes Miller. "It may increase the client's comfort level if you 'speak' their 'language.'" If all else fails, Miller suggests getting samples by "volunteering to write for a local effort you believe in."

THE COLD CALL

Peter Bowerman prefers to approach clients by telephone. "If people aren't expecting your correspondence, chances are excellent it'll go into the trash unopened. You really need to establish that connection with someone so that they know what your package is when it shows up on their desk," he notes. Here's his approach to the "cold call":

Your Script. Know exactly what you're going to say when your prospect answers the phone. Write it out word-for-word on a 3″ × 5″ card and keep it in front of you. Always say it, and never say anything but. In my opinion, this is a critical secret to staying focused during prospecting, while removing one potential source of anxiety from the process. Keep it brief (fifteen seconds or less), simple, and to the point.

My basic version goes like this: "Good morning, my name is Peter Bowerman, and I'm a freelance writer, making contact with local banks [for instance], to determine whether you have any ongoing or occasional needs for a good freelance writer to help create marketing collateral material: brochures, newsletters, ads, etc. Who might be the best person to talk with?" The word "collateral" is industry standard. Use it, and you'll fit in.

Ideally, you'll have a name to ask for, but if not, this'll do, and it's always enough to get some reaction, which then drives the rest of the call. Hopefully, you know what to say if they respond, "Great! Your timing couldn't be better." It happens.

How To Talk. Slowly, clearly, and evenly. When you get someone on the phone, don't just chat away like you normally would. Adjust to accommodate people who don't know you and weren't expecting your call. Make it easy for them to switch gears.

What Not to Say. Refrain from cuteness, like an ultracheerful, "How are you today!?" unless they ask you first. Coming from you, it fairly screams "Salesman Butter-Up Line!!" If they ask, it can be like a cool drink of water. Simply reply politely, "Very well, thank you. Yourself?" Resist the urge to jump all over them with dirty paws like a golden retriever greeting its master after a two-week absence.

THE MEETING

Whether your initial approach is by telephone or letter, you will ultimately need to arrange a face-to-face meeting with potential clients. This is one of the key differences between business writing and magazine freelancing. In the latter case, you never have to leave your desk (or change out of your fuzzy bunny slippers). When dealing with businesses, however, you'll need to present a businesslike image, not only on your letterhead, but in person.

Don't make the mistake of treating a client meeting like a job interview, however. You are a professional, not an applicant, and you should dress and act the part. Display confidence in your skills and in your ability to handle the type of work you're trying to solicit. Don't convey the impression that you will be humbly grateful for whatever crumbs the client cares to toss your way—at whatever salary they might choose to offer!

Create a portfolio to bring to your meetings. Invest in a good-quality binder (preferably leather) and plastic sheet-protectors. Include copies of any clips or materials that are relevant to the services you're trying to pitch. If you don't have any "real" clips yet, consider dummying up a sample brochure or newsletter to show the type of service you can provide. Include a few writing samples from magazines if that's all you have, but don't expect a client to be impressed; business samples will be much more useful.

You'll also want to prepare a package to leave behind. Bowerman recommends the following: "Take a regular manila file folder (or better yet, a colored one to stand out) and, on the tab, affix a printed label with four lines: your name, 'Freelance Copywriter' in big letters, your company name, and phone number. Into the folder go a resume/client list, three business cards, and appropriate samples. Now they have your stuff all in one place, in a folder that's ready for easy accommodation into their system. And, you'll instantly impress them with your organizational skills."

BIDDING ON A JOB

Making contact is only half the battle. Once you've convinced a potential client that you can offer a useful service, you must still convince that client to hire you.

Usually, you won't be invited to a meeting unless the client has a specific project in mind and believes that you might be a likely candidate to handle it. The client may be considering several freelancers—or you may be the only one. Either way, you will still have to convince the client that you can handle the project in a reasonable amount of time, at a reasonable price. This means preparing a bid.

A bid should present your client with the following information:

- What you will do
- How long it will take
- What you will charge

On the surface, that all sounds simple enough! In practice, however, developing an effective bid can be quite a challenge—especially if you're not accustomed to setting your own rates or estimating how long a project will take. The most common beginner mistakes are failing to clearly define the project, underestimating the time factor, and setting rates too low. Here are some ways to avoid those mistakes.

DEFINING THE PROJECT

The first step in submitting a bid (or in determining whether to bid in the first place) is to determine exactly what the project involves. This means finding out what the client wants. If, for example, the client wants a brochure, find out how much information will be provided, how much you'll have to dig up on your own, how it should be presented, and whether you are expected to provide a finished product or just written copy. Determine the goal of the brochure, including its audience and the image the company wishes to project.

Similarly, if you're asked to edit a document, review the material first. Find out what level of editing is desired: proofreading for typos, copyediting for grammar and style, or content editing for readability and accuracy. Does the copy need a lot of work, or is it fairly clean?

Don't settle for statements like, "I want you to make this report sing," or "I want a brochure that will generate more sales." Don't play mind reader; ask questions until you're sure that both you and the client have the same idea as to what constitutes "singing copy." If necessary, use your interview training as a writer to draw out more information: "What would make *you* want to buy this product?"

Once you've determined what is expected of you, spell that out in your bid (in writing). In other words, tell the client what the client has told you. This is your only protection against unexpected demands, changes, or requests for endless revisions.

DETERMINING A TIMELINE

Once you have defined what a project entails, you'll need to determine when it can be delivered. In many cases, the client will set the deadline, whereupon you'll have to determine whether you can meet it. In other cases, however, the client will ask you how long the project will take. You may be required to offer a completion date, an estimated number of hours, or both, depending on how you will be billing the client (see below).

Think carefully before you answer this question! It is easy, especially in the beginning, to underestimate how many hours a project will require. Be sure to leave room for unexpected delays, difficulties, changes in direction, and people who don't deliver their part of the work (such as instructions, information, or reviews) on schedule. If you have to submit the project for corporate approval at various stages before completion, remember that this can also add significant delays.

Also consider any other projects you have (or hope to have). Can you fit this project into your existing schedule? Will you have to drop or postpone other projects or clients? Will you be able to take on new projects? Again, budget extra time for the unexpected: If problems arise in another project, will they delay this project?

Resist the temptation to underestimate the amount of time required in an effort to impress the client with your speed and efficiency. Often, this can backfire: Too short an estimate can convey the impression that your work is hasty and slipshod. Though clients value speed, they also want to know that you are giving their work your full attention.

As a writer, you may be accustomed to thinking only about writing time. As a business writer, however, you'll be billing for all the time you spend on that project—including telephone time, meetings, research, errands, revisions, more revisions, etc. Be sure to include all those hours in your estimate.

SETTING FEES

Many writers find this the most difficult aspect of business freelancing. We're used to being told what we can hope to receive—and not a penny more! We're *not* used to attempting to determine what our time is worth or what to charge for a particular task.

One place to check for going rates is the current *Writer's Market,* which lists fees for a wide range of writing services, such as copyediting, copywriting, speechwriting, brochures, and so forth. In some cases, these fees are listed by hour; in others, they're listed by project. You can also find fee information on the sites listed in the section 5 resources.

Most fee listings offer a range of fees—usually somewhere between $20 and $100 per hour. Where you should place yourself on that range depends on a variety of factors, including your experience *and* your geographic location. Freelancers based in New York City, Los Angeles, or Silicon Valley will be able to charge higher rates than freelancers doing the exact same work in Kansas or Nebraska.

Don't assume that you have to start at the bottom of the rate scale. Instead, call around and try to determine the going rate in your area. Look for editors online (run a search on "business editors," and refine it by including criteria such as your city and/or state), and contact them to determine their rates. (If you're not comfortable admitting that you want to know how much the competition charges, pretend you're a potential customer.)

Another way to determine your fee is to determine how much you need to earn. First, determine how much income you'll need in a year. Then, determine how much of that income will come from other sources, such as freelance articles. Divide the remainder by the number of *billable* hours you believe you'll be able to devote to business freelancing. (Keep in mind that you'll be spending a fair amount of time on nonbillable tasks, such as prospecting for clients.) If the resulting number is in line with general and local rates for the type of service you're offering, use it!

Just as you shouldn't underbid on hours, you should also avoid underbidding on price. It's tempting to bid low, on the assumption that a client will prefer to hire the cheapest contractor available. In reality, clients tend to avoid contractors who price themselves too cheaply; just as you might wonder why something is marked down to a bargain price, your client may also wonder why your rate is too low. Also, avoid the temptation to underbid the competition. It's wiser to build good relationships with other business freelancers, who may then refer clients to you when they're overloaded.

Once you've determined your hourly rate, you can calculate how much a project is worth. Your final decision, as you prepare your bid, is whether to price the project on an hourly basis, a flat rate, or some other rate scale. Each has advantages and disadvantages.

If you are concerned that a client will think your hourly rate is too high, a flat rate may work best. The advantage of a flat rate (e.g., "$300 per brochure") is that you get the same fee even if you put in fewer hours than you originally estimated— more profit to you! The disadvantage, obviously, is if the reverse occurs: If the project runs longer than you anticipated, you won't get any more money. (You will, however, get an education on how to price future projects, which is worthwhile.) Some clients like flat rates; others don't. Often, this is something you'll need to determine by working with the client.

An hourly rate has the advantage of being more open-ended. If the client wants revisions, makes changes, or adds extra tasks, you just add extra billing hours. The disadvantage of billing by the hour is that some clients have no understanding of how long things really take and may assume that you're padding your bill. Again, it may not be possible to determine the best approach until you've actually discussed the project with the client.

A third approach is to bill by some other measure, such as per page (which is how I bill for editorial services). The way to determine this type of rate is to simply estimate how many pages you can edit in an hour, and then divide your hourly rate by that number! The advantage of this approach is that it is easy to calculate: The client only has to count the number of pages in the project to determine the final cost. Another advantage is that, like the flat rate, you'll get paid the same amount even if the work goes more quickly than expected. The disadvantage, of course, is also the same: If the work goes more slowly than you expected, you get paid less.

The final element you'll need to calculate into the billing portion of your bid is expenses, if any. If you will need to purchase special software to handle the job, or subcontract portions of the job to others (such as artists or designers), be sure to include an estimate of those amounts in your bid. Make sure that these are listed separately from your own billing hours. Try to determine exactly what those costs will be, so that you don't surprise the client at the end of the job with an unexpected list of outside expenses.

GET IT IN WRITING

When you bid on a project, submit your bid in writing. E-mail is often acceptable. Don't be surprised if you have to negotiate before your final bid is accepted. Don't start the project until the client has accepted your bid in writing. Here's a sample bid on a book-editing project:

Dear _____:

Thanks for sending the manuscript. I've reviewed it, and here is how I would like to proceed:

First, a clarification of terms.

RATES:

1) I charge $5 per double-spaced page for basic copyediting and proofreading, with suggestions regarding content as needed. (Only pages that actually require editing are counted. Pages that contain less than ten lines of actual text are not counted. Pages that consist of figures or tables, or other nontext material, that do not require editing are not counted.)

2) We never discussed the rate for formatting the manuscript. As this will be a separate process, I'd like to add $1 per MANUSCRIPT page for formatting the manuscript through Pagemaker to Adobe PDF files. (In this case, all pages are counted, as formatting involves manipulating the entire document.)

DEADLINE:

You haven't mentioned when you want this. Did you have a date in mind when you'd like to be able to post the final draft? Let me know, and we can work backwards from there.

PROCESS:

1) I will separate the book into chapters, double-space the chapters, and print them. Once I've done this, I will go over the printout to determine the exact number of "edit" pages and e-mail you an estimate of total cost for the editorial stage.

2) I will edit the hard copy, making all notations on that copy, and mail it to you for review.

3) You may either make changes on your files or, after reviewing suggested changes (and making any additional changes), mail the copy back to me, and I can input them into the file. I will not actually make changes to the electronic file without prior approval.

4) Once all changes and corrections have been made, I will create a sample formatted chapter and e-mail it to you (in PDF format) for approval.

5) Once we've agreed on a format, I will format the entire document in Pagemaker and Adobe and return both (a) the edited Word file and (b) the formatted files to you.

OPTIONS:

1) If you prefer, I can send you the edited pages on a chapter-by-chapter basis. This might streamline the process so that you can look at one chapter's suggestions while I work on the next, rather than getting it all at once. In that way, too, once I finish the entire manuscript, I can begin immediately on corrections and formatting.

PAYMENT:

Once I have gone through the manuscript and provided an estimate of the total payment (edit plus format), my preference would be to receive one-third of the payment in advance, one-third upon delivery of the fully edited manuscript, and the final third upon delivery of the formatted files. Would that be acceptable?

If so, let me know, and I'll dive into the book this week.

Best,

Moira Allen[2]

You also need to determine exactly when and how you will get paid. If you're undertaking a large job (e.g., worth more than $500 or $1,000), you may wish to ask for payment in installments. Some writers ask for payment in thirds: one-third when the bid is accepted or the contract is signed, one-third halfway through the project, and one-third on completion. Others ask for half down and half at the end. If you have to buy materials or software to complete the project, ask for payment for those items in advance. If you need to subcontract part of the work, you'll usually ask for reimbursement of those expenses after the work has been completed.

---

[2]Before submitting this bid, I asked for a sample chapter to review and edit. This enabled me to determine how much editing would be required and enabled the author to determine whether he liked my editing style. Even then, my "$1-per-page" formatting bid did not account for the possibility that the author would submit an endless stream of format changes, and my offer to input editorial changes did not take into account the difficulty of reading the author's handwriting (or my own!). However, when all was said and done, I earned my preferred hourly rate—and some valuable lessons about bidding at the same time!

Business clients expect to be invoiced. Accounting departments are more likely to respect a professional-looking invoice; it's worth going to the office supply store and buying a pack of preprinted forms. Find out whether you need to provide a purchase order number to get paid.

FOLLOW UP!

Once you've completed a job, follow up! Find out whether the work was considered satisfactory, and remind the client that you would welcome other projects. Ask the client to refer you to other companies, and ask whether the client is willing to be used as a reference when you contact other prospects.

A word of warning, however: Not every corporate client is easy to work with. A bad customer can waste your time—and in the business of corporate freelancing, time is money. Don't spend time dealing with clients who don't know what they want and are never satisfied with what you give them. Don't let such clients deter you; just finish the job and move on. There are lots of other prospects available; use your newly gained clips and go after them!

23

GRANTS FOR WRITERS
by Kelleen Zubick and Maryo Ewell

M any opportunities are available for writers of fiction, poetry, drama, journalism, nonfiction, children's books, and screenwriting that offer cash stipends of $500 or more. These opportunities generally fall into two (imprecise) categories: awards and grants.

- **Awards** are cash prizes given to writers in recognition of outstanding promise or accomplishment. Fellowships and scholarships for writers should also be considered awards, because these are also often cash stipends given in recognition of talent, as is the case with fellowships awarded by the National Endowment for the Arts. (In cases like this, "fellowship" is often used interchangeably with "award.") However, sometimes this type of award is restricted. For example, most fellowships and scholarships awarded by academic institutions and artists' colonies are meant to recognize talent *and* to be used for a specific purpose, such as a course of study or residency expenses at a particular colony.

- **Grants** differ from awards in that they are usually funds given to writers to accomplish a particular project described in a proposal. Many arts agencies and organizations offer grant-funding categories that are open to individual writers. Sometimes individual writers are funded directly, but more often they are funded as part of a team proposal in which an organizational partner is the actual applicant (more about that later). Limited opportunities exist for "emergency grants," which are short-term funds available to writers experiencing hardship and which require a statement of need rather than a proposal.

Grants and awards are usually offered by publishers, foundations, arts organizations, and academic institutions. They provide an invaluable source of both income and recognition for writers. Nearly all have an application process involving the submission of an application and an excellent manuscript. This chapter will show you how to develop a successful application.

SOURCES

The best sources to consult for information on awards and grants to writers are the annual editions of the PEN American Center's *Grants and Awards;* the F&W Publications' directories, such as *Poet's Market, Writer's Market,* and *Children's Writer's Market;* and the Theater Communications Group's *Dramatists Sourcebook.* Monthly or bimonthly publications, such as *Poets and Writers Magazine, The Writer, The Writer's Chronicle* (published by Associated Writing Programs), and *Writer's Digest,* are good professional resources, containing updated information on opportunities for writers as well as application deadlines. Other good resources are the publications of writers' associations, such as the American Society of Journalists and Authors, the Modern Language Association, and the Editorial Freelancers Association.

State arts councils or commissions, which can be found in every state or territory (see section 5 resources), usually sponsor grants, fellowships, or residencies for writers residing within their states. These state agencies can also provide writers with leads for additional resources, both locally and nationally.

TYPES OF SUPPORT

AWARDS

Awards are generally made to writers in recognition of outstanding promise or accomplishment. Many of the awards for accomplishment, such as the Heinz Awards or the American Academy of Arts and Letters Awards, are determined by internal nomination only. However, publishers often hold contests and give awards as a means of acquiring new material, and organizations often give awards as a means of raising the visibility of particular groups of writers or genres or the mission of the organization.

For emerging writers, first-book awards such as those offered by Bantam Doubleday Dell (Books for Young Readers), the National Poetry Series, or the Academy of American Poets, provide new talent with remuneration, publication, distribution, and lots of visibility. Even magazine contests like the River City Writing Awards in Fiction or the *Highlights for Children* Fiction Contest offer a chance to get published with more visibility and remuneration than sending a query and work directly to an editor at the same publications.

FELLOWSHIPS

Fellowships are often just another label for awards of recognition. The National Endowment for the Arts and many state arts councils/commissions award individual fellowships in recognition of exceptional talent. These awards include cash amounts to be used for general career advancement. Other significant recognition fellowships include Princeton University's Alfred Hodder Fellowship, which is given (usually) to those from outside academia and in early stages of their careers for independent work in the humanities, and the Pope Foundation's Journalism Awards, an open-ended working fellowship given to mid-career investigative journalists or social commentators.

Some fellowships and/or scholarships are restricted in terms of use, but they can still be wonderful opportunities for writers, furthering both careers and finances. For writers of fiction, nonfiction, poetry, and play/screenwriting, many residency opportunities offer space and a literary community within which to create. In addition to room and board, a small number of residency fellowships also include modest living stipends.

For writers who have the ability to live away from home "in residence" from two weeks to two years, these are wonderful opportunities to build relationships with other writers and to produce work in a supportive environment. Some fellowships, such as those to colonies such as Yaddo or the Fine Arts Work Center in Provincetown, make no other demands on the writer's time. Others, like the Jerome Playwright-in-Residence at the Playwrights' Center in Minneapolis or the Wallace Stegner Fellowships at Stanford University, require fellows to participate in some institutional activity.

Other examples of restricted awards are scholarships offered by many institutions to writers to produce works of particular institutional foci. For example, the Schomburg Center for Research in Black Culture offers stipends of up to $30,000 for scholars studying black history and culture, and the American Institute of Physics gives an annual Science Writing Award in Physics and Astronomy to writing (including journalism and children's) that improves public understanding of physics and astronomy.

GRANTS

Project grants are different from fellowships/awards in that they require a proposal for work to be completed in the future (often within a specific time period), while awards are based on the perceived excellence of past work. Here, again, it is important to ask the staff for clarification. Generally, by "project grant," an agency means "community-oriented project," which lets you know that you need to be collaborating with others, putting your literary skills to work in the service of some community end. (While many agencies do offer grants to individuals, in most cases grants are offered to teams that have an organizational sponsor as the actual applicant.)

For example, a community project might involve offering writing workshops for underserved kids in a particular housing project. In this case, you would want to write a proposal that demonstrates that you and the housing authority people have been collaborating to make this happen—that this isn't just a brainstorm of yours that doesn't already have the approval of the housing authority. Or, a community project might involve a series of readings commemorating special occasions, or a first-ever literary series within an ongoing performing arts festival.

Since the term "grant" typically refers to funds received for an event that you have projected for the future, your idea cannot be judged simply on the merit of work you have already done. Instead, it will be judged on the degree of careful, detailed planning evident in your proposal. What, precisely, will happen, and when? Who will be involved in each phase, as artists, participants, and audience members? What will be the impact on the artists, the participants, and the audience, and how will you know if that impact has happened? How, in short, will you evaluate the project? What is your project timeline for the grant period? Who will be your partners, and how will each partner be involved? It's important to demonstrate up front that these partners are working with you.

Many grants require "matching funds," meaning that for every dollar you hope to receive, you must raise a certain number of dollars elsewhere. It is important to be specific about your sources of matching funds. Even if you don't have them in hand yet, you can show that you have done your homework by saying that you will receive "$500 from the XYZ Trust, to be applied for on December 15" or income from "four hundred chapbooks to be sold at $5" or "freewill donations averaging $100 per reading." Never say just that your funds will come from unspecified "local businesses" or "individual donors," because reviewers will dismiss this as wishful thinking. Find out if the match needs to be cash, or if it can include donated ("in-kind") goods and services.

Most arts agencies that fund projects in which writers are involved will want to see work samples as described below (the same kind of work samples you'll need to prepare for fellowship applications). They will also want to see evidence of collaboration with your community partners and evidence of community need. Ask the staff of the funding organization what kind of support materials are most appropriate.

EMERGENCY FUNDS

These are the rarest of grants for writers, but foundations do exist that provide *professional* writers with short-term grants to help in situations of hardship caused by medical conditions, disability, advanced age, or professional crisis. Among those organizations accepting applications for this type of assistance are the American Society of Journalists, the Authors Charitable Trust, and the Actors Fund of America.

A WORD ABOUT ENTRY FEES

Many awards, including contests and fellowships, require entry fees. This is becoming standard practice for organizations trying to cover hefty reading fees and in-house processing costs. At $15 to $25, these entry fees can add up, so it is important to research the organizations giving the awards and be familiar with their past winners' work. Paying entry fees is nothing to be worried about once:

1) You are sure you've found an appropriate market for your work—i.e., you have a reasonable chance at receiving the award, and

2) The potential benefits (significant prize money, publication by a well-known press, or honor conferred by a venerable institution) exceed the cost.

Note that the presence or absence of an entry fee is *not* an indication of an awarding agency's credibility or merit. It is important to research any organization thoroughly before applying for an award or fellowship.

CRAFTING SUCCESSFUL APPLICATIONS

Not all grants and awards applications require the same materials. However, the requirements are often similar, and eventually you'll need some basic application materials on hand so that when a sudden opportunity arises that's just right for you, your application materials are ready. These include a writing sample, a curriculum vitae (CV), and letters of recommendation/support. These core materials take time to develop, and consequently tend to be of better quality when prepared well in advance.

WORK SAMPLES

Regardless of the kind of award or grant for which you are applying, having an excellent work sample of between ten and thirty pages will be crucial to your success. But how do you know when your work sample is excellent? If your work is being published regularly in standard journals and magazines, chances are your writing is consistently well received. If you're not seeking publication in journals and magazines, start doing so, because in addition to giving you feedback on the "readability" of your work, this will also help you develop a track record as a writer that you can cite in your CV. Since few editors have the time or inclination to comment on submissions, and those that do don't necessarily do so *quickly,* this is obviously something that you'll need to begin well in advance. Getting feedback from publication is an important but long-term strategy for developing a critical sense of your work.

In the short term, joining a writers group can be a way of receiving immediate reaction to new work. Just make sure that the members of your group can offer constructive criticism in addition to being supportive and nurturing. If your group is not doing this for you, or if your group members are not seasoned writers, it may be time to attend a writer's conference or festival that offers manuscript review by established writers, agents, or editors.

By following these strategies for determining what others perceive as good examples of your work, you should be able to identify at least three to five work samples for your application file. Pick and choose from these based on the guidelines of specific applications. Having published as well as unpublished strong work (for publication awards) is also important.

When your work samples are excerpts of longer pieces, try to include sections in which characters are introduced (as in novel excerpts) or that include the thesis of the piece (for nonfiction). Sections of longer work that include a limited number of characters or ideas are often more successful, because readers don't have to rely on context to follow the narrative. Including one brief paragraph of context for the reader—*à précis*—with the work sample or manuscript is also acceptable and helpful for panelists evaluating your application.

THE WRITER'S CURRICULUM VITAE

For both grants and awards, but especially for fellowship and scholarship applications, conveying your professionalism and commitment as a writer is critical to your success. Every writer's CV should have a section for publications; a section for literary activities, including readings and public appearances, coursework or workshops attended or given, and teaching or volunteer activities; and a section listing honors. Beyond your talent as a writer, the people evaluating your applications are often trying to discern the appropriateness and the benefit of an award to a writer. If you're applying for a fellowship appropriate to someone in mid-career, your CV should reflect five to ten years of steady publishing and literary activity. If you're an emerging writer, the prominence of your honors or publication and presentation venues won't be as important, but you'll still be expected to demonstrate that you're actively seeking to participate in your literary community. If you're just starting out, attend local readings and writing workshops, share your work and knowledge with the organizers, and let them know you'd like to participate. There should also be room on your CV for professional experience and education information, but these should generally be included at the end of the CV, rather than at the beginning.

LETTERS OF RECOMMENDATION AND/OR SUPPORT

Hopefully, you will have met a few other writers or editors (a teacher at the very least!) who've had great things to say about your work. Stay in touch with these people, because sooner or later, you'll need letters of recommendation for some of your applications. When that time comes, and as far ahead of the application deadline as possible, ask your recommender for a letter. Be sure to explain what you're applying for and why you're asking for his or her recommendation. Go ahead and remind that person what he or she found so attractive about your work: the more specific the praise, the more convincing the letter.

Similarly, if you're writing a project proposal for a grant, you might benefit from having three to five potential "letters of support" sources in mind. Ideal sources are prominent individuals and key organizations relevant to your project, who can write a letter of support for your proposal that demonstrates knowledge of and enthusiasm for your project. For grant proposals where such testimonies are permitted, letters of support can move the judges' perception of a project from possibility to actuality—a subtle but powerful edge in the competitive grants arena. Just be sure to give your sources as much advance notice as possible (once you've established that including support letters with your proposal is permissible). You might also want to share a rough draft of your proposal with the source, and then look over the letter to make sure there are no errors or inconsistencies with your proposal *before* the letter gets signed.

PREPARING APPLICATION-SPECIFIC MATERIALS

MAKE SURE GUIDELINES ARE CURRENT

After obtaining general information on an award or grant and deciding that your work is a good match for the opportunity, contact the granting organization for current guidelines. Send a brief note of request along with an SASE. Current guidelines may also be available on organizational Web sites, but always check posting dates to be sure you're not looking at last year's forms. Call or send an e-mail with any questions or concerns about the application, and always use an organization's official application form, if required.

Make several copies of the form, and complete a practice copy to make sure your information can be concisely and clearly presented. When you're satisfied with your answers, type them neatly onto the original. The staff—especially in public agencies—is responsible for assisting you to the best of its ability; don't be shy about asking questions on anything you want clarified.

Here are a few questions that are worth asking, for they will guide you in providing information:

- What is the ideal formatting? Very often, the guidelines won't give you details like spacing, margins, minimum type size, or binding, so don't hesitate to ask.
- Who will be reviewing the proposals (e.g., staff, publishers, fellow writers, etc.)?
- What types of support materials would be helpful to include with the application?
- Can you expect feedback on your work samples?
- How many submissions are anticipated by the organization, and how many awards will be made?

Once you've determined exactly what is required for a particular application, you're ready to write any application-specific materials necessary, such as the creative purpose statement, the needs statement, or the grant proposal. The key to all of these materials is keeping them brief, accurate, specific, and relevant to the particular opportunity for which you are applying. Add these to your impressive core materials and your impeccable application forms, and you've got a winning combination for success in the grants-and-awards arena.

THE CREATIVE PURPOSE STATEMENT

Creative Purpose Statements, or Artist Statements, are often required for fellowship and scholarship award applications. Outstanding creative purpose statements are concise and specific statements focused on the anticipated outcomes for a writer receiving a particular grant. In less than two pages, try and capture your development as a writer to date. Briefly include your achievements, and then describe the benefits that would be afforded to you as writer-in-development as a result of receiving the award for which you are applying.

For example, an emerging fiction writer who has published three stories, has six others finished, and is applying for a fellowship for a residency at the Atlantic Center for the Arts, could emphasize the benefit of working closely with a "master" fiction writer. (The Atlantic Center for the Arts has a mentoring program that pairs emerging and established writers.) The applicant might propose that working with a "master" writer would allow him or her to learn how to develop and organize a book of short stories, and include his or her vision for what that book might be. The applicant could also compare and contrast his or her work with the "master" writer's and offer an explanation as to how both writers would benefit from working together. Lastly, the applicant, knowing from the guidelines that financial need should be established along with artistic merit, could explain specific financial obligations or limited annual income that prevents him or her from taking advantage of the residency opportunity to advance his or her development as a writer without the assistance of a fellowship.

STATEMENT OF NEED

Foundations and associations providing emergency funds for writers in need will scan an applicant's statement of need for two main qualities: evidence that the applicant is a professional writer, and evidence that the applicant is indeed experiencing hardship for which he or she has no other recourse. To establish yourself as a professional writer, you should describe the span of your career, and back this description up with your CV. You may even want to include a tax return on which "writer" or "author" is listed for occupation. You want to make a clear connection between writing and your livelihood in order to motivate the reviewer to read on about your case.

The best case for hardship is built with a specific detailing of events in chronological order, ending with your current circumstance and documented need. Do you have medical bills that exceed your ability to pay for them? Including a tax return, annual budget, and copies of the bills and a documented medical diagnosis will establish this case.

TIPS FOR GRANT PROPOSALS

The acronym "PLEASE" is an organizing principle and "secret recipe" for a successful grant proposal:

P is for Passion—Don't be afraid to let it show

We're often asked about using a professional grant writer, and we recommend against it. No one can tell your story with the same passion that you can, and in your own words. Use a forceful tone (you *know* you're going to do that project, right?).

L is for Literally Follow Every Direction

One state arts agency estimates that over a third of the proposals they receive don't follow the guidelines. Common mistakes include: exceeding the page limit, using a typeface that's too small, or submitting one big essay instead of answers to each question. There's a reason for every requirement. If you don't follow all instructions to the letter, it can really hurt you. Take the example of one grant writer who called the National Endowment for the Arts to see whether "no more than ten pages" meant ten single-sided or double-sided pages—and was glad she did. Half of her proposal would have been thrown out.

E *is for Easy to Understand*

What, exactly, will you spend the money on? It's amazing how many proposals go on for many pages and never say, exactly, what's going to happen or how the money will be used. Find someone on your team who can write a good freshman composition. This includes a topic sentence, active verbs, and paragraphs that relate. Use action verbs and the active voice. Make sure your proposal tells your story in a way that anyone will understand it, including someone who doesn't know you at all. There's no need to write a proposal that resembles a government document—the reviewers will probably be writers like you.

A *is for Accuracy in All, from Assertions to Arithmetic*

Make sure that your assertions of what will happen and how many people will be involved are grounded in reality—and that your budget figures are, too. Make sure that your claims relate to your budget. For instance, if you say that your total attendance will be five thousand, and your organization sells tickets to events, then income should reflect five thousand times a reasonable ticket price. The reviewers are likely to know what is realistic. Budget-padding is too easy to spot. By the same token, don't undervalue your work, hoping that if it's cheap, it will be funded.

S *is for Show Me with Specifics and Examples*

We're talking about arts proposals that will probably be reviewed by artists. Assuming that the guidelines allow you to provide sample work, it's more powerful to give people sounds rather than a description of sounds. An image of a painter's personal work can help the reviewers imagine the mural she would create with kids. Many a grant-writing error has been forgiven if the art is inspired.

Consider these examples:

Instead of this . . .

Music of great quality and diversity will be performed for underserved audiences in locations convenient for them.

. . . try saying it this way:

A chamber group from the Big Apple Symphony will perform short selections from contemporary composers on Sunday afternoons for three hundred senior citizens gathered in the dining room of their nursing home. (See Attachments 1 and 2 for a tape of the chamber group and three possible programs.)

The second version provides a mental picture that a reviewer can see, and music that a reviewer can hear.

E *is for Easy to Read—Margins, typeface, and white space*

Think about it. The reviewers may be reading fifty proposals, skimming them again at the last minute to refresh their memories. The agency may limit each review to a very few minutes. So, make it easy for the reviewers—use white space, bullets, a clear organizational scheme, a typeface that's large and clean, good margins, and underlines for key points.

WHEN TO GIVE UP

As long as you find satisfaction in your work, the answer is, *never.* Ultimately, grants and awards are only a means to spur and sustain writers, and not a measure of the value of a writer's work. Competition for grants and awards is fierce, and the subjective nature of evaluating "excellence," "talent," and "merit" means that an application that "fails" with one jury may find success with the next. Walt Whitman published his own work (and wrote his own favorable reviews) for lack of patronage. Recognition is not a requirement for excellent work.

SECTION 5 RESOURCES

BUSINESS AND TECHNICAL WRITING

GENERAL
Business and Technical Communication
www.cohums.ohio-state.edu/english/areas/bizcom.htm
Links to business and technical communications journals, organizations, discussion lists, and related pages.

Business Writer's Free Library
www.mapnp.org/library/commskls/cmm_writ.htm
An extensive collection of links, resources, and references for business and technical writers, including correspondence and document samples, reference materials, basic writing skills, and "general advice."

The National Writers Union (NWU)
www.nwu.org
Offers a variety of services to members, including a job hotline.

Society for Technical Communication
www.stctoronto.org
Articles, links, and other resources for technical writers and communicators.

Technical Writing
http://techwriting.miningco.com
Gary Conroy's extensive coverage of business and technical writing.

The Well-Fed Writer
www.wellfedwriter.com
Peter Bowerman's home page. In addition to excerpts from his book, *The Well-Fed Writer,* and an excellent FAQ on business writing, Bowerman offers a section "for women only" on women in business and a wide selection of links to other business writing (and general writing) resources.

WritersWrite: Business Communications
www.writerswrite.com/buscomm
A selection of links to business writing resources online.

Writers Write Resources for Technical Writers
www.writerswrite.com/technical/techlink.htm
Links to information on book publishing, electronic publishing, desktop publishing, medical writing, "RoboHelp," software, standards references, technical dictionaries, technical news, translation, and more.

SETTING FEES
Fee and Scheduling Guidelines
www.tiac.net/users/freelanc/fees.html
A handy guide from the Freelance Editorial Association on how to set fees for different types of freelance writing and editorial jobs.

National Survey: Freelance and Contract Writer's Rates
www.nwu.org/hotline/hotsurv.htm
An overview of average pay rates in different areas of the writing business, including business writing, Web authoring and design, ghostwriting, journalism, copyediting and proofreading, grant writing, and more.

Putting a Price on Your Capabilities: How to Set Your Fees as a Freelance Writer
www.writedirection.com/rprt300e.htm
A complex examination of how to figure your fees, based on your expenses, cost of living, etc.

Salary.com
www.salary.com
Use the "Salary Wizard" to determine typical rates for business/writing jobs in specific regions.

What to Pay a Writer
www.writers.ca/whattopay.htm
A good overview of freelance fees and rates for such jobs as advertising, business writing, editing, ghostwriting, magazine writing, technical writing, translation, and more. Though the rates are listed in Canadian dollars (this page is from the Periodical Writers Association of Canada), the same numbers are applicable to U.S. writers.

SITES FOR EDITORS AND COPYEDITORS
CopyEditor: Language News for the Publishing Profession
www.copyeditor.com
Includes an extensive job board for copyeditors.

Editorial Freelancers Association
www.the-efa.org/main.html
Events, links, articles, and benefits for editorial freelancers.

Editorial Freelancers' Home Page
http://server06.nerc.com/freelancer
Links for editorial freelancers, plus a selection of articles on the "freelancing life."

The Writers-Editors Network
www.writers-editors.com
A membership organization of writers and editors. The Web site offers a good selection of free tips on marketing and business writing.

JOB SITES
American Journalism Review Job Link for Journalists
http://ajr.newslink.org/joblink/
Usually offers an interesting selection of jobs around the country, as well as international listings.

Authorlink Jobs Available
www.authorlink.com/jobavail.html

Avalanche of Writing Jobs
www.sunoasis.com

craigslist
www.craigslist.com/wri/
This site focuses primarily on job listings in the San Francisco/Peninsula/Bay Area.

Cassell Network of Writers
www.writers-editors.com
List yourself in the Writer Data Bank, or join the network to find market information. The site also has some handy tips.

Editor and Publisher Classifieds
www.editorandpublisher.com/ephome/class/classhtm/employment.htm

Freelance Online
www.FreelanceOnline.com/faqs.html

JobsPage: Your Link to Newspaper Careers
www.freep.com/jobspage/high/NAAguide.htm

MediaBistro.com (formerly HireMinds)
www.mediabistro.com

NewsJobs Network
www.newsjobs.net
Editing and writing jobs for the U.S., Canada, and the U.K. Free newsletter and discussions.

Telecommuter's Digest
www.tdigest.com
An e-zine for telecommuters.

Telecommuting Jobs
www.tjobs.com/index.shtml

University of California/Berkeley J-Jobs
www.journalism.berkeley.edu/jobs/
Though this site focuses primarily on journalism-related jobs, you'll also find listings for magazine positions and freelance writing.

The Write Jobs
www.writerswrite.com/jobs

WritersWeekly.com
www.writersweekly.com
A weekly e-mail newsletter that lists a variety of writing positions.

Writing Job Center
www.poewar.com/jobs.htm

SPEAKING AND TEACHING OPPORTUNITIES

CONFERENCES
The Guide to Writers Conferences and Workshops
http://writing.shawguides.com

CLASSES
The Guide to Writers Conferences and Workshops
http://writing.shawguides.com

2001 Colleges, College Scholarships, and Financial Aid Page
www.college-scholarships.com/
You can find a listing of colleges in every state on this page. However, the listing doesn't pro-vide mailing addresses, and in many cases doesn't give a phone number, so you can't easily determine what area the college may be in. It does give an e-mail address for the admissions department, but this often won't be the address you need to find out more about continuing education sources.

American Universities
www.clas.ufl.edu/CLAS/american-universities.html
Lists colleges alphabetically. Does not provide an opportunity for regional searching.

Canadian Universities
www.uwaterloo.ca/canu/
Lists universities by province. Does not provide e-mail addresses or a more detailed regional search ability.

College and University Homepages—Geographical Listing
www.mit.edu:8001/people/cdemello/geog.html
Links to universities around the world.

Community College Web
www.mcli.dist.maricopa.edu/cc/
Allows you to search for community colleges by region, college name, or keyword. Gives the city in which the college is located and a link to the college Web site.

The University Pages
http://isl-garnet.uah.edu/Universities/universitiestx.html
Lists universities and colleges by state.

CHATS
About.com
http://home.about.com/arts/chat.htm
Visit the "Art/Entertainment Area" for a list of guides that host chats and forums. Java required.

America Online
www.aol.com
Chats are held in several areas, including "Writers Club Romance Group" (Keyword: WCRG), "Fictional Realm" (Keyword: Books), "Book Central" (Keyword: BC), "Other Side of Creativity" (Keyword: OSC), and "Amazing Instant Novelist" (Keyword: Novel).

Byron's Romance Port
www.geocities.com/Athens/8774
Chats for writers include "Bookaholics," "Kensington Interactive," and "NovelTalk."

The Chat Hole
www.geocities.com/SouthBeach/Breakers/5257/Chathole.htm
A site listing links to a wide range of chat topics, along with useful articles on how to participate in a chat.

CNN Interactive Interviews
www.cnn.com/chat/
"Multimedia interviews with your favorite authors."

Compuserve
www.compuserve.com
"Litforum" offers several areas and chat groups for writers.

Delphi
www.delphi.com
Look for writer chats (in both Java and HTML) in the "Creative Arts" area, which includes the Painted Rock Writer's Colony.

From the Heart Online
www.delphi.com/FTH
Romance Writers of America holds a weekly public chat on Thursdays at 9:00 p.m. EST. It also hosts a number of workshops open only to members.

The Literary Times
www.tlt.com/news/itiner.htm
Provides a place for romance authors to post events such as chats and book signings.

Reader's Choice Book Chat
www.thegrid.net/dakaiser/books/chat.htm
"An online community created by book lovers for book lovers."

Romance Central
http://romance-central.com/chat.htm

Romance Club
www.theromanceclub.com
A "writer's chat" hosted every Thursday from 9:00 to 11:00 P.M. EST.

TalkCity
http://talkcity.com/neighborhood/entertainment.htmpl
A site dedicated to talk and discussion, including author chats and general reading chats (e.g., "SF&Lit Chat, a discussion of the best and brightest in SF&F literature"). Transcripts of previous chats are also available.

Word Museum
www.wordmuseum.com
Word Museum's Friday chats (10:00 P.M. EST) frequently feature guest authors, agents, and editors. Transcripts from such sessions are often available.

WordsWorth
www.wordsworth.com/www/present/interviews/
A bookstore that hosts author interviews and author promotional pages.

The Writer's BBS
www.writers-bbs.com/chat.html
Offers chat rooms, discussion forums, and an e-zine titled, "Fish Eggs for the Soul."

Writers Write Chat
www.writerswrite.net

ONLINE CLASSES
Coffeehouse for Writers: Workshops
www.coffeehouseforwriters.com/courses.html

CourseBridge.com
www.coursebridge.com

Freelance Success Institute
www.freelancesuccess.com

MagazineWriting.com
www.MagazineWriting.com
"Online study for aspiring magazine writers," featuring beginning and advanced classes.

Painted Rock Writers and Readers Colony
www.paintedrock.com/conference/wrtclass.htm

Romance Writers Homepage
www.simegen.com/out-t/school/OnlineLessons/index.html
Chat-based courses on romance writing and other topics.

School for Champions
www.school-for-champions.com/writing.htm
Courses on writing methods, technical writing, and fiction writing.

UCLA
www.onlinelearning.net/

Word Museum
www.wordmuseum.com

WritersBureau
www.writersbureau.com/wxx.html
A U.K. school, apparently based on correspondence.

WritersCollege.com
www.WritersCollege.com
Offers almost 60 online courses in a variety of genres and fields.

Writers.com
www.writers.com/writing-classes.htm
For individual tutoring, see *www.writers.com/tutors.htm*.

WritersOnlineWorkshops.com
www.writersonlineworkshops.com
Writer's Digest online workshops and classes.

Writer's Village University
http://4-writers.com

Writers Workshops
www.nwu.org/links/lnkwks.htm
A list of online and offline workshops, seminars, writers' groups, and discussion lists

WritingClasses.com (formerly Gotham Writers' Workshop)
www.writingclasses.com/
This is an excellent place to acquaint yourself with how online classes work. It offers a "sample" class that enables one to explore a syllabus, posted lectures, student forums, homework assignments, etc.

Writing Corner
http://writingcorner.com/courses/main.htm
Links to writing courses and schools.

WritingSchool.com
www.WritingSchool.com

GRANTS AND PROPOSALS

GENERAL RESOURCES
Money for Writers, edited by Diane Billot (Owl Books)

FundsforWriters
http://groups.yahoo.com/group/FundsforWriters
A mailing list with announcements of contests, awards, grants, and other sources of funding.

Newswise Guide to Journalism Grants and Fellowships 2000–2001
www.newswise.com/grants.htm

Online Grant Writing Workshop (by Maryo Ewell)
www.umass.edu/aes/grantscript8AB2.htm
More tips from the coauthor of chapter 22.

State and Jurisdictional Arts Agencies
www.pixi.com/~cpac/saas.htm
List of state, national, and regional funding agencies.

FUNDING AGENCIES—U.S. NATIONAL AND REGIONAL
National Endowment for the Arts
1100 Pennsylvania Avenue NW
Washington, D.C. 20506
PH: (202) 682–5400; FAX: (202) 682–5721
http://arts.endow.gov

National Assembly of State Arts Agencies
1029 Vermont Avenue, NW, Second Floor
Washington, D.C. 20005
PH: (202) 347–6352; FAX: (202) 737–0526
http://nasaa-arts.org

Americans for the Arts
1000 Vermont Avenue, NW, Twelfth Floor
Washington, D.C. 20005
PH: (202) 371–2830; FAX: (202) 371–0424
www.artsusa.org

Hennepin Center for the Arts
528 Hennepin Avenue, Suite 310
Minneapolis, Minnesota 55403
PH: (612) 341–0755
www.artswire.org/Artswire/artsmidwest/home.htm

Mid-America Arts Alliance
912 Baltimore Avenue, Suite 700
Kansas City, Missouri 64105
PH: (816) 421–1388; FAX: (816) 421–3918
www.maaa.org

Mid Atlantic Arts Foundation
22 Light Street, #330
Baltimore, Maryland 21202
PH: (410) 539–6656, ext. 105; FAX: (410) 837–5517
www.charm.net/~midarts/

New England Foundation for the Arts
330 Congress Street, Sixth Floor
Boston, Massachusetts 02210–1216
PH: (617) 951–0010; FAX: (617) 951–0016
www.nefa.org

Western States Arts Federation
1543 Champa Street, Suite 220
Denver, Colorado 80202
PH: (303) 629–1166; FAX: (303) 629–9717
www.westaf.org

Guam Council on the Arts and Humanities
Office of the Governor
Post Office Box 2950
Agana, Guam 96910
PH: 011–671–647–2242
www.guam.net/gov/kaha

Commonwealth Council for Arts and Culture
Post Office Box 553
CHRB, CNMI Convention Center
Commonwealth of the Northern Mariana Islands
Saipan, MP 96950
PH: 011–670–322–9982
www.nasaa-arts.org/new/nasa/gateway/NorthernM.html

U.S. STATE ARTS COUNCILS
Alabama State Council on the Arts
1 Dexter Avenue
Montgomery, Alabama 36130
PH: (334) 242–4076
www.arts.state.al.us

Alaska State Council on the Arts
411 West 4th Avenue, Suite 1E
Anchorage, Alaska 99501–2343
PH: (907) 269–6610
www.educ.state.ak.us/ASCA/home.html

Arizona Commission on the Arts

417 West Roosevelt
Phoenix, Arizona 85003
PH: (602) 255–5882; FAX: (602) 256–0282
http://az.arts.asu.edu/artscomm

Arkansas Arts Council

1500 Tower Building
323 Center Street
Little Rock, Arkansas 72201
PH: (501) 324–9766
www.arkansasarts.com

California Arts Council

1300 I Street, Suite 930
Sacramento, California 95814
PH: (916) 322–6555, (800) 201–6200; FAX: (916) 322–6575
www.cac.ca.gov

Colorado Council on the Arts

750 Pennsylvania Street
Denver, Colorado 80203–3699
PH: (303) 894–2617
www.coloarts.state.co.us

Connecticut Commission on the Arts

755 Main Street
One Financial Plaza
Hartford, Connecticut 06103
PH: (860) 566–4770; FAX: (860) 566–6462
www.cslnet.ctstateu.edu/cca/

Delaware Division of the Arts

State Office Building
820 North French Street
Wilmington, Delaware 19801
PH: (302) 577–3540
www.artsdel.org

District of Columbia Commission on the Arts and Humanities
410 8th Street NW, Fifth Floor
Washington, D.C. 20004
PH: (202) 724–5613; FAX: (202) 727–4135
http://dcarts.dc.gov/about/main.shtm

Division of Cultural Affairs
Florida Department of State
The Capitol
Tallahassee, Florida 32399–0250
PH: (850) 487–2980; FAX: (850) 922–5259
www.dos.state.fl.us/dca/

Southern Arts Federation
1401 Peachtree Street, Suite 460
Atlanta, Georgia 30309
PH: (404) 874–7244
www.southarts.org

Georgia Council for the Arts
530 Means Street NW, Suite 115
Atlanta, Georgia 30318–5730
www.arts-ga.com

State Foundation on Culture and the Arts
44 Merchant Street
Honolulu, Hawaii 96813
PH: (808) 586–0300; FAX: (808) 586–0308
www.state.hi.us/sfca

Consortium for Pacific Arts and Cultures
2141C Atherton Road
Honolulu, Hawaii 96822
PH: (808) 946–7381

Idaho Commission on the Arts
Post Office Box 83720
Boise, Idaho 83720–0008
PH: (208) 334–2119; FAX: (208) 334–2488
www.state.id.us/arts/

Illinois Arts Council
100 West Randolph, Suite 10–500
Chicago, Illinois 60601
PH: (312) 814–6750; FAX: (312) 814–1471
www.state.il.us/agency/iac/

Indiana Arts Commission
402 West Washington Street, Room 72
Indianapolis, Indiana 46204–2741
PH: (317) 232–1268; FAX: (317) 232–5595
www.state.in.us/iac/index.html

Iowa Arts Council
600 East Locust
State Capitol Complex
Des Moines, Iowa 50319
PH: (515) 281–4451
www.culturalaffairs.org/iac/index.html

Kansas Arts Commission
Jayhawk Tower
700 Jackson, Suite 1004
Topeka, Kansas 66603
PH: (785) 296–3335
http://arts.state.ks.us

Kentucky Arts Council
31 Fountain Place
Frankfort, Kentucky 40601
PH: (502) 564–3757
www.kyarts.org

Division of the Arts
Louisiana Department of Culture, Recreation, and Tourism
1051 North Third Street
Post Office Box 44247
Baton Rouge, Louisiana 70804
PH: (225) 342–8180; FAX: (225) 342–8173
www.crt.state.la.us/crt/ocd/doapage/doapage.htm

Maine Arts Commission
55 Capitol Street
State House Station 25
Augusta, Maine 04333–0025
PH: (207) 287–2724; FAX: (207) 287–2335
www.mainearts.com

Maryland State Arts Council
601 North Howard Street, First Floor
Baltimore, Maryland 21201
PH: (410) 767–6555; FAX: (410) 333–1062
www.msac.org

Massachusetts Cultural Council
120 Boylston Street, Second Floor
Boston, Massachusetts 02116–4600
PH: (617) 727–3668; FAX: (617) 727–0044
www.massculturalcouncil.org

Michigan Council for Arts
and Cultural Affairs
525 West Ottawa Street
Post Office Box 30705
Lansing, Michigan 48909
PH: (517) 241–4011
www.commerce.state.mi.us/arts

Minnesota State Arts Board
Park Square Court
400 Sibley Street, Suite 200
St. Paul, Minnesota 55101–1949
PH: (612) 215–1600
www.arts.state.mn.us

Mississippi Arts Commission
239 North Lamar Street, Suite 207
Jackson, Mississippi 39201
PH: (601) 359–6030; FAX: (601) 359–6008
www.arts.state.ms.us

Missouri State Council on the Arts
Wainwright Office Complex
111 North Seventh Street, Suite 105
St. Louis, Missouri 63101
PH: (314) 340–6845; FAX: (314) 340–7215
www.ecodev.state.mo.us/moartscouncil

Montana Arts Council
316 North Park Avenue, Room 252
Helena, Montana 59620–2201
PH: (406) 444–6430; FAX: (406) 444–6548
www.state.mt.us/art/default.htm

Nebraska Arts Council
Joslyn Castle Carriage House
3838 Davenport Street
Omaha, Nebraska 68131–2329
PH: (402) 595–2122, (800) 341–4067; FAX: (402) 595–2334
www.nebraskaartscouncil.org

Nevada Arts Council
Capitol Complex
602 North Curry Street
Carson City, Nevada 89710
PH: (702) 687–6680
http://dmla.clan.lib.nv.us/docs/arts

New Hampshire State Council on the Arts
40 North Main Street
Concord, New Hampshire 03301–4974
PH: (603) 271–2789; FAX: (603) 271–3584
www.state.nh.us/nharts/

New Jersey State Council on the Arts
Post Office Box 306
20 West State Street, #306
Trenton, New Jersey 08625–0306
PH: (609) 292–6130; FAX: (609) 989–1440
www.artswire.org/Artswire/njsca

New Mexico Arts Division
228 East Palace Avenue
Santa Fe, New Mexico 87501
PH: (505) 827–6490

New York State Council on the Arts
915 Broadway
New York, New York 10010
PH: (212) 387–7000
www.nysca.org

North Carolina Arts Council
Department of Cultural Resources
Raleigh, North Carolina 27601–2807
PH: (919) 733–2821
www.ncarts.org

North Dakota Council on the Arts
418 East Broadway Avenue, Suite 70
Bismarck, North Dakota 58501–4086
PH: (701) 328–3954; FAX: (701) 328–3963
www.state.nd.us/arts

Ohio Arts Council
727 East Main Street
Columbus, Ohio 43205–1796
PH: (614) 466–2613; FAX: (614) 466–4494

Oklahoma Arts Council
Post Office Box 52001–2001
Oklahoma City, Oklahoma 73152–2001
PH: (405) 521–2931; FAX: (405) 521–6418
www.state.ok.us/~arts

Oregon Arts Commission
775 Summer Street, NE
Salem, Oregon 97310
PH: (503) 986–0082
http://art.econ.state.or.us

Commonwealth of Pennsylvania
Council on the Arts
Finance Building, Room 216
Harrisburg, Pennsylvania 17120
PH: (717) 787–6883; FAX: (717) 783–2538
www.artsnet.org/pca

Institute of Puerto Rican Culture
Apartado Postal 4184
San Juan, Puerto Rico 00902–4184
PH: (809) 723–2115

Rhode Island State Council on the Arts
95 Cedar Street, Suite 103
Providence, Rhode Island 02903
PH: (401) 277–3880; FAX: (401) 521–1351
www.risca.state.ri.us

South Carolina Arts Commission
1800 Gervais Street
Columbia, South Carolina 29201
PH: (803) 734–8696; FAX: (803) 734–8526
www.state.sc.us/arts/

South Dakota Arts Council
Office of Arts, Department of Education and Cultural Affairs
800 Governors Drive
Pierre, South Dakota 57501–2294
PH: (605) 773–3131; FAX: (605) 773–6962
www.state.sd.us/state/executive/deca/sdarts/sdarts.htm

Tennessee Arts Commission
Citizens Plaza
401 Charlotte Avenue
Nashville, Tennessee 37243–0780
PH: (615) 741–1701; FAX: (615) 741–8559
www.arts.state.tn.us

Texas Commission on the Arts
Post Office Box 13406
Austin, Texas 78711–3406
PH: (512) 463–5535; FAX: (512) 475–2699
www.arts.state.tx.us

Utah Arts Council
617 East South Temple Street
Salt Lake City, Utah 84102–1177
PH: (801) 236–7555; FAX: (801) 236–7556
www.dced.state.ut.us/arts

Vermont Arts Council
136 State Street, Drawer 33
Montpelier, Vermont 05633–6001
PH: (802) 828–3291; FAX: (802) 828–3363
www.vermontartscouncil.org/index1.htm

Virginia Commission for the Arts
223 Governor Street
Richmond, Virginia 23219
PH: (804) 225–3132
www.artswire.org/~vacomm

Virgin Islands Council on the Arts
41–42 Norre Gade, Second Floor
Post Office Box 103
St. Thomas, Virgin Islands 00802
PH: (340) 774–5984
www.nasaa-arts.org/new/nasaa/gateway/VI.html

Washington State Arts Commission
234 East Eighth Avenue
Post Office Box 42675
Olympia, Washington 98504–2675
PH: (360) 753–3858; FAX: (360) 586–5351
www.wa.gov/art/

Arts and Humanities Section
West Virginia Division of Culture and History
1900 Kanawha Boulevard East
Capitol Complex
Charleston, West Virginia 25305–0300
PH: (304) 558–0220
www.wvculture.org/arts/index.html

Wisconsin Arts Board
101 East Wilson Street, First Floor
Madison, Wisconsin 53702
PH: (608) 266–0190; FAX: (608) 267–0380
www.arts.state.wi.us

Wyoming Arts Council
2320 Capitol Avenue
Cheyenne, Wyoming 82002
PH: (307) 777–7742; FAX: (307) 777–5499
http://commerce.state.wy.us/CR/Arts/

COLONIES AND RESIDENCIES
Written By: Writers' Colonies
www.wga.org/WrittenBy/1998/0298/colonies.html
Article about writers' colonies, with a list of colonies and links at the end.

Villa Montalvo Artist Residency Program
Box 158
Saratoga, California 95071

PEN Northwest
Boyden Wilderness Writing Residency
c/o John Daniel
23030 West Sheffler Road
Elmira, Oregon 97437

University of Arizona Poetry Center
Summer Residency Program
1216 North Cherry Avenue
Post Office Box 210410
Tucson, Arizona 85721–0410
PH: (520) 321–7760
www.coh.arizona.edu/poetry/index.htm

Japan-United States Friendship Commission
1120 Vermont Avenue NW, Suite 925
Washington, D.C. 20005
PH: (202) 275–7712; FAX: (202) 275–7413
www.jusfc.gov/commissn/commissn.html

Millay Colony for the Arts
East Hill Road, Box 3
Austerlitz, New York 12017
PH: (518) 392–3103

Ragdale Foundation
Frances Shaw Fellowship
1260 North Green Bay Road
Lake Forest, Illinois 60045
PH: (847) 234–1063

Vermont Studio Center
Fellowship Competition
Post Office Box 613PW
Johnson, Vermont 05656
PH: (802) 635–2727
www.vermontstudiocenter.com

Lucky Dog
Studio #11
Post Office Box 65552
St. Paul, Minnesota 55165
PH: (651) 776–1738

Inroads Arts International
809 United Nations Plaza
New York, New York 10017
PH: (212) 984–5588

EMERGENCY FUNDING
Gottleib Foundation
380 West Broadway
New York, New York 10012

The Awards Secretary
Society of Authors
84 Drayton Gardens
London SW10 9SB, England

INTERNATIONAL
Arts Council of England
14 Great Peter Street
London SW1P 3NQ, England
PH: 011–44–0171–973–6472
www.artscouncil.org.uk

The Awards Secretary
Society of Authors
84 Drayton Gardens
London SW10 9SB, England

Australia Council
Post Office Box 788
Strawberry Hills, New South Wales
2012 Australia
PH: 011–02–9950–9000; FAX: 011–02–9950–9111

Arts Council of New Zealand
Third Floor, Southern Cross Building
Corner High and Victoria Streets
Post Office Box 1425
Auckland, New Zealand
PH: 011–09–373–3066; FAX: 011–09–377–6795
www.creativenz.govt.nz/main.html

Canada Council for the Arts
350 Albert Street
Post Office Box 1047
Ottawa, Ontario
Canada K1P 5V8
PH: (613) 566–4414; FAX: (613) 566–4390
www.canadacouncil.ca

A Final Word:
Capitalizing on Success

M uch of this book has focused on how to prepare a pitch or proposal in such a way as to minimize your chances of rejection. But what happens when you succeed? What comes next?

Don't let success take you by surprise. While it's unwise to count your chickens before they're hatched—or spend your advance before your proposal has been accepted—you should have some ideas about what you will do when you get that letter you've been hoping for. Here are some tips on what to do after the celebration:

- **Read the acceptance letter carefully.** Make sure you understand what is expected of you. Has an editor made any changes to your proposal? Are you being asked to make changes to your work or idea? If so, are those changes acceptable?

- **Review any terms that have been offered with care.** Don't be so overcome with joy at the thought of getting published that you throw caution to the winds. Book contracts, in particular, tend to be written in dense legalese (though I have also seen a four-page magazine contract). If you have any doubts about the rights you're being asked to grant, or the compensation you will receive, have your contract reviewed by a qualified contract or copyright lawyer.

- **Make sure you can provide what you have promised** (or what is being asked of you) by the specified deadline. If you've promised to hand in a complete novel in one month, and you really *haven't* finished the final draft, it's time to get writing.

- **Make sure that you deliver exactly what the editor, publisher, or agent expects.** Don't do a "bait and switch." Fulfill your end of the agreement to the letter, and then some.
- **If you have any doubts about anything, call the editor or agent for clarification.** Get all important terms and agreements in writing.

Finally, perhaps the most important step of all is to *follow up!* You will never be as "hot" as you are right now. Follow up that magazine query with another query. Follow up your book proposal with another idea. Go back to that editor or agent *now,* while s/he remembers you and is impressed with your work. Keep the queries and proposals flowing. Establish yourself as a regular, reliable, high-quality contributor. If you're writing for a business client, go back for more business, or ask for referrals.

That's the way to keep work—and checks—flowing across your desk. By following up immediately on a positive response, you'll not only land more assignments, but you're also likely to find that, before too long, editors start calling *you* with ideas. And then you'll be in the ideal position to decide whether to accept—or to write a rejection letter of your own!

CONTRIBUTOR BIOS

PETER BOWERMAN (quoted in chapter 22) is the author of *The Well-Fed Writer: Financial Self-Sufficiency as a Freelance Writer in Six Months or Less*. For more information on corporate and business freelancing, visit his Web site at *www.wellfedwriter.com*.

ROBIN CATESBY, whose comments on speaking with an agent at a writing conference appear in chapter 14, is a short-story writer, novelist, and author of ten plays, including three highly successful children's musicals. She is a member of Willamette Writers and assists in the agent/editor pitch area during their annual conference. For more information, visit *www.sff.net/people/catesby*.

AMY CHAVEZ ("Newspaper Queries," "How to Become a Syndicated Columnist," "How to Become an International Columnist") writes a humor column for *The Japan Times*. Her work has appeared in humor magazines, in-flight magazines, anthologies, ESL textbooks, and newspapers around the world. She is currently working on a new book, *Getting in Touch with Your Inner Bonsai*. Visit her Web site at *www.amychavez.com,* or subscribe to her weekly *Japan Times* column at *www.egroups.com/subscribe/JapanLite*. She can be reached by e-mail at *amychavez@excite.com*.

A.C. CRISPIN ("Display Sites") is the author of twenty novels and works with The Write Connection to identify and warn aspiring authors about the dangers of various types of scams.

MARYJANICE DAVIDSON ("Chat Your Way to Sales") has sold ten books to five different publishers in the last three years. She writes across a variety of genres, including young adult, romance, nonfiction, and paranormal. Her latest release, *Escape the Slush Pile,* is available from The Fiction Works. Davidson's column, "Book Promotion on a Budget," is featured on Inkspot. For more information, visit her Web site at *www.usinternet.com/users/alongi/index.html*. Davidson welcomes e-mails at *alongi@usinternet.com*.

MARYO EWELL ("Grants for Writers") has been an associate director at the Colorado Council on the Arts since 1982. Prior to that, she worked for the Illinois Arts Council and for two community arts councils in Connecticut. In 1995, she was awarded the Selina Roberts Ottum Award by Americans for the Arts, acknowledging leadership in the community arts field.

DEBBIE FARMER ("How I Became a Syndicated Columnist") is a contributor to *Chicken Soup for the Soul*. Her family humor essays have been published in over five hundred publications throughout the United States, Canada, and Australia. Her award-winning weekly family humor column, "Family Daze," is internationally syndicated by Paradigm-TSA and is available to run in newspapers, magazines, and newsletters, or on Web sites. For information contact *Features@familydaze.com* or visit the Family Daze Web site: *www.familydaze.com*.

LYNN FLEWELLING ("The Fiction Query Letter") is the author of several internationally acclaimed fantasy novels, including *Luck in the Shadows* and *Traitor's Moon*. She also writes short fiction and works as a freelance journalist and editor. For more information, visit her Web site at *www.sff.net/people/Lynn.Flewelling/*.

HUW FRANCIS ("Pitching to International Book Publishers") worked for eight years in the United Kingdom and Hong Kong as an engineer, communications consultant, and business manager before moving his family to Ankara, Turkey, where he became a freelance writer and consultant. Francis has been published in a variety of international magazines and newspapers (in six countries) and is a contributing editor to Suite101.com. His first book, *Live and Work Abroad—A Guide For Modern Nomads,* was published in June 2001. To find out more, visit *www.huwfrancis.com*.

TARA K. HARPER ("Writing the Agent Query") is the author of eight science fiction novels, including the best-selling and critically acclaimed *Wolfwalker* series and *Cat Scratch* series. Harper has worked for over twenty years as a science editor and writer in a diverse range of scientific and technical fields. For more information, visit *www.teleport.com/~until/*.

SHARON IHLE ("Sample Novel Synopsis") is a best-selling and award-winning author of western historical romances, including *Maggie's Wish, The Marrying Kind,* and *The Bride Wore Spurs. Untamed* is her latest release, from Kensington. Visit her Web site at *romance-central.com/SharonIhle/* for her current book release news.

TINA MILLER, whose advice is quoted in chapter 22, is a freelance writer, editor, corporate writer, instructor, and motivational speaker. For more information, visit *www.tinalmiller.com*.

AMY D. SHOJAI (whose sample proposal appears in chapter 11) is a nationally known authority on pets and is the author of sixteen nonfiction books and more than three hundred articles and columns. Amy frequently answers questions about pets—and about writing—during television appearances, in-person lectures, and "virtual" chats. She can be reached via her Web site at *www.shojai.com*.

VICTORIA STRAUSS ("Display Sites") is the author of five fantasy novels, most recently *The Garden of the Stone* (HarperCollins Eos). She's an active member of the Science Fiction and Fantasy Writers of America, where she serves as cochair of the Writing Scams Committee, and maintains the Writer Beware literary scams warning Web site (*www.sfwa.org/beware/*).

REBECCA VINYARD ("The Basic Elements of a Synopsis," "Anatomy of a Synopsis"), a former journalism major and e-zine editor, is published in poetry, fiction, and nonfiction. Her two novels are *Diva,* a historical romance, and *Deadly Light,* a romantic suspense. Ms. Vinyard is a member of the Dallas chapter of the Romance Writers of America and the Webmaster of Romance Central at *romance-central.com/*.

KELLEEN ZUBICK ("Grants for Writers") is an associate director at the Colorado Council on the Arts. She has also served as associate director of the Academy of American Poets, program coordinator at the Folger Shakespeare Library, and executive director of Writers' Conferences and Festivals (now Writers' Conferences and Centers). Her poems have appeared in numerous literary magazines, including *The Antioch Review, Doubletake,* the *Massachusetts Review,* and *5 AM*.

"Anatomy of a Synopsis," © 1998 by Rebecca Vinyard. Originally published online.

"The Basic Elements of a Synopsis," © 1998 by Rebecca Vinyard. Originally published online.

"Chat Your Way to Sales," © 2000 by MaryJanice Davidson. Originally published on Inkspot.

"The Cold Call" (quoted in chapter 22), © 2000 by Peter Bowerman. Excerpted from "Corporate Writing: Getting in the Door," published on Inkspot.

"Display Sites: An Alternative to the Query/Synopsis Process?" © 2000 by A.C. Crispin and Victoria Strauss. Originally published in *Writer's Digest*.

"The Fiction Query Letter," © 1998 by Lynn Flewelling. Originally published in *Speculations*.

"Grants for Writers," © 2000 by Kelleen Zubick and Maryo Ewell.

"How I Became a Syndicated Columnist," © 1999 by Debbie Farmer. First published online in the Writers Guidelines Database.

"How to Become a Syndicated Columnist," © 2000 by Amy Chavez. Originally published in *Inklings*.

"How to Become an International Columnist," © 1999 by Amy Chavez. Originally published in *Global Writers' Ink*.

"Newspaper Queries," © 2000 by Amy Chavez.

"Pitching to International Book Publishers," © 2000 by Huw Francis. Originally published in *Global Writers' Ink*.

"Sample Novel Synopsis," © 1998 by Sharon Ihle. Originally published online.

"Writing the Agent Query," © 2001 by Tara K. Harper. Originally published online.

INDEX

BOOKS FROM ALLWORTH PRESS

writing.com: Creative Internet Strategies to Advance Your Writing Career by Moira Anderson Allen (paperback, 6 × 9, 256 pages, $16.95)

Marketing Strategies for Writers by Michael Sedge (paperback, 6 × 9, 224 pages, $16.95)

Writing for Interactive Media: The Complete Guide by Jon Samsel and Darryl Wimberly (paperback, 6 × 9, 320 pages, $19.95)

Business and Legal Forms for Authors and Self-Publishers, Revised Edition by Tad Crawford (paperback (with CD-ROM), 8½ × 11, 192 pages, $22.95)

The Writer's Legal Guide, Second Edition by Tad Crawford and Tony Lyons (paperback, 6 × 9, 320 pages, $19.95)

The Writer's Guide to Corporate Communications by Mary Moreno (paperback, 6 × 9, 192 pages, $19.95)

How to Write Articles That Sell, Second Edition by L. Perry Wilbur and Jon Samsel (hardcover, 6 × 9, 224 pages, $19.95)

How to Write Books That Sell, Second Edition by L. Perry Wilbur and Jon Samsel (hardcover, 6 × 9, 224 pages, $19.95)

Writing Scripts Hollywood Will Love, Revised Edition by Katherine Atwell Herbert (paperback, 6 × 9, 160 pages, $14.95)

So You Want to Be a Screenwriter: How to Face the Fears and Take the Risks by Sara Caldwell and Marie-Eve Kielson (paperback, 6 × 9, 224 pages, $14.95)

The Screenwriter's Guide to Agents and Managers by John Scott Lewinski (paperback, 6 × 9, 256 pages, $18.95)

The Screenwriter's Legal Guide, Second Edition by Stephen F. Breimer (paperback, 6 × 9, 320 pages, $19.95)

Writing Television Comedy by Jerry Rannow (paperback, 6 × 9, 224 pages, $14.95)

Please write to request our free catalog. To order by credit card, call 1-800-491-2808 or send a check or money order to Allworth Press, 10 East 23rd Street, Suite 510, New York, NY 10010. Include $5 for shipping and handling for the first book ordered and $1 for each additional book. Ten dollars plus $1 for each additional book if ordering from Canada. New York State residents must add sales tax.

To see our complete catalog on the World Wide Web, or to order online, you can find us at *www.allworth.com.*